THE EVOLUTION OF
THE SAILING NAVY,
1509–1815

RICHARD HARDING

M
St. Martin's Press

First published in Great Britain 1995 by
MACMILLAN PRESS LTD
Houndmills, Basingstoke, Hampshire RG21 2XS
and London
Companies and representatives
throughout the world

A catalogue record for this book is available
from the British Library.

ISBN 0–333–59604–8 hardcover
ISBN 0–333–59605–6 paperback

10	9	8	7	6	5	4	3	2	1
04	03	02	01	00	99	98	97	96	95

Printed in Malaysia

First published in the United States of America 1995 by
Scholarly and Reference Division,
ST. MARTIN'S PRESS, INC.,
175 Fifth Avenue,
New York, N.Y. 10010

ISBN 0–312–12407–4

Library of Congress Cataloging-in-Publication Data
Harding, Richard, 1953–
The evolution of the sailing navy, 1509–1815 / Richard Harding.
p.   cm. — (British history in perspective)
Includes bibliographical references (p.   ) and index.
ISBN 0–312–12407–4
1. Great Britain—History, Naval. 2. Sailing ships—Great
Britain—History—16th century. 3. Sailing ships—Great Britain–
–History—17th century.   4. Sailing ships—Great Britain–
–History—18th century. 5. Great Britain.   Royal Navy—History.
I. Title.   II. Series.
DA85.H37 1995
359'.00941—dc20   94–31972
                                                              CIP

British History in Perspective
General Editor: Jeremy Black

PUBLISHED TITLES

Please see overleaf for forthcoming titles

FORTHCOMING TITLES

John Belcham *Nineteenth-Century Radicalism*
Eugenio Biagini *Gladstone*
Peter Catterall *The Labour Party, 1918–1940*
Gregory Claeys *The French Revolution Debate in Britain*
Pauline Croft *James I*
Eveline Cruickshanks *The Glorious Revolution*
John Davis *British Politics, 1885–1931*
David Dean *Parliament and Politics in Elizabethan and
Jacobean England, 1558–1614*
Susan Doran *English Foreign Policy in the Sixteenth Century*
David Eastwood *England, 1750–1850: Government and Community
in the Provinces*
Colin Eldridge *The Victorians Overseas*
S. Fielding *Britain and the Impact of World War II*
Angus Hawkins *British Party Politics, 1852–1886*
H. S. Jones *Political Thought in Nineteenth-Century Britain*
D. E. Kennedy *The English Revolution, 1642–1649*
Anthony Milton *Church and Religion in England, 1603–1642*
R. C. Nash *English Foreign Trade and the World Economy, 1600–1800*
W. M. Ormrod *Political Life in England, 1300–1450*
Richard Ovendale *Anglo-American Relations in the Twentieth Century*
David Powell *The Edwardian Crisis: Britain, 1901–1914*
Robin Prior and Trevor Wilson *Britain and the Impact of World War I*
Brian Quintrell *Government and Politics in Early Stuart England*
Stephen Roberts *Governance in England and Wales, 1603–1688*
W. Stafford *John Stuart Mill*
Alan Sykes *The Radical Right in Britain*
Ann Williams *Kingship and Government in Pre-Conquest England*
Michael Young *Charles I*

History of Ireland

Toby Barnard *The Kingdom of Ireland, 1641–1740*
Sean Duffy *Ireland in the Middle Ages*
Alan Heesom *The Anglo-Irish Union, 1800–1922*
Hiram Morgan *Ireland in the Early Modern Periphery, 1534–1690*

History of Scotland

I. G. C. Hutchinson *Scottish Politics in the Twentieth Century*
Roger Mason *Kingship and Tyranny? Scotland 1513–1603*
John McCaffrey *Scotland in the Nineteenth Century*
John Shaw *The Political History of Eighteenth-Century Scotland*
Bruce Webster *Scotland in the Middle Ages*

History of Wales

Gareth Jones *Wales, 1700–1980: Crisis of Identity*

CONTENTS

PREFACE

The purpose of this work is to present the reader with a particular perspective of British history. The maritime connection is so important that it is usually well embedded in studies of British political, economic, cultural and social history. However, the Royal Navy, the organ of government that projected maritime power and eventually protected global interests, is seldom the subject of much study on history courses. Older histories of the Royal Navy, which concentrate on operations and personalities, are neglected, whilst the new research which appears in specialist publications is unevenly absorbed into the mainstream of historical studies. This small volume is intended as a manageable overview of the newer works with a focus on the navy as an evolving organisation, contributing to and being shaped by the political, economic, diplomatic, social and technological changes in British society. It is intended to show that although much research has been done in recent decades, there are still many gaps in our understanding of the navy. Far from being an exhausted field, the history of the navy still provides the researcher with important and potentially fruitful avenues to explore.

In the desire for brevity detail has had to be sacrificed. The endnotes list only the most relevant items and are intended to direct readers to works which contain fuller details and bibliographies. Quantitative information is notoriously misleading in early modern naval history, so I am very grateful to Professor Jan Glete for permission to use the figures from his *Navies and Nations* which are listed at intervals throughout the text. Readers are strongly recommended to read Professor Glete's work, rather than rely too heavily upon the very limited statistical information presented here. Where the average tonnage of vessels is noted, this is my calculation from the data. The project would not have been possible without the valuable criticisms of fellow historians. I owe a great debt to Dr Jeremy Black for his editorial guidance and wide knowledge of diplomatic history. Dr Peter Le Fevre gave me a great deal of his time in discussion. I have also benefited from the comments of Professor David Loades, Professor Geoffrey Parker, Professor Daniel Baugh, Dr David Davies, Dr Michael Duffy, Mr Philip Woodfine and Mr Tim Bean. These scholars gave up their time and saved me from many errors. They also suggested many improvements, not all of which could be included in such a short work. I am nevertheless grateful to them. The omissions and errors remaining are entirely my own. I am also grateful to Anne, Rebecca and Hannah for cheerfully putting up with the sailing navy.

R. Harding

ABBREVIATIONS

Econ. H. R.	*Economic History Review*
EHR	*English Historical Review*
HJ	*Historical Journal*
MM	*Mariner's Mirror*
TRHS	*Transactions of the Royal Historical Society*

A Note On Dating

All dates are Old Style, unless otherwise noted. The new year is assumed to commence on 1 January.

1

1509–1603: MARITIME RESOURCES, THE NAVY ROYAL AND NAVAL POWER

Anyone purporting to present a single-volume history of the Royal Navy up to 1815 must expect to have to justify the endeavour. There are already many histories of the navy accessible to the general reader. As a subject for undergraduate study, institutional history in general and that of the Royal Navy in particular has slid into disfavour. Institutions have been largely replaced as the main foci of historical study by analyses of the social, economic and political forces that shaped them. The Royal Navy, which figured so prominently in the jingoistic imperial history that dominated syllabuses around the turn of the century, seems to have little to offer British students in a post-imperial age. There are, however, at least two reasons for presenting a new history of Britain's navy.

The first of these reasons is that as an organ of government the navy was probably second only to the Treasury in forming the relationship between the state, English society and the outside world. The navy became the largest spending department of state, the largest organisation of its kind in the world, a major direct consumer of all kinds of industrial and agricultural products, the major weapon in foreign policy, and it had a significant impact upon the evolution of Britain's maritime commerce. The navy is intimately tied up with the evolution of British political ideology, from the assertion of liberty of the individual to the claim to an imperial destiny. To ignore the navy is to neglect a major thread in the development of Britain.

The second reason for presenting this history is that in recent decades so much new work has been done by historians and archaeologists that our understanding of this important institution has deepened. The bald claims of the nineteenth-century navalists and propagandists have been subjected to close examination by historians equipped with the techniques of the social sciences and modern underwater archaeology. The relationship between the navy and society has come under greater scrutiny. New conclusions have been reached and fruitful areas of study have been opened up, which are marked advances upon the still common impressions inherited from the beginning of this century.

The English Crown, Society and Naval Requirements to 1509

Any explanation of the role of the navy in British history must start with an understanding of what a navy is. A navy can be described as a maritime force designed primarily to secure the advantages of free passage across the sea.[1] These advantages are numerous. The possessor of maritime forces can carry commerce wherever ships can go. Military forces can be transported by sea or fresh water to apply pressure to the enemy by destroying or obstructing commerce, ravaging coasts and landing armies to occupy territory. Last but by no means least, sea-power prevents the enemy from doing the same. With this in mind, it is possible to see navies as highly variable organisations, consisting of ships, seamen, fighting men, weapons, dockyards, repair facilities, stores and victuals, all underpinned by money and an administrative machine capable of converting that money into effective force. Accordingly, the organisation of navies varies in relation to the resources they possess and the tasks they need to carry out.

Modern navies, with their highly specialised vessels and weapons systems, their need for rapid action and reaction, are fully owned and supported by the state. This is one response to the increasing intensity and decisive effect of war at sea. It was a response that was recognised by the beginning of the sixteenth century, but it was to be decades before it became politically or administratively practicable. Nor was it for contemporaries the only or natural solution.

An early modern navy could be the personal property of the monarch, maintained out of the King's purse, and utilised for his benefit, quite incidental to the material interests of his subjects. A navy could be improvised from the maritime community. It could be created by royal agreement with ports. The Cinque Ports were an association of Dover, Hastings, Romney, Hythe, Sandwich and later Winchelsea and Rye, dating from at least 1278. In return for their charter privileges these towns were obliged to provide the Crown with men and ships in times of war. A navy could also be created by hiring vessels from domestic or foreign merchants to act as warships.

Navies such as these were common in the Middle Ages. In northern Europe the savagery of the elements prevented the development of specialised fighting vessels. In the Mediterranean, where tidal movements are small and the weather is relatively benign, the broad-beamed, square-rigged trading vessel had been supplanted for war since classical times by the sleek, oared galley. These ships were built for speed, manoeuvrability and ramming the enemy. Although galleys regularly ventured into the Atlantic, the advantages of oared propulsion were greatly diminished there by the rough and unpredictable seas. Indeed, their low build and relatively poor buoyancy made galleys extremely vulnerable.[2]

In northern waters galley tactics were impracticable. The most effective method of fighting at sea was to shower the enemy vessel with arrows and follow up by boarding. Northern ships, built for strength and carrying capacity, served equally well for commerce and war. The cog, and from the fourteenth century, the similar hulc, were capacious, broad, flat-bottomed vessels, carrying a single mast, square-rigged with a single sail, which dominated northern carrying trades. They sailed poorly, but were fairly stable in the rough northern waters. It was easy for merchant vessels to be hired or requisitioned by the monarch, and put to sea for military purposes. The changes required for service were usually minimal. Some ships might need to be internally strengthened and have their fore-and-aft structures built-up into so-called 'castles' to give archers an advantage over the enemy. Beyond this little needed to be done.[3]

England's position, firstly as a Norman possession off the coast of

Europe (1066–1154), and later as part of the Angevin empire (1154–1224), ensured that the Channel was always important for the Norman and Plantagenet monarchs. There was, however, little need for a large-scale naval force. When kings wanted substantial naval forces they called upon the merchant community to provide the ships. It was only at the end of the fifteenth century that changing conditions compelled English monarchs to establish a navy of permanently available vessels, supported by an administration and shore-based facilities which, in turn, led to the creation of a standing professional naval force.

Although Normandy had been lost by 1204, there were no significant naval forces in the Channel and North Sea to deprive monarch or merchants of free passage. Piracy was endemic and its impact on individual merchants or seafarers catastrophic, but it was too disorganised and spasmodic to be of critical importance to the merchant community as a whole or to the monarch. In any case, rulers seldom, if ever, thought it their duty to protect their subjects' commerce. The monarch could keep a small number of vessels which differed little in their essentials from the common trading cog.

The military need for naval forces was not great, but monarchs were not indifferent to the military importance and potential of the waters between England and the Continent. There were occasions when fighting on the water could assume an importance to the Crown. The wars against Wales (1277–95) and Scotland (1296–1328) relied substantially upon seaborne transport and supply. The ultimate failure of English attempts to subdue Scotland has been attributed to the rupture of English seaborne communications with the north. The conquest of Normandy by King Philip II of France in 1204 had given him the capacity to intervene directly in the political strife that marked the last years of King John and the early minority of Henry III (1213 and 1215–17). In 1340, Edward III's freedom to reinforce his army in Flanders and Picardy was confirmed by the action of Sir Robert Morley's English fleet, which destroyed a much smaller French force in Sluys harbour in June of that year. However, naval action was seldom decisive in itself. The victory at Sluys had little impact on the campaign at large or on the truce that was concluded at the end of that year. Six years later, Edward resumed the war in Normandy by landing his army in the rear of the French army operating against the

English possessions in Gascony. However, once ashore, Edward did not need continuous naval support. His army was small enough to be supplied locally and to manoeuvre freely, and the campaign ended with the crushing victory at Crécy.[4]

Cross-Channel raiding had been a feature of Anglo-French relations for many years, but the political upheavals in England during the 1370s brought chaos, a collapse of English power in France and a determined attempt by the French to strike at England. The result was destructive raids upon Hastings, Rye, Gravesend and the Isle of Wight, but the French had not got the forces to make a sustained campaign in England.[5]

In 1415, when Henry V began his determined effort to make good his claim to the French throne, his army had to be carried to France, but he relied primarily upon the chronic weakness of the French monarchy and an alliance with Burgundy to secure the sea passage and the campaign. Nevertheless, Henry purchased vessels and created the largest royal navy in Europe at that time. He established a roadstead for his vessels in the River Hamble, near Southampton. The spectacular results of his campaigns between 1415 and 1420 not only established him as Regent of France and heir to the French throne, but secured the Channel coast from Normandy to Picardy. When Henry died in 1422, he left a situation in which, for the first time since 1204, both sides of the Channel coast were in English hands. With England's Burgundian allies controlling the Flanders coast, free passage seemed to be secure.

Within a few decades of this highpoint of English power and prestige on the Continent, events were to refocus English attention on the security of the Channel. Perhaps the principal cause of this was financial. Despite the apparent success of his campaigns and diplomacy, Henry V bequeathed to England a war which had become bogged down in expensive sieges in the interior of France. These could not be sustained by Crown revenues, or by parliamentary grants, or by the political acumen and administrative skills of the Regent to the young King Henry VI, the Duke of Bedford. Therefore, while the coasts were secure, Henry's navy was deemed unnecessary. His ships were sold to pay off the mounting Crown debt and the Hamble roadstead fell into disuse.[6]

This reversion to the traditional practice of hiring naval forces when required might not have mattered had not other dramatic changes occurred. Parliament became disenchanted with the war in France, popular resistance against the English in conquered areas mounted and, in 1435, the Duke of Burgundy defected to the French side. These factors combined with a resurgence of French morale, symbolised by Joan of Arc, and led to the complete collapse of English power in France. By 1453 only Calais remained of the great empire. The sea was no longer the route to English possessions. There was no immediate threat to the integrity of the Lancastrian inheritance in England, but by 1490 England had only the sea as a buffer between her and a resurgent France. The sea had become vitally important to the security of the new Tudor regime.

The sea was also becoming economically more important. During the fifteenth century the Channel was becoming much more of a highway than it had ever been. The wine and wool trades had expanded dramatically between 1300 and 1500, and although the protection of trade was not a prime concern of the Crown's navy, the growing wealth of the merchants was not a matter of indifference. At least part of the Lancastrian political difficulties in the civil war between 1450 and 1485 was caused by the Yorkist sympathies of the expanding maritime community.[7] Henry VI's failure to control piracy soured trading relations with Flanders and the North German Hansa League, whilst his inability to pay merchants and seamen made the monarch increasingly unpopular.

Until the 1490s the seas to the west of Ireland had little attraction for merchants and seamen, beyond a little fishing or whaling. From the 1470s Portuguese vessels were exploring and trading down the coast of Africa, but after 1492, and the discovery of the New World, the Atlantic became a new highway to previously unimagined wealth and unlimited possibilities. This had been made possible by important developments in maritime technology. Despite its carrying capacity, the medieval cog was difficult to manoeuvre. The Portuguese were the first to marry this basic design with the finer lines and fore-and-aft rig of the Mediterranean galley. These small caravels employed square-set sails on two masts, with a fore-and-aft-, or lateen-rigged sail on a mast towards the stern. This latter rig made it easier to adjust the vessel to drive to windward. The caravels were excellent vessels for exploration of the coastal waters of Africa. Another type of vessel, the carrack, evolved from the cog. It retained the latter's sturdy build and high defensive castles, but was larger and had two or three masts carrying square- and lateen-rigged sails. The good cargo capacity and sturdiness, combined with the manoeuvrability conferred by the mix of sails, made the carrack an excellent vessel for long-distance trade and exploration.

As the long-distance trades began to flourish, all kinds of maritime industries were stimulated. Finance, insurance, ship design, building, provisioning and storing, were all influenced by the profits and employment of the trade to the Americas and Asia. Spain and Portugal dominated these trades and developments and, initially, English merchants were not heavily involved. England remained, like all countries in this period, predominantly agrarian, and her maritime trade remained dominated by the Flanders wool market. However, very soon the horizons of English merchants were literally expanded. West Country merchants of Bristol and Plymouth were quick to participate in the American trade, building up a tradition of interloping on the American and African monopolies claimed by Spain and Portugal. England was no longer on the fringes of the main European trade routes, but lay athwart the northern fringes of the route to a new and vitally important source of wealth.

These changes also had implications for military forces at sea. The improved sea-keeping of the carrack made it possible to maintain forces at sea and employ those forces in Atlantic waters in a way which would have been unthinkable in previous centuries. Military forces could be taken further and brought back more easily than before, and it was but a short step to recognise that more decisive military action might take place afloat. The sea was becoming a conduit for valuable American cargoes, vital to a state's military capacity. Intercepting those cargoes could have an important impact upon an enemy's ability to make war.

The traditional methods of fighting, by arrow and boarding, were suited to the construction of the evolving oceanic carrack. It was also well suited to a new weapon – the cannon. At first small guns were used as a means of defence against boarding, but over the first decades of the sixteenth century both the size and number of artillery pieces on ships grew to line the broadsides of the vessels. The capacity of ships to deal highly destructive blows against other vessels, without boarding, had a growing impact on the conduct of war at sea. Ships would have to be organised to provide mutual support and make the best use of this new firepower.[8]

By the early decades of the sixteenth century, sea-power was of greater importance to England than it had ever been before. As the century progressed, its importance grew as England's ability to compete with her rivals on the battlefields of Europe declined. The feudal armies of armoured knights, supported by peasant levies, that had fought each other in the latter stages of the Hundred Years War (1340–1450) were gradually being replaced by professional mercenary forces, capable of handling the pike and firelocks. These disciplined professional infantrymen broke the ascendancy of the armoured horseman. As the century progressed, the wars between France and the Habsburgs encouraged the retention of these professional soldiers in increasing numbers as standing forces loyal to the monarch.[9]

This was a slow and uneven process everywhere in Europe, but nowhere more so than in England. The transference from a feudal force to a professional army was complicated by the fact that social changes in England strained and broke the feudal system long before an acceptable and effective alternative military structure was in place. Fears of a standing force were quickly perceived in England and the Crown was compelled to compromise with those opposed to the extension of its military power. Henry VIII's campaigns in France between 1513 and 1545 consciously evoked memories of Edward III and Henry V, but both the French and English forces were very different from those of previous centuries. Henry still relied upon a feudal type of levy, but increasingly he was forced to supplement it with a more general or 'national' levy. His army was both technically and organisationally inferior to that of Francis I, and his main hope for victory lay not in decisive action, but in using allies to draw off the main enemy force to fight elsewhere.[10]

The belief that naval power could and should be used to compensate for this inability to meet Continental adversaries on equal terms on land, was to become a central theme in British naval, military and political history. By the eighteenth century the relative weakness of England's military forces and the strength of her navy compared to the Continental powers were being seen as the keystone of her world power and domestic liberties. It was a theme upon which Disraeli embellished in the 1860s and was to be an article of faith in public opinion by the end of the nineteenth century. It is not surprising therefore, that the question as to whether English strategy ever was, or should be, exclusively 'Continentalist' or 'Blue Water' has been central to the historiography of the Royal Navy and foreign policy and it is an issue that will never be far from the centre of this work.

Thus the period beginning in the 1450s saw both the start of a qualitative change in the nature of sea-power and a growing need for the English Crown to concentrate more of its resources upon ensuring that it had secured for itself the advantages of free passage around the British Isles. Whilst the Wars of the Roses, between the houses of York and Lancaster, continued, little was done, but with the death of Richard III at Bosworth in 1485 the effective struggle for the Crown ended, and the victor, Henry Tudor, now Henry VII, could look out beyond the English coasts to make the adjustments to his navy demanded by these changing conditions.

1485–1546: The Emergence of a Navy Royal

During Henry VII's reign (1485–1509) the changing needs of the state in relation to its navy were not entirely obvious and very little changed. This was largely because the legacy of the civil war and Henry's foreign policy made significant change in the immediate term difficult and unnecessary. During the civil war rivals had used the sea to escape defeat and assault the kingdom. This continued as the Burgundians supported the Yorkist attempt to place the pretender, Lambert Simnel, on the throne in 1487 and fostered the Irish rebellion of 1491.[11]

Faced with the need to establish his authority, Henry did not have the resources to build up his naval forces at speed. He relied upon the traditional expedient of hiring domestic and foreign merchantmen as warships as the need arose. He was, however, aware of the importance of using the sea to accomplish his aims. He looked to Spain, not just as a potential ally, but as the exemplar of modern maritime practices. He followed Spanish practice in trying to stimulate domestic production of large vessels by offering a bounty on the building of vessels of about

100 tons or over. Almost immediately after his accession he hired a storehouse at Greenwich to supply vessels that would protect the Thames and the east coast. In the same year an act was passed to encourage English shipping by prohibiting the import of wines except in English or Welsh holds. A further act in 1489 reinforced this policy.[12]

Henry's main problem was his lack of support in Europe. Scotland remained a threat in the north. Burgundy was a broken reed and antipathetic to the Tudors. France, having destroyed the English empire in Europe, remained an expansionary and hostile power. With the ports along the Channel coast, Charles VIII was ideally placed to seek advantage in the seas to the west or north of England. Henry attempted to secure himself at home and to prevent French power extending into Brittany and Biscay by allying himself with Spain (1489). In 1492 Henry mounted a small campaign to besiege Boulogne. Both the siege and the attempt to keep Brittany out of Charles VIII's hands failed. France could now exploit substantial Breton maritime resources well to the west of England. The generally prevailing westerly winds gave the French a significant advantage in being able to descend upon England whilst English vessels lay wind-bound far to leeward in the Thames estuary. Henry countered this threat by developing Portsmouth, in order to concentrate naval forces nearer the Western Approaches. At Portsmouth he built the first dry dock in English history for the repair and maintenance of the ships.[13]

By the time the dry dock was ordered in 1495, the European situation had taken a dramatic turn in Henry's favour. Charles VIII had committed his forces to Italy, which absorbed the majority of French energies in a struggle for mastery of that peninsula until 1559. Henry's diplomacy aimed at keeping French attention focused on Italy, since whilst it was he had little need for maintaining expensive maritime defences.

Relieved from this pressure, Henry's ambitions were directed to securing appropriate dynastic marriages with the Scottish and Spanish royal families. Naval organisation assumed a much lower priority. Even the interests of maritime commerce, which continued to expand and which Henry encouraged, were subordinated to these ends. Henry showed some interest in the discoveries in the New World by sponsoring a number of voyages, including those by John Cabot

(1497–8) and Juan Fernandez (1501–2), to reach Cathay by a westward voyage and settle heathen lands. However, Henry was careful not to alienate his Spanish allies and his patents demanded that the adventurers respect the lands occupied by other Christian powers, nor should they cross the ocean in latitudes more southerly than England. English trade continued to expand, but it had little impact on Henry's foreign policy or his views about his navy.[14]

Historians are divided on Henry VII's contribution to the evolving naval power of England. He is seen by some as the initiator of a maritime defensive policy that lasted some 400 years. Others argue that the navy developed very little, either qualitatively or quantitatively. Henry was not faced with the need to develop the Crown's naval power much beyond what he had inherited.[15] The changes being wrought in the exercise and importance of sea-power in the decades after 1450 had not become apparent by the time Henry died in 1509. He did what his predecessors and successors tried to do – direct the state's naval resources to the threats and opportunities as they appeared to him at the time. He was not deficient in this, but neither his prescience nor his abilities were tested in action. His son's use of the navy royal suggests that he had done enough for the times in which he lived and to permit development when those times changed.

It is with the accession of Henry VIII in 1509 that most histories of the Royal Navy commence. The reason for this is simple. During his reign (1509–47) the navy developed the basic features which identified it for the next 300 years. The ultimate symbol of the Crown's power at sea, the warship, emerged as a powerful and valued weapon. During a series of crises with France, between 1512 and 1546, Henry greatly expanded the number of his warships in the royal fleet. At his death in 1547, 84 vessels had been added to the navy, at one time or another, of which 46 had been specially built for him. The rest had been either purchased or captured. Although the vessels varied in size, from the 30- or 40-ton *Hare* and *Brigandine*, to the *Henry Grace a Dieu*, at over 1000 tons, 52 of the 85 vessels were over 100 tons. The basic tactical objective of these warships remained the boarding of enemy vessels, but the cannon being carried in the vessels were getting larger and, from the evidence of the *Mary Rose*, placed upon carriages that made them handier than the guns on continental warships. Ships were still built high for defence and dramatic effect. They were

	N° of warships	Average displacement (tons)
1500	9	550
1505	6	666
1510	7	714
1515	23	565
1520	25	520
1525	18	500
1530	11	636
1535	10	700
1540	11	636
1545	32	468
1550	37	459

Source: Glete, J., *Navies and Nations*, I, 130.

increasingly decorated and gilded as floating bastions and symbols of Tudor might.[16]

Part of this large investment in the navy resulted from Henry's personal interest in the splendour of his fleet. Henry was, like his contemporaries, a Renaissance monarch, acutely aware of the importance of reflecting his own power and glory in the physical artifacts of the Crown. The warship was a magnificent vehicle for this symbolism. However, his interest was also stimulated by the changing requirements of naval defence. Although only about 8 years of Henry's 37-year reign were war years, his rivalry with Francis I of France, the uncertain English position with regard to Ireland and Scotland, and the domestic dislocation created by the Reformation meant that Henry spent most of his energies ensuring England's security.

Increasingly, the Crown needed a large and permanent navy. The ships were the embodiment of Henry's quest for security, and they required increased administrative support. The great yards in the Thames, at Deptford (1517) and Woolwich (1518), with a dock at Erith, were established or expanded. Towards the end of the reign, Portsmouth was expanded. In these yards and those which built Henry's warships, there was a small but growing proportion of the maritime community who drew a livelihood from the Crown.

When Henry came to the throne in 1509, it did not take him long to appreciate the importance of his fleet. Unlike his father, he determined to heal the wounds of civil war by adopting the posture of chivalric tradition by which the monarch achieved true glory and acclaim by force of arms. In 1510 he planned an expedition in the crusading tradition against the Moors. By 1512, his diplomacy had brought him into an alliance with Spain against France. His ships, under the Lord Admiral, Lord Thomas Howard, cleared French shipping from the Channel, for an expedition under Dorset to sail to join the Spaniards besieging Bayonne. The land campaign was a failure, but the success of the English ships in securing the Channel provoked James IV of Scotland into war against England.[17]

The war dragged on until 1514, as Henry exhausted his treasury in an indecisive campaign in northern France. The death of James IV at Flodden in 1513 secured the northern borders of England, while English ships raided Brittany and the Normandy coast, to little effect. French interests were too little tied up with the sea to have any impact on Louis XII's ability to maintain his war. The peace brought Henry the towns of Tournai and Thérouanne and a pension from France, in exchange for the marriage of his sister, Mary Tudor, to Louis XII. Henry's navy had performed well enough in the war and seemed perfectly able to maintain the sea passage to Calais and its expanded hinterland. The death of Louis XII in 1515 and the accession of the energetic young Francis I reopened Anglo-French antagonism. Francis' skill in creating discontent in Scotland and his advance in Italy aroused Henry's envy and anger. Over the next 10 years Henry was involved in diplomatic activity which relied upon his naval power to bring assistance to potential allies against Francis.

When war broke out its focus was in northern France. The Duke of Suffolk led a small expedition on a raid in 1522. More ambitious plans, involving a coordinated attack upon France in 1523 by England, Spain and the rebellious Duke of Bourbon, came to nothing.[18] Henry had strengthened his fleet in expectation of war, but financial strain was already becoming apparent. His attempts to revive a combined offensive in the wake of Francis' defeat and capture at Pavia in 1525 foundered on his inability to collect adequate funds.

In the years that followed 1525, Henry's own succession problems absorbed him, and although the Reformation triggered a series of domestic rebellions and crises, he was not pressed by powerful enemies abroad. Italy remained the focus of both French and Habsburg ambitions, whilst the impact of the Reformation and the eruption of Turkish power into Central Europe kept attention focused upon eastern and southern Europe. This comparative calm in Henry's foreign relations was shattered in 1538, when Francis and the Holy Roman Emperor, Charles V, concluded their war over Italy and looked westward to schismatic England. Francis had been building up his naval forces and facilities on the Atlantic coast at Le Havre and Brest. These enlarged ports could receive vessels from the Mediterranean sent to reinforce Francis' naval efforts in the Channel. There was, therefore, for the first time the prospect of a substantial hostile force in the Western Approaches, the Channel and the North Sea.

Henry's reaction to the crisis of 1538–9 was not unlike that of his predecessors. He embargoed merchant ships for defence and ordered the building of additional royal warships. Perhaps the most interesting development was his decision to build a series of about 20 low fortifications to defend the Thames and the Kent coast, including the magnificent examples at Deal and Walmer. These were positioned to defend the anchorages with artillery and to be themselves poor targets for gunners at sea. Here was an indication that artillery was beginning to be used as a decisive weapon in both the attack and defence of ships.

In the event, Francis' plans came to nothing, but Henry determined to revive his own scheme for the conquest of France. Four years of diplomatic activity led to a plan to attack France in concert with Charles V, to revive the old English empire in the north of France, Normandy and Guienne. By 1544, negotiations and planning with Charles V had led to an ambitious scheme to advance on Paris with a combined force of 80,000 troops. Henry took the field in July and besieged Montreuil and Boulogne, while the Habsburg army sat down in front of St Dizier. At the same time Henry's tense relationship with Scotland once more broke into open war as the pro-French and Catholic faction assumed political control of the Regency of the infant Mary Queen of Scots. English forces ravaged the lowlands, whilst Lord Lisle took a fleet to sack Edinburgh and Leith. Within five weeks, Lisle had devastated the port and capital, illustrating the potential of growing English sea-power in its relationship with Scotland.[19]

In September Boulogne fell to the English, but Charles V had had enough of the campaign and made a separate peace with Francis.

Within a month, the English expeditionary army was disintegrating and weakened garrisons were concentrated in Boulogne and around Calais. The frailty of the English position now became painfully apparent. The war in Scotland rumbled on. The army for France had been put together only with the utmost difficulty and it was unlikely another could be assembled for 1545. The French were concentrating over 50,000 soldiers and a powerful naval force of about 150 sailing vessels, together with rowboats, and 25 galleys at Le Havre. The militia of local people was mobilised to repel an invasion that seemed imminent, but just as Henry's navy had been used to great effect against Scotland in 1544, he hoped that it would again justify its existence by preventing a French landing. Hired merchantmen stood out to the west, while Lord Lisle took a fleet of 80 vessels, including the royal warships, to attack the French in the Channel. Lisle was driven back by bad weather, but the French fleet, which took advantage of his withdrawal to put to sea, was unwilling to pursue him into the shoal waters off the English coast. The campaign at sea settled down to a French cruise off the southern coast of England, with the English fleet seizing what opportunities it could to attack at an advantage.

This campaign is chiefly remembered today for the dramatic loss of the *Mary Rose* in the Solent on 19 July, as she put out with other great ships to challenge the French fleet in the offing. It was, however, in the opinion of Sir Julian Corbett, a campaign that 'best marks the birth of English naval power'.[20] The tactics planned by both sides still reflected the dominance of ramming and boarding, and the performance of the French galleys so impressed Henry that he ordered galleys for his own fleet. However, there were signs which, in retrospect, could be seen to have presaged changes. The fleets seem to have manoeuvred with a conscious tactical formation, reflecting the organisation of land forces. Despite the value of the galleys in calm and confined waters, it was the cannon that made the biggest impact on the campaign. The galley captains dared not make way in the calms which could leave them far from the supporting gunfire of the sailing ships.

Corbett probably overstated the significance of this campaign. The events of 1545 were indecisive both for the military situation at the time and as markers for the future evolution of naval power, but equally there is good reason to see the year as significant. Both sides had assembled large naval forces of over 100 vessels – royal ships, converted merchantmen, rowboats and galleys. There was a plan to invade England and the decisive action occurred at sea. With the presence of a growing French naval power and the disorganised state of the English land forces, England could not afford to neglect her maritime resources. It was vital that Henry retained the ability to call into being a large navy, and in 1546, probably drawing upon his experience of setting up an administrative board to expand the production of cannon in England, Henry established a board of administrators to manage the process. Since the thirteenth century the modest numbers of King's ships were in the care of a Clerk of the Ships. By the early sixteenth century, he was assisted by the Clerk Controller and the Clerk of the Storehouses. The fighting at sea was under the nominal control of an aristocratic soldier, the Great Admiral of England, but the disjointed nature of war at sea seldom demanded the presence of such an august person. By the time of Henry's death in 1547 there had been a small but significant change in the military and administrative control of the navy. Henry's Lord Admirals were needed both at sea and as administrators. The administrative tasks of maintaining the expanded fleet for long periods demanded an expansion of the professional administrators who supported it. In 1546, a board of officials with broadly defined functions replaced the overworked Clerks. This broad functional definition of responsibility was the basis for greater role clarity as the century progressed and from it emerged the Navy Board, which was to have responsibility for the management of ships, yards and seamen until it was abolished in 1832.[21]

The importance of these changes was that over time it would be possible for the administrators and military seamen to define and advocate the needs of the fighting navy. It would be many decades before a naval officer corps evolved, and centuries before the formal recognition of the career naval seaman. Indeed, it would be even longer before the recognition of a career administrator, or civil servant. However, an established board, and the acceptance of military service afloat as important, requiring a *corpus* of expertise, laid the foundations for the influence of interested 'experts' in the development of the navy. From the first half of the sixteenth century the navy was to be established as a permanent organ of the state, which the army, lacking these foundations and depending upon the will of the sovereign, did not achieve until centuries later. The significance of this in English attitudes to the two services over the centuries can hardly be emphasised enough.

1547–1585: Consolidation and Opportunity

Henry VIII has been universally praised for his development of the navy. The foreign policy that caused him to rely upon his fleet so heavily has been less charitably received by historians. When Henry died in 1547, he left a war which England could not win against Scotland. The peace agreed with France in June 1546 was unstable. Financial crisis and the inability to organise land forces or allies to renew a war in France left Henry on the defensive, and the navy was for him essentially a defensive weapon. In this respect Henry was reactive to the situation around him, rather than an innovator. He invested in his navy to meet his personal needs for a symbol of his power, and to fulfil the increasingly pressing need to counter the French in the narrow seas. He was very energetic and clear-sighted in this, but he did not require or organise any major social changes to achieve it. Trade and fishing were growing, so that there were ships and seamen enough for Henry's needs. Soldiers were expected to fight on the ships and the military nobility was expected to command. Henry's naval activities demanded no new social organisation to manage the improved administrative structure of the navy. However, his success in organising his naval forces, combined with the social changes that made the raising of land forces more difficult, gave the navy a sense of purpose that it had lacked up to that point.

During Henry's reign the Crown had recognised the growing importance of the sea in foreign policy. It was not lost by his successors. Whilst the war with Scotland continued until 1550, the requirements for sustaining a navy were met. The navy was vital to supply the Protestant rebels and limit French assistance reaching the Catholic party in Scotland. Although some of the smaller and weaker vessels were sold off, the number of sailing ships of force remained largely unchanged. The administrative organs that had slowly evolved under Henry VIII continued to expand and take a more permanent form, particularly the victualling service. Ultimately, England failed to sustain the anti-French party in Scotland, but when peace came there was no question of reverting to fifteenth-century practice and dismantling the navy. Gillingham, at the mouth of the Thames, had been established as a safe anchorage where the ships could be laid up until required for action – a condition known as having the ships 'in ordinary'. The administrative structure that was required to provide vessels for war in the future remained intact.[22]

	N° of warships	Average displacement (tons)
1550	37	459
1555	26	384
1560	26	500
1565	24	583
1570	20	700
1575	20	700
1580	21	714
1585	22	680

Source: Glete, J., *Navies and Nations*, I, 130.

The English Crown had established a navy second to none in northern waters. A large part of this achievement can be attributed to the context in which the navy evolved. English maritime trade expanded rapidly during the first half of the century. England's staple exports, wool and woollen cloth, found a growing market in Flanders. Exports of cloth increased by 300 per cent between 1475 and 1550, producing within the maritime community an expansion of manpower and know-how.[23] The French threat, which reached its height in 1545, was a continual stimulus to Henry's determination to develop his naval strength, but never, until 1545, so great or sustained as to demand radical departures from precedent or the commitment of an unobtainable level of resources. The navy could develop within known parameters and acceptable resources.

This stable evolutionary process largely continued until the early years of the seventeenth century, punctuated on the one hand by periodic demands to reduce the financial burden of the fleet, such as during the years 1550 to 1556, and on the other hand, by frenetic activity to meet an enemy, as happened in the years 1556 to 1564, 1570 and 1585 to 1588. Despite the period 1548 to 1585 being years full of domestic crisis, revolving around the succession, religion, and relations with Scotland and Ireland, England's interests were not immediately threatened by her continental neighbours. France was successively distracted by war with the Habsburgs (1552–9), bankruptcy, and the Wars of Religion (1562–98), which were completely to change her relationship with England in the next decades. The transformation of Spain from an ally to an enemy took decades (1558–85). In the meantime, the English navy drew increasing strength from the expanding maritime community. It was a symbiosis that established a solid naval infrastructure to maintain a war at sea and exploit the offensive potential of such a war.

The critical feature of this evolutionary process was the strengthening ties of the men occupying the administrative offices of the navy with the expanding merchant community. These administrators, such as Benjamin Gonson, William and George Winter and, most famous of all, John Hawkins, were merchants with experience of investing and participating in overseas trade. The growing number of state papers relating to the navy suggests that such men had an active interest in developing an understanding of what the navy was capable of doing. Likewise, the monarchs and their advisers saw the virtue of drawing such men into the administrative apparatus.[24] Undoubtedly, a partial stimulus to this association of merchants and adventurers in the royal administration was based upon mutual private profit. For example, in 1561 Benjamin Gonson, Treasurer of the Queen's Navy, was part of a group of merchants who hired four royal ships to participate in a trading venture to the Guinea coast. John Hawkins was a very active trader in slaves to the Caribbean. Aristocratic investment in these ventures was an established feature of their financing from the 1560s. By the end of the century this community of interest in trading activities was an essential link between the administrative control of the navy, the aristocratic policy-makers in government, and the expanding and voluble mercantile interests in England.[25]

Major changes were going on within the patterns of English trade. London, which dominated English overseas trade in the sixteenth century, had historically concentrated upon the trades to north-west

Europe, leaving oceanic trading to the outports such as Bristol, Southampton and Plymouth. The experience of these outport merchants was invaluable, but from the middle of the century London merchants invested more heavily in the distant trades to Guinea and the Levant, giving the administrators of the navy a pool of expertise close at hand.[26] The benefits that this relationship between the royal administration and the merchant community as a whole bestowed upon the English navy were numerous. As early as the 1540s, it seems that by appointing capable and knowledgeable administrators some idea of a naval policy was beginning to evolve. In 1558, when Elizabeth I came to the throne, the naval administrators presented her with an outline, not just of the state of her navy, but also of their opinion of the strength at which it should be maintained and the funding it required. By and large their recommendations formed the basis of Elizabeth's naval forces and the administrators were confirmed in their posts.[27] In the 18 years before the Armada crisis of 1588, the English naval administrators' knowledge of the maritime environment made possible a series of surveys of shipping to identify the resources that would be available to the Crown in an emergency.[28]

As oceanic travel increased, there were some significant improvements in ship design, which were incorporated into new ships built for the Crown. The name of John Hawkins, Treasurer of the Navy from 1577 to his death in 1595, is particularly connected with these improvements. During this period there was a growing movement towards distinguishing between the merchantman, which retained a relatively broad beam for carrying capacity, and the warship, which was being built with a longer keel relative to beam, to mount more cannon along its sides and improve its manoeuvrability at sea. Finer underwater lines were used, and the high fo'castles and sterncastles were cut down. Although these flush-decked or 'race-built' vessels were constructed only after the invasion scare of 1571, their performance at sea greatly enhanced the fighting power of the English fleet.[29]

Whilst royal vessels were taking on more of the appearance of specialised fighting vessels, the merchant vessels, venturing further afield, were themselves becoming more formidably armed as private men-of-war. Although there was a conflict between carrying heavier armaments and the loss of cargo capacity, merchant vessels trading to the Levant, Barbary, Guinea and the Indian Ocean had to carry adequate defensive armament against strong local maritime opposition.[30] Furthermore, on English vessels at least, operating these cannon was increasingly a part of the seaman's job. The period was therefore one which witnessed a significant change in the relationship between the seaman and the soldier. As the use of cannon was replacing boarding as the major naval tactic, so the role of the foot soldier in the fleet diminished and the role of the seaman trained in gunnery increased.

This period of relative peace, between 1555 and 1585, is therefore highly significant for the navy. It permitted the administrative machinery set up during Henry's lifetime to consolidate around a growing number of capable merchant administrators who could combine a knowledge of ships, trade and the maritime resources of England. By the mid 1580s, England possessed not just an impressive merchant marine, but also a naval potential which exceeded that of any of her neighbours. The diplomatic changes that took place in this period, culminating in the Armada crisis of 1588 and an indecisive war with Spain for the next 16 years, were to illustrate the extent and limitations of that potential. Moreover, although monarchs and counsellors had long been aware of the importance of naval power, the expansion of English maritime resources and wealth was to embed the idea of naval power deeply in the political consciousness of the English people.

The main change in England's relationships with Europe was, undoubtedly, the growing hostility with Spain. Whilst England's main adversary had been France the Crown's navy had a limited role to play both as a cause of hostility and as a weapon in the struggle. Hostility with Spain was very different. It cannot be argued that the tension between the two powers at sea was fundamental to the growth of hostility, but it was certainly an important factor. Relations between the two former allies had become strained by the build-up of Spanish forces in the Netherlands following the revolt there in 1567. Elizabeth, troubled by domestic Catholic opinion, could not fail to be concerned by the most powerful Catholic power in Europe ferrying soldiers and money to suppress the revolt on the other side of the North Sea. Tension between the Spanish Regent in Flanders and the English grew and in 1568 the two states almost came to war over a diplomatic tangle that included Elizabeth seizing Spanish pay ships and the Spaniards closing Antwerp to English merchants. This latter act not only struck at the most important branch of English overseas trade but also damaged royal revenues that accrued from export taxes.[31]

If growing Spanish military power in northern Europe was causing Elizabeth concern, English maritime expansion was also causing Spain anxiety. Throughout the 1560s and 1570s English interlopers, tolerated and indeed sponsored by the English Crown, were trading and raiding in the Caribbean. These raids were more than just a nuisance. Drake's voyage through the Caribbean in 1572–3 and his raid of 1585 effectively disrupted the flow of bullion to Spain, causing a serious strain on the treasury. After years of penury, the Spanish Crown relied on silver from the Americas to finance its military activities in Europe. French, English and Dutch raiders posed a real threat to this lifeline.[32] English ships appeared in almost all the waters of importance to Spain. With the Dutch Protestant rebels they dominated the Channel; a major route to the theatre of operations in the Low Countries. They were active in the Baltic, from which Spain drew vital supplies of grain and naval stores. From about 1570 heavily armed English vessels began to reappear in the Mediterranean.[33]

These conflicts were the effects, not the principal cause, of hostility between England and Spain. However, it was the sea, which for years had done much to create bonds of mutual benefit by the trade between England, Flanders and the Iberian peninsula, which was now the environment in which the dynastic territorial and confessional antagonism could be articulated.

1585–1603: Conflict with Spain

By the early 1580s Spain seemed to be gaining, inexorably, the upper hand in the struggle for power in western Europe. The civil war in France had rendered that country impotent. Philip II of Spain no longer had to fear French disruption to his reconquest of Flanders and the success of the Catholic League seemed likely to make France a steady ally of Spain. Peace with the Turks released more resources for that reconquest. The Spanish annexation of Portugal in 1580 brought

Philip wealth, colonies and significant naval resources. English assistance to the Dutch and the Portuguese had angered Philip. He reacted by supporting assassination plots against Elizabeth, as well as providing troops and money for anti-English revolts in Scotland and Ireland.

By 1585 relations between England and Spain had all but broken down. Philip's seizure of English grainships in Spanish harbours united the merchant community against Spain and precipitated a destructive raid by Francis Drake through the Caribbean. Plans for an invasion of England had been laid before Philip for many years, but in 1583 serious consideration began to be given to the idea. By 1586 plans were laid and resources prepared: war had broken out.

This war has had a major impact on British naval historiography. The defeat of the Spanish Armada in 1588 has been the focus of attention. It was a clear case of a major threat to national independence being foiled at sea. The role of English naval power in this victory is debatable, but contemporaries and later generations have seized upon it as evidence of the maturity and effectiveness of the navy. It was also the first occasion on which the naval administration left behind valuable collections of documents to record the events. It is not surprising that when the Navy Records Society was formed in 1893 some of the first and most impressive collections of documents published concerned the Anglo-Spanish war of 1585–1604. In recent decades, historians have put the naval achievement of the war and the events of 1588 into clearer perspective, but nonetheless, these 19 years remain critically important to the development of the navy.[34]

	N° of warships	Average displacement (tons)
1585	22	680
1590	36	694
1595	35	657
1600	34	794
1605	30	766

Source: Glete, J., *Navies and Nations*, I, 130.

What cannot be denied is that this was the first occasion on which naval activity had a major impact on both the defensive and the offensive strategies of England. It demonstrated both the strength and the weakness of English naval power at that time. The strength of the English navy is most clearly seen in the events of 1587–8. This strength lay in an ability to mobilise at short notice and at minimal cost to the Treasury large numbers of private ships that could easily serve as warships. The number of royal ships remained fairly stable after an initial expansion, but the growth of England's merchant marine had equipped it with large, sturdy vessels, manned by seamen who could navigate their vessels and handle cannon in a manner second to none. The Crown's naval administration had built up close contacts with these merchants and seamen and for years had utilised them to pursue policy. So long as the Crown's foreign policy could demonstrate the prospect of achieving a return for their investment, the merchants were at the service of the state.

By the end of 1586 Elizabeth knew of Philip's intention to invade. She hoped to contain the increasingly dangerous rift but by early March 1587 it was impossible to ignore the great preparations being made in Spanish ports for a naval expedition. Drake was ordered to sea with four of the Queen's warships, and two smaller pinnaces. To these were added 12 more ships and 5 pinnaces provided by the Levant Company and individual adventurers, including Drake himself. These latter ships were victualled and paid for by the owners in expectation of booty from a successful voyage. Drake arrived at Plymouth on 23 March and sailed with the fleet within nine days. On 29 April this force entered Cadiz, the main supply port for the assembling Armada. The galleys which had been thought ideal to defend the sailing ships in the shallow and confined waters of the bay were unequal in firepower to the English warships. By the time Drake left the next day, he had captured 6 vessels and destroyed 18 more.

Drake moved out and took up a position at Sagres, west of Cape St Vincent. From here his vessels intercepted about 50 vessels intended to supply Lisbon, the port from which the Armada was to depart. By these actions and the threat he posed to the treasure fleet returning from the Americas, Drake completely foiled the Spaniards' plans for an invasion in 1587. It was a victory made possible by the availability at very short notice of sound and equipped warships in greater numbers than the Queen could have afforded herself.

This mobilisation was repeated in 1588. Although the manpower of the fleet was reduced by half during the winter months it was agreed to have the whole navy concentrated at Portsmouth by the end of March 1588, except for a squadron of 30 ships, including 7 royal warships, under Drake at Plymouth. The fleet stood ready to intercept the Armada as it proceeded up Channel, to mount a diversionary raid in the rear of the Spanish fleet against Portugal, and to have vessels ready to cruise off the Spanish coast or intercept the treasure fleet off the Azores. To Sir Julian Corbett, one of the first great historians of the Royal Navy, this was a critical moment in English naval history; Drake's denunciation of this strategy is a 'despatch deserving to be treasured for a sacred document of the nation as the first enunciation of the doctrines which made [England] mistress of the seas'.[35] Drake planned to take the offensive and to make the object of his attentions to seek out and destroy the main battle fleet of the enemy at sea. Drake was not permitted to undertake this offensive at the time, but in April the Lord Admiral, Lord Howard of Effingham, was ordered from Portsmouth to join Drake at Plymouth, to form a combined force of over 100 vessels. A journey to London in May had enabled Drake to convince the Queen of the necessity for a pre-emptive strike at the Armada, and back in Plymouth at the end of May he persuaded Howard to undertake the operation. On 4 July the fleet left Plymouth to seek out the Spaniards.

This excursion by a major fleet demonstrated not just a changing strategic understanding of sea-power in England, but a tactical change as well. Corbett noted that the fleet was divided into three divisions to cover the approach of the Armada, which he speculated might be the first occasion for the use of what was to be the classic divisional formation of the age of sail. However, a critical weakness of the navy soon became apparent. Although it was possible to mobilise warships from the merchant community with relative ease, provisioning them with food – victuals – particularly away from the great London markets, was a major problem. Even before the fleet set sail, complaints about scarce victuals were common. As contrary weather hindered the fleet's progress victuals began to run out and the decision had to be made to return to Plymouth. Throughout the rest of the campaign, a lack of victuals was to dog the English ships.

The story of the Armada itself is well known, although the conclusions drawn from the campaign by modern historians are less familiar. It is now clear that the English fleet was far from unprepared.

English ships were not significantly smaller or carrying less weight of shot than the Spaniards. The manoeuvring of a large fleet of ships and galleasses in coherent formation up the Channel to Calais was a magnificent piece of seamanship, but many of the Spanish ships were not ideal warships and their crews were, on the whole, not such experienced oceanic seamen or naval artillerists as their English adversaries. Philip had been planning such an invasion since 1583, and the plan that was eventually adopted in 1587 was much more limited in resources and objectives than that discussed two years earlier. Nonetheless, the forces that were eventually assembled in the Tagus, under the Duke of Medina Sidonia, in the early summer of 1588 represented a remarkable administrative achievement. About 130 vessels, carrying 19,000 soldiers, were to proceed up Channel to cover the landing of about 17,000 battle-hardened troops from the Duke of Parma's Army of Flanders.

The Armada left Lisbon on 18 May, and after a struggle against contrary winds reached Corunna in northern Spain. After repair and restocking, the Armada sailed for the Channel on 12 July. On 19 July the Armada sighted the Lizard. Forewarned, Howard took the main body of the English fleet out into the Channel to allow the Armada to pass by. This gave Howard the windward position from which he could bear down upon or fall off from the Spaniards as he chose. From the first contact, which occurred off Plymouth on 21 July, Howard exploited his position. He kept his distance and utilised the gunnery expertise of his seamen, by proceeding in line around the rearward vessels on the great crescent-shape that was the Armada proceeding up Channel.[36] Little damage was done. Further clashes on 23 and 24 July produced few losses to the Armada.

The critical point was reached on 25 July, when the Armada approached the Solent. The English did not know that Medina Sidonia's instructions were to cover the landing of Parma's army rather than to effect an invasion himself. If the Armada could put into the Solent and effect a landing a Spanish foothold would be established in England. For his part, Medina Sidonia, who had not heard from Parma in Flanders, considered the Solent a good anchorage in which to await Parma's confirmation of readiness to sail. Should Parma be unready, there was nowhere east of the Solent that the Armada could safely wait for him.

To defend against this possible landing, the English fleet divided into three parts. Martin Frobisher stood in to shore, Howard and Hawkins harried the rear of the Armada, and Drake stood out to seaward. Whether the Armada was forced to bear away from the Solent by Drake's vigorous attack on its seaward flank, which threatened to push the Spanish formation on to the Owers Banks, or if it was delayed for a critical period to miss the tides by the astute positioning of Frobisher's vessels, is unclear. The result was, however, decisive. The Spanish fleet bore off to the east and missed its last safe refuge west of Parma's army in Flanders.

By 26 July the Armada was anchored off Calais, still undefeated. On the night of 27 July an attempt to burn the Spanish fleet by fireships caused the Spaniards to put to sea in a great hurry, cutting cables and losing anchors. For the first time the English ships closed in to attack the scattered formation at close range, causing substantial damage to some vessels and sinking one. The Spaniards were severely hindered in their reply by lack of training in the handling of cannon at sea and by the poor quality of their guns, some of which, as the recent archaeological discoveries of Colin Martin have shown, were incapable of being fired.[37] By the next day they were drifting with the wind to the north, powerless to cover the planned invasion by the Duke of Parma's army of Flanders.

There was national rejoicing in England as the Armada scattered and struggled to regain the ports of Portugal and Spain by the hazardous passage around Scotland and Ireland. However, it was not a victory bought by superior sea-power, nor was it a victory of the small plucky English vessels against the vastly superior fighting ships of Spain. The English fleet was powerful enough to cause damage to the Armada but not to defeat it at close quarters. The English tactics and strategy had worked as far as they went. Despite this, the Armada was still capable of covering Parma's landing when it anchored off Calais and Gravelines. If communications with Parma had been better they might still have achieved their objective. The delay at Calais and the fireships largely decided the issue.

England was undoubtedly saved from an invasion which she was probably too weak to resist on land. Whether a Spanish foothold in England was sustainable is impossible to establish, but the defeat of the Armada was in the immediate term vital for England and important for the Protestant cause.[38] In the longer term, the campaign did not secure either for the future. Philip was devastated by the defeat, but patiently set about building another Armada, which by 1596 almost matched that of 1588. It did not greatly hinder the Spaniards in their activities in Flanders and France.

The distinctive features of English sea-power demonstrated in 1587–8 can be seen in the years that followed. For Elizabeth the most important objective was to keep the Protestant rebels in the Low Countries and France from succumbing to Spain and her Catholic allies. This could most effectively be done by supporting the Dutch and Huguenot land forces with men or money.[39] However, despite great efforts, Elizabeth had too little of either to make a decisive impact on the campaigns. Encouraging a war at sea, on the other hand, was relatively cheap. English shipowners speculated on the rewards of privateering against the Spanish empire. These privateers were privately financed but officially sanctioned ships sent out on expeditions of plunder. Over 15 years, groups of merchants invested together with policy-makers, such as Sir Robert Cecil and the Lord Admiral, the Earl of Nottingham, and wealthy seamen, to build powerful warships for this business.[40]

This was the only substantial offensive action England could take. Whereas the Tudor state failed to tap, effectively, national resources by taxation or the organisation of military manpower, it managed to create an administrative structure to mobilise the nation's maritime resources. There is some debate as to the effectiveness of this policy. It is undoubtedly true that the damage to Spain was far less than contemporaries had hoped, or later propagandists claimed. Spain managed to reorganise her defence of the Americas in the 1590s and the raids of this decade did not have the *éclat* of the 1570s, yet privateering continued to be a thorn in the side of the Spaniards until the peace of 1604. On one occasion, in 1596, a large fleet was put together and a damaging attack upon Cadiz was launched. Furthermore, it enabled Elizabeth to concentrate the scarce manpower and financial resources she possessed on preserving the Protestant cause in France and the Netherlands.[41]

The weaknesses of this very close relationship between state naval power and the merchant community were also apparent in these years. Primarily, the weakness sprang from the inability of the state to direct the naval resources. Naval action was the result of a negotiation between the Queen's representative and the syndicates that contributed some of the vessels. In 1589 Drake and Sir John Norreys laid a plan before the Queen to strike at Spain by a large-scale raid upon Lisbon. It was to be financed by the Queen, a syndicate led by Drake and City investors. A large force was put together of 85 warships, including seven of the royal navy, and 11,000 soldiers. The expedition reached Corunna, but quickly found its resources for the much larger target of Lisbon to be inadequate. Drake and Norreys therefore agreed to sail instead to the Azores, where they might stand a good chance of recouping their losses by taking Spanish vessels returning from the Americas. The Azores proved an irresistible attraction to English commanders and investors. In 1597 the Earl of Essex was commissioned to lead a large portion of England's mobilised sea-power to attack Ferrol, where another Armada was assembling. The attraction of the Azores proved too strong for Essex. In the meantime, that Armada had left to make a landing at Falmouth, only to be dispersed by gales.[42]

When the Crown recognised the damaging dichotomy of interest that existed between its objectives and those of the merchant investors and abandoned further grandiose expeditions, this particular form of English sea-power reached its apogee. Investors were freed to take their picking wherever they saw best, and with increasing numbers of French and Dutch privateers they infested the waters of the Caribbean, contributing to the bankruptcy of the Spanish Crown by 1596.

By the time Queen Elizabeth died in 1603, a tradition, a philosophy and an organisation for the exercise of sea-power had become well established. Many of the beliefs and values underlying later political debate and decisions regarding the use of the navy had already been expressed. Naval forces had proved an effective weapon in defence and attack against a powerful state like Spain. English seamen were the equal of any in the world. Despite the limited sea-keeping capabilities of sixteenth-century ships, the belief that the defence of the realm could be entrusted to a naval force had been tested. The idea that blockade could be effective in the West Indies or in Europe had been expressed not just by Drake, but by the Earl of Essex and later by Sir Francis Bacon and Sir Walter Raleigh.[43]

In practice the exercise of sea-power was difficult and fragile, but the organisation of English naval resources had proved adequate for the crises it was called upon to surmount. The state did not possess much of the basic infrastructure for prolonged maritime activities, particularly in matters of financing and victualling. However, it mobilised adequate numbers of powerful ships, manned by experienced seamen, more effectively than any of its European neighbours. Major changes in the power structures of Europe and in maritime conditions during the early seventeenth century destroyed England's supremacy, but the bones of a central administration, which understood the nature of naval power, remained. The absence of sustained maritime crisis for 40 years and the existence of real maritime resources enabled this administration to make constructive modifications which led to the resurrection of English naval power in the 1630s.

2

1603–1642: Decline and Recovery

1603–1619: A Navy in Decline

With the death of Queen Elizabeth in March 1603, the new king, James I, ushered in a new dynasty and a new foreign policy. The fact that both dynasty and policy changed has had an impact upon historical judgements about the Royal Navy.

The war that Elizabeth had waged against Spain since 1585 had become bogged down. The Wars of Religion in France had come to an end in 1598 with Protestantism apparently secured within a Catholic state. France and Spain made peace in the same year. The Irish revolt, that had been a major drain on English resources since Hugh O'Neill revived Irish resistance in 1594, came to an end in 1603 but left the long-term drain of garrison costs. Philip II of Spain, who had personified the Catholic claim to the English throne, died in 1598. The war of the Dutch rebels against Spain, that England had been supporting since the 1580s, appeared stalemated. The financial strain of these conflicts left the English Crown indebted and uncertain of its ability to continue a significant conflict in future years. For James, there was little to be gained by continuing the war. Apart from the lack of obvious advantage, James saw himself much more as a mediator than a chivalric prince and was personally predisposed towards peace.[1]

During the Queen's final years the efforts of her navy, both directly owned by the Crown and hired, had not made a decisive impact upon Spain. However, the opportunities open to private adventurers to profit from the plundering of the Queen's enemies were highly destructive to Spain's American trade, and had a major effect upon the English maritime community. The system stimulated a great demand for relatively large, well-armed and heavily manned private men-of-war. These vessels were ideal traders in the dangerous waters of the Mediterranean, and excellent privateers to prey upon Spanish trade to and from the Americas. Although the Spanish defences had become more organised since Drake's raids of the 1570s, major Spanish ports in the West Indies, such as Campeche, Santa Marta, Porto Rico, Tabasco, Porto Bello and Porto de Caballos, were sacked by English raiders between 1597 and 1603.[2]

James was determined to end the war, and sea-power, exercised by private raiders, was exploited by his chief minister, Sir Robert Cecil, later first Earl of Salisbury, to bring a bankrupt Spain to peace.[3] This peace was signed in August 1604, and although the threat of an intensified campaign in the Caribbean was probably not a decisive factor in Spanish considerations – indeed the peace left English pretensions to trade in the West Indies highly ambiguous – there was a strong belief in English minds, informed by articulate City and merchant interests who had links with prominent courtiers, that sea-power had been effective in bringing Spain to a satisfactory treaty.

With the advent of peace, this fairly effective private sea force naturally ceased to exist, as shipowners sought different employment for their vessels. It was not to be conveniently or quickly recalled to support the Crown's foreign policy objectives. When James's son, Charles, tried to exercise a more bellicose policy against Spain and France between 1625 and 1629, the merchant community were mobilised only with great difficulty and responded to their duties in conjunction with the Crown's ships with extreme reluctance and ill-will.

Partly, this was the result of a long peace which lasted almost until James's death in 1625, during which the understanding between the Crown's navy and the merchant shipping community withered. However, it was not just the relationship with private shipping that seems to have suffered in the peace. Contemporaries noted a marked decline in the quality of the royal vessels. Commissions of enquiry, in

1608 and 1618, exposed the Crown's vessels as being poorly constructed and maintained. The stores were found to be of poor quality and much decayed. Corruption in the administration of the navy seemed rife. Fraud and theft were seen as endemic, whilst the sale of offices seemed to have undermined the ability of the administration to provide any remedy.[4] Contemporaries noted a decline in the status and condition of seamen, and a deterioration in the quality of ships' officers, from which they deduced a decline in the general capability of English seafarers.[5] English trade seemed insecure even in English waters, with Barbary corsairs, Dunkirk and even English pirates, cruising unchecked about the coasts.

The period suffers greatly from a lack of scholarly interest and research. It has been described by historians as a 'definite regression' or the 'administrative nadir' of the navy.[6] Research by scholars such as Alan McGowan, and more recently by Michael Young, Linda Peck and David Hebb, has greatly improved our understanding of the early Stuart navy, but it is still difficult to provide a sound answer to the vitally important question of why this apparent decline occurred so soon after the flowering of English sea-power under Queen Elizabeth. In part the decline is relative. The number of royal ships remained almost unchanged, but the naval power of Spain, France and the United Provinces increased as shown in J. Glete's figures for 1605–40. Lists of Spanish and Dutch vessels are unreliable, but their naval strength was growing as they fought each other for control of the vital North Sea area.

	N° of ships	Average displacement (tons)	N° of French ships
1605	30	766	–
1610	30	800	–
1615	29	793	–
1620	29	827	3
1625	34	911	17
1630	38	815	57
1635	41	878	50
1640	43	883	53

Source: Glete, J., *Navies and Nations*, I, 130.

There was also an absolute decline in the quality of the navy and its administration. For some historians this was just a manifestation of the congenital incompetence of the Stuart dynasty. Others have placed these maritime failures in the context of the broader political or policy failure of James himself. His inability to come to terms with Parliament over the issue of political authority in the realm and his profligacy broke his financial resources. His willingness to turn a blind eye to the corruption of officials, exposed by commissions of inquiry, undermined attempts to reform the navy. His concentration of scarce resources upon large warships, unsuited to combat the fast, small pirate craft in the Channel and North Sea, wasted effort and left the trade of the nation in jeopardy.[7]

There is much truth in this. Whatever James may have inherited in terms of a large Crown debt and pent-up political frustration on behalf of the nobility and gentry, his own actions increased that debt and intensified the political rift between himself and the political nation. However, to conclude that England's naval decline was largely, if not completely, attributable to James, is pushing the point too far. Much of the evidence related to this matter is derived from the State Papers and the two commissions of inquiry into the navy of 1608 and 1618. These sources tend to relate problems rather than accurately describe causes. Blame was laid upon policy and people which were thought to be in the power of the Crown to change, rather than on any wider issues. This is unfortunate, because the period of the early decades of the seventeenth century probably marks one of the most significant and intensive phases of change in English maritime and naval history.

Perhaps the most significant change was that occurring in English overseas trade. Although the 1610s were generally years of depression and falling wages in the merchant marine, following the end of the war with Spain the period between 1580 and 1630 as a whole saw a steady expansion of English shipping. Two national surveys of shipping, in 1582 and 1629, indicate that the total tonnage rose by about 70 per cent during these years. Both in size and numbers English ships were steadily growing. Although East Anglia retained its position of having the largest volume of shipping, there was a noticeable increase in the concentration of large ships in the Thames.[8]

Part of the growth in shipping was in response to the improved prospects for short-haul cargoes as the Dutch carrying trade was disrupted from the 1570s by war with Spain. English trade to the Baltic in flax, tar, hemp, corn, iron and timber doubled between 1580 and 1640. The growth of London expanded the demand for coal from the north of England. The long-haul trades also grew rapidly. English trade into the Mediterranean in fish and draperies grew steadily in the vacuum left by the decline of the Dutch and, in the 1620s, by the collapse of the Spanish and Italian cloth industries. In 1600 the East India Company was established which rapidly opened an important trade to Asia. America and the Caribbean also offered opportunities to trade. Virginia and the Chesapeake were precariously settled between 1609 and 1624. Bermuda was occupied in 1609, Barbados in 1624–5, Nevis, Antigua and Montserrat between 1627 and 1632.

Although the great expansion of these oceanic trades lay in the future, the significance of these developments for the navy lay in the fact that the type of vessels best suited to these trades, large, well-armed ships, were also the vessels upon which the navy had relied for its expansion in times of crisis. Although the navy still needed these ships, it was less clear that the merchants still needed the navy. Trade provided a better and more secure return on investment than privateering. By the end of the 1590s privateering, which had interested merchants and courtiers alike since the 1570s, was looking less attractive. The Spanish defences were reorganised and French and Dutch adventurers demonstrated the demand there was in Spanish America for European goods.[9] With employment prospects for their large vessels looking sound, few merchants looked forward to privateering, still less did they relish poorly paid and dangerous employment as auxiliary warships in the Crown's navy.

The second important feature of the opening decades of the century was the ambiguous legacy of the war for the evolution of the warship itself. Since the 1570s the merits of low race-built ships, which were relatively manoeuvrable but vulnerable to boarding, had been argued against the less seaworthy but high-sided Great Ship. The war in the last quarter of the sixteenth century had not resolved the debate. Operations at sea, even the fate of the Armada, had not clearly pointed to the superiority of one design over the other. Nor had a clear tactical deployment based upon the advantages in naval gunnery or ship manoeuvrability evolved. The Armada had shown that controlling a heterogeneous force of ships in narrow waters was fraught with danger, but the success of the galleons of the escort for the Indies convoys also showed that the high-sided men-of-war remained a formidable force at sea.[10]

It is hardly surprising therefore, that in England there was little clarity in the ship-building policy for a future conflict. Although England seemed threatened by growing French, Dutch and resurgent Spanish power, the end of the war in 1604 had actually removed the pressure to resolve the ambiguity in the evolution of the navy. It was only when active naval operations were again planned, in 1625, that the weakness of the Crown's decisions became apparent.

In the absence of the pressure of active service, the evolution of the navy depended on other factors. The most important of these were the King and his advisers on naval matters. The nominal administrative head of the navy since 1557 had been the Lord Treasurer. Mary and Elizabeth had the good fortune of possessing two Lord Treasurers, the Marquis of Winchester (1550–72) and Lord Burghley (1572–99), whose administrative abilities and interest in naval affairs ensured a good relationship between the naval administrators and the court.[11] Their successors, Lord Buckhurst (the Earl of Dorset from 1604) (1599–1608), the Earl of Salisbury (1608–12) and the Earl of Northampton (1612–13), seemed less interested. In part they took their cue from the King, in part the ending of the war and the financial crisis changed their priorities, and in part, the longevity of Lord Howard of Effingham, Earl of Nottingham, who held the senior sea-going appointment as Lord Admiral from 1585 until 1619, provided a point of stability and expertise upon which to rely. Nottingham's advancing age – he was over 80 when he gave up his post – and his lack of interest in administration meant that his supervision of the navy was minimal.

James himself had little interest in his ships. Until the last years of his life, his foreign policy did not demand a strong fleet. Until the final year of his life he achieved his primary objective – to avoid war. Some contemporaries bemoaned the decline of England's reputation at sea since the death of Elizabeth, but James and his advisers could afford to view his navy with some detachment. Between 1604 and 1621

England was not immediately threatened by invasion. Her trade was growing. Barbary corsairs caused losses around the coast of Britain, but it was only in the 1620s that the intensity of privateering increased so as to put England's claim to sovereignty of the seas in doubt. Nor was it a clearly held axiom that the Crown had a duty to defend merchant vessels. In 1619 it was decided to try to solve the Barbary piracy problem by raising a naval force to attack Algiers. The financing of these ships was to come from the seaports of England and the London merchant companies. The force spent some months in the Mediterranean and longer in the Channel, but when the money from these sources dried up in 1622 the ships were laid up. Enthusiasts such as Sir Francis Bacon and Sir Walter Raleigh might see the state's interest in protecting the commerce of the realm, but it was by no means a universal view. Sir William Monson, a man with long experience in the service of the Crown at sea, was well aware that in some people's minds there was a clear distinction between the interest of the subject and the interest of the monarch in the maintenance of a navy. His proposition to Parliament, probably written in the 1630s, to provide financial support for the King's navy, acknowledged the monarch's right to direct the navy, making no reference to the protection of the subjects' commerce, but justifying funding by Parliament on the grounds of a common security.[12]

Nevertheless, the idea that England had a claim to sovereignty in the seas around the British Isles was a view that gathered strength during the first half of the seventeenth century as the importance of the sea became more clearly absorbed into both the political and economic culture of English society. By the 1650s, the concept formed a clear part of an ideological as well as commercial hostility to the Dutch.

James possessed the traditional royal attitude to his fleet. He concentrated what resources he had on the construction and rebuilding of the large ships; well-armed almost impregnable vessels, ideal for defending the realm against enemy men-of-war and for diplomatic display. In 1610, the building of the *Prince Royal* of about 1000 tons, carrying 55 cannon on three decks, represented the high point of that policy. Of the 30 ships built or rebuilt during James's reign, 12 were over 600 tons, whilst a further 9 were classified as 'Middling', between 450 and 600 tons.[13]

With operational demands and James's own ambitions for his navy limited, the priorities of domestic politics and the administrative system impinged more closely upon the development of the Crown's fleet. The first of these was financial. Elizabeth had left a debt of about £428,000 and only £60,663 in her coffers. The greatest part of the subsidies voted by Parliament in 1601 remained to be collected, but whilst the war continued, this money would be required for funding current expenditure.[14] James also brought his own priorities for state finances, principally in expanding the household expenditure. He was a new monarch in a kingdom which expected him to be generous and he spent heavily on items of the royal account on which the elderly Elizabeth had been very frugal. Historians still debate the wisdom of James's decision, but the result of it is indisputable. Substantial economies had to be found in other items of royal expenditure. The need for economies became even more pressing as the years progressed. Despite action to increase revenues and reduce costs the debt continued to mount, standing at £597,000 when Lord Salisbury became Lord Treasurer in May 1608. From 1610 James and his Westminster parliaments failed to agree on future subsidies, which signalled even greater need for financial stringency. From this point until his death in 1625 James's financial position was extremely precarious. In 1621 the debt stood at about £900,000. From 1610 commissions of enquiry, 'projects' and expedients were sought to resolve the financial crisis, and the navy, the second biggest single item on the Crown's account, could not escape unscathed.[15]

The peace had enabled annual expenditure on the navy to be pushed down from about £70,000 in the 1590s to £30,000 in 1606, but the need for retrenchment went further. The commissions of enquiry into the navy of 1608 and 1618 were part of a much larger administrative effort based upon royal commissions to secure savings in Crown expenditure.[16] The effectiveness of these commissions is questionable, in terms both of their procedures and of the principles upon which they operated, but many shortcomings in the administration of the navy were uncovered. The declining fortunes of the navy in this period were not just owing to a government demanding draconian cuts in funding. The decline in the quality of naval administrators was remarked upon by Oppenheim, and Paul Kennedy has observed that a Hawkins might have spent that money much more effectively than his successors.[17] There was, undoubtedly, an administrative dimension to the problem as well. Money might be short, but one can still ask, was it well spent?

Although one must be cautious in that much of the evidence was generated by commissions of enquiry politically hostile to the incumbent administrators, it does seem that the money was not well spent. Responsibility for this must lie with James and the administrators he appointed, and here both were found wanting. In the absence of a reliable system for appointing public officials by open competition, patronage was the universal system. It could work efficiently and reasonably fairly, when patrons demanded and could measure effective performance from their clients. With the pressures of war Elizabeth and Burghley did both. James seems to have done neither. Untested by military crisis and hamstrung by increasing debt, which may have lowered expectations of activity, the naval administrators paid greater attention to the demands of the client network than to the provision of an effective navy. James has some defence in that the predominance of financial pressures over military demands made measuring effectiveness difficult, but James's unwillingness to take action when those officials were shown to be wanting by the commissions of enquiry is far less defensible.

In 1604 Sir Robert Mansell was appointed Treasurer of the Navy, by the favour of the King and the Lord Admiral Nottingham. Mansell was an experienced seaman, and might have been expected to bring a seaman's knowledge to the administration of the navy, but he did not. In partnership with the Surveyor, Sir John Trevor, he created a clientage system in the administration, perpetrated fraud and was generally negligent of the responsibilities of the posts. In 1608, political enemies of the Lord Admiral, led by Lord Howard, managed to have a commission of enquiry appointed to look into the operation of naval administration. The report laid before the King in June 1609 was a catalogue of inadequacy and fraud. However, James stood by Mansell and the latter's assistants. In 1611 Mansell effectively prevented a further commission of enquiry, although not before landing himself in the Marshalsea Prison for a time for querying the royal prerogative. It was only after Mansell's resignation from the Treasuryship in 1618 that major changes in the administration of the navy occurred.[18]

Finally, the political situation at court cannot be ignored. The navy was the most expensive organ of the state. It was a political prize of considerable value. The commissions of enquiry, which had important financial objectives, were also weapons in the political struggles at the Stuart court. The commission into the navy of 1608 was moved by the Earl of Northampton, the Lord Privy Seal, as part of his campaign against his cousin Nottingham. The commission of 1618 became a vehicle for the ambitions of the Marquis of Buckingham.[19] Buckingham had established himself in James's regard by 1616, and by 1618 had definite ambitions for political office. The office of Lord Admiral seemed open to him as his protégé, Lionel Cranfield, headed the commission of enquiry into abuses in the navy and uncovered a series of major failings. With his reputation under severe attack, Nottingham agreed to share his post with Buckingham. In January 1619 Nottingham finally conceded and Buckingham was appointed Lord Admiral. Buckingham seems to have been genuinely interested in reform and changes did, at last, begin to take place, but the political motivation, as opposed to the administrative or operational imperatives, must be kept in mind when viewing both the instigation and the outcomes of the change within the navy.[20]

In the years between 1603 and 1619 the effectiveness of the navy declined. It was a period in which, by any definition, it was badly managed. It was also a time when, in retrospect, some wrong-headed decisions were taken in regard to the investment of scarce funds in the navy. When war came again, England was deficient in the small ships necessary to combat the privateers and pirates that posed the main threat to English commerce. The reasons for this are unclear. Financial crisis, negligence and corruption were complicated and stimulated by a divergence of Crown and commercial maritime interests. They were extenuated by the lack of an immediate task for the navy, by technical change which gave no decisive direction, and by the growth of Dutch and Spanish naval forces in the North Sea, as both sides prepared for the end of the 9 years truce. In the first 15 years of James's reign the navy certainly lacked clarity of direction. A new and militant foreign policy provided the direction but exposed the weaknesses of the immediate past.

1619–1628: Buckingham as Lord Admiral

The changes in foreign policy and to the navy are closely associated with the growing influence of George Villiers, Marquis of Bucking-ham (Duke of Buckingham from 1623). Buckingham assumed the title of Lord Admiral in 1619, probably as a means of strengthening his influence with James. He was not particularly versed in naval or military matters, but his tenure of office was highly significant for the navy. First, he was strongly associated with men such as Lionel Cranfield and Sir John Coke, who were leading figures in the move-ment for financial and administrative reform. Second, he had a strong desire to play an active part on the larger European scene, in which the navy was required to play a prominent role.

On assuming the title of Lord Admiral Buckingham grasped the opportunity to reorganise the administration of the navy. The 1618 commission of enquiry had produced a damning report on the administration. The commission offered to take over from the Principal Officers – the Treasurer, the Surveyor, the Comptroller and the Clerk. The offer was accepted and the commissioners were given 5 years to complete their task of containing the naval budget whilst increasing the size of the fleet. Buckingham led the commission but it retained its principal reformers, Cranfield and Coke.

The tighter supervision and the clear objective of this commission to reduce expenditure brought a greater effectiveness to the naval administration. The commission claimed at the end of its 5 years of administration that it had increased the number of serviceable ships from 23 to 35, it had ordered the building of 10 new vessels and had built up a reserve of stores. During this period, the Crown probably acquired more ships and stores of higher quality than it had done under the previous system. Other decisions were taken which in the longer term added to operational effectiveness, such as the suppres-sion of the galleys and the building of vessels to a constant draught. However, these achievements must be looked upon with caution. The commission's claim of establishing financial control and greater oper-ational efficiency is not supported by other evidence. In 1621 it was not able to fit out a fleet in response to the crisis over the Palatinate. By 1623 there were growing suspicions of corruption within the commission, admittedly fostered by those officers who had served under Nottingham and Mansell.[21]

Despite the enthusiasm with which the commission went to work, the basic function of English naval administration remained as it had been since Elizabeth's reign – to provide facilities for a number of large and small warships to defend the realm and to call upon merchant vessels either to supplement this defence or to undertake offensive operations. Like the commissions of enquiry, it was not the direct responsibility of Buckingham's commission to reorganise or reconsider this function, but simply to ensure that the traditional role of the administration was done more cheaply and efficiently. Nothing significant was done with regard to the crucial relationship between the navy and the merchant marine. In 1624 the bounty instituted by Henry VII, paid for the building of ships over 100 tons, was abolished, possibly in the belief that the changed nature of English overseas trade ensured the provision of adequate numbers of these vessels without the bounty. However, enough had been done by the commission to convince Charles I in 1625 of the need to extend its existence indefinitely. The financial difficulties of the Crown had called attention to the efficiency of the administration of the navy, and, almost co-incidentally, improved its organisational effectiveness, but this was still only a small, if significant, aspect of sea-power in the early seventeenth century. Therefore, despite these changes, the Crown's naval power remained extremely fragile.[22]

This fragility became painfully apparent between 1625 and 1627. The truce between Spain and the United Provinces of the Netherlands came to an end in 1621. James's initial policy had been to lean towards Spain but remain neutral. By the end of 1624, Buckingham and Charles, the Prince of Wales, had ambitious plans to enter the anti-Habsburg war. Their diplomatic, political and strategic skills, however, in no way matched this aim. When on 27 March 1625 James died, the restraint that Buckingham and Charles felt regarding a direct assault on Spain disappeared. Without allies or significant land forces, the navy was the means of this assault. In May 1625, the Privy Council agreed to a naval expedition to Spain. In organisation, assumptions and approach it differed very little from the large operations of Essex in the 1590s. The Crown would supply 14 warships, to be supported by 30 merchantmen and 40 colliers to transport 10,000 troops for an enterprise against Spain. The principal objective was to destroy Spanish shipping and if possible seize or destroy harbours, although, as was usual, considerable latitude was permitted the council of war to determine the objective closer to the scene of operations.[23]

Although it seems that the Crown anticipated few differences from the precedents of the last war with Spain, the passage of time had wrought significant changes. The close cooperation between the Crown's military leaders and the merchant seafaring community which had built up from the mid sixteenth century was just a memory by 1625. The navy had not required this exchange of expertise and authority in the decades of peace, so it was not surprising that the principal naval commanders appointed to the expedition were all soldiers. The only significant change was that the Crown undertook to supply all the ordnance stores for the expedition, rather than relying upon the merchants and counties to supply their own stores.

The expeditionary force assembled under Sir Edward Cecil (Viscount Wimbledon) during the summer of 1625 at Plymouth. The difficulties of mobilising such a large force in the West Country after so long a peace soon became apparent. The ships defending the Channel had to be reduced to a minimum, exposing merchantmen to the Flemish privateers based at Dunkirk. The merchant ships conscripted to fight alongside the royal vessel were slow to arrive and the crews sullen and mutinous. The victuals were poor and inadequate. The stores were rotten. The most effective means of remedying this miserable situation – ready cash – was simply not available. Parliament could not be induced to provide money. Charles was eventually forced to use the Queen's dowry to meet the mounting costs of the operation. However, money alone would not have solved every problem. The stores, victuals and the infrastructure to deliver them were all inadequate. Supply and resupply in the far west was not easy. The ordnance stores at the Tower of London were stripped to supply the expedition. This department was probably the most comprehensively organised since the days of Henry VIII, but even it had no mechanism for controlling the distribution and quality of stores at such a distance from London. The provision of victuals and naval stores, which had not developed beyond the creation of a central post of responsibility in London, was even less subject to control at a distance.

The expedition sailed on 8 October 1625, in company with about 20 Dutch vessels, which joined the expedition as a result of a treaty of alliance against Spain, signed in September. The council of war decided upon an assault on Cadiz, a secure harbour conveniently close to the mouth of the Guadalquivir, up and down which the rich Indies vessels made their way to and from Seville. After a bombardment and surrender of the Puntales fortifications, which defended the inner Bay of Cadiz, an English squadron got into the bay but was unable to proceed up it owing to sunken ships obstructing its path.

Wimbledon decided to reduce the town of Cadiz on the point of the isthmus at the seaward edge of the outer bay. The isthmus was largely devoid of water and the troops quenched their thirst with large quantities of wine. Wimbledon soon found his army unmanageable and after three days, on 27 October he withdrew, leaving some hundreds of stragglers to be captured or killed by the Spaniards. On 16 November Wimbledon ordered the fleet home. The ships, their crews weakened by disease, lacking water and food, straggled home to English and Irish ports.

This disaster has received substantial attention from contemporaries and historians. Much of it has focused upon Buckingham, both as the architect of the strategy and as Lord Admiral. Wimbledon blamed the inexperienced troops and a lack of ammunition. The naval commissioners were also suspected of providing inadequate vessels, stores and provisions. Wimbledon and his council of war have been blamed for a ponderous approach unsuited to the demands of speed and surprise in amphibious warfare. Their attitude has been unfavourably compared to the spirit of expeditionary forces of the 1580s and 1590s.[24]

While all these factors played a part, it is too facile to make comparisons between apparent success under Elizabeth and disaster under the Stuarts. The problems went beyond the incompetence or inexperience of individuals to the changes that had taken place in the navy's relations with the merchant marine since 1604. The Crown's administrative capabilities, its demands and expectations, had changed little since 1604 but the expectations of the merchants and seamen had altered. This was becoming apparent in the 1590s but peace prevented it from developing. Charles opened the campaign with an administrative system as weak as that of Elizabeth, but whereas the Queen could rely upon merchant auxiliaries which had learned how to cope and profit from their enforced cooperation with the Crown, Charles was faced with unwilling, resentful and increasingly desperate owners, masters and seamen.

English squadrons were still highly significant in the balance of naval power in the Channel and the North Sea. Small expeditions to the North African coast against Barbary corsairs had shown that it was possible for England to keep ships in distant waters, but the attack upon Spain in 1625 demonstrated that the English navy no longer had the capacity for operations of such size, speed and distance that it possessed in the last quarter of the sixteenth century. The structure of the English navy had changed. There were about as many royal warships in 1625 as in the 1590s. During the 1590s the Crown warships were smaller and carried fewer cannon, but the principal offensive strength of English naval power lay in merchant privateers seeking their own advantage as well as that of the state. In 1625 this offensive power was no longer available. There were voices in England calling for an attack upon Spain's American empire, but the redirection of private shipping towards privateering was not to be easily achieved, and was dependent upon the judgement of the merchants over a period of time. In the immediate term the Crown had little choice but to recreate a grand expedition like those which had achieved so little in the 1590s. Once again, an expedition failed to achieve its anticipated objectives.

As this breakdown was not the fault of any individual, so it was not in the capability of any individual to resurrect the relationship between merchant and royal fleets. A new means of rebuilding English sea-power had to be found. It was not long before the expansion of the state's own professional naval forces became the focus of naval policy.

The Cadiz expedition had opened a war with Spain which left England exposed to the possibility of invasion and the certainty of increased depredations by the Dunkirk privateers. Although Buckingham and Charles planned another expedition for 1626 they lacked troops, stores or money. Mutinies wracked the south coast ports as ships were prepared for sea. Even in London, Buckingham was threatened by sailors demanding their arrears in pay, and the

Treasurer of the Navy, Sir William Russell, had to have his house put under guard. Eventually a squadron under Lord Willoughby was assembled at Portsmouth and sent to cruise off the Spanish coast. It got no further than the Bay of Biscay, where a storm forced it to return to England.

1626 had been disastrous and Buckingham organised an enquiry into the state of the navy, which led the Privy Council to appoint a new commission, again headed by Buckingham. Meanwhile, Buckingham's political survival was increasingly dependent upon his success in preserving the Huguenot enclave around La Rochelle. Proceedings for Buckingham's impeachment were under way in Parliament and the navy was in turmoil after he had lent Louis XIII warships which had been used to attack the Huguenots. La Rochelle had to be saved and in 1627 Buckingham decided that he would lead an expedition himself. There was too little money to secure adequate victuals, stores and arms but Buckingham provided some funds from his own pocket and a cruise by Captain John Pennington with a small squadron off the French coast netted about 70 prizes. The proceeds provided adequate funds to enable the expedition to go ahead.[25]

The force of about 100 vessels, including only 10 royal warships, sailed in June 1627. The army landed on the Ile de Ré, off the French coast, apparently in the hope of establishing a secure permanent base from which to support the Huguenots at La Rochelle. Hopes of successfully besieging the citadel of St Martin gradually faded during the summer of 1627, as the French succeeded in evading the naval blockade of the island. Attrition by sickness within the English army and the delays in sending the promised resupply of victuals and troops caused Buckingham to attempt an escalade, which ended in complete failure. The retreat and re-embarkation occasioned further losses.

Another year of failure only hardened Parliament's opposition to Buckingham's strategy. The reinvigorated naval administration under Buckingham's new 'Council at Sea' did, marginally, improve the prospects of getting an effective fighting force to sea and maintaining it there. The bounty on vessels over 100 tons, abolished in 1624, was restored in 1626. Portsmouth, which had gone into relative decline in the early seventeenth century with the expansion at Chatham and the consolidation of Deptford as the Crown's principal yards, was given renewed attention. Plymouth had not been a successful assembly point for the fleet in 1625 and Portsmouth was, once again, assuming its role as a major anchorage, well positioned between the stores and yards of the Thames and operational areas to the west of France and Spain. Henry VII's dry dock had been filled up in 1623. A new dock was started to replace it. A new building programme, begun in 1627, created 10 'Lion's Whelps', small vessels of about 180 tons which, manoeuvrable and capable of being propelled by wind or oars, were to be used to combat the Barbary and Dunkirk raiders.[26]

These changes, stimulated by the impact of war, all helped but could not mitigate the fundamental effect of changes within the maritime community. The interests of the merchant marine and the Crown with regard to naval power had significantly diverged. The monopoly companies provided their own trade protection and did not welcome the employment of their vessels on formal campaigns in Atlantic waters. Entrepreneurs looking to America for opportunities thought in terms of private investment in trade or war rather than joint operations with the Crown. Operations against the coast of Spain or France offered limited prospects of compensation for lost opportunities and only very poor rates of pay offered by the Crown.

Buckingham planned a further relief operation to La Rochelle in 1628. Although it employed a greater proportion of royal warships it suffered from the same lack of money, victuals and stores as its predecessors. After putting down another mutiny by seamen, Buckingham was murdered in his lodgings at Portsmouth in August. The expedition then sailed under the Earl of Lindsey but was even less successful than the previous year's operation. Whilst the fleet lay off the coast in October 1628 La Rochelle finally surrendered to Louis.[27]

As Lord Admiral and director of Charles's strategy Buckingham had a major influence on both the domestic and the foreign policies that shaped the navy and its employment. Although Charles carried on the war, his advisers, particularly the new Lord Treasurer, Richard Weston, gave little support and in May 1629 the French war was brought to a close by the Treaty of Suza. The Treaty of Madrid concluded the war with Spain in November 1630. The Channel and the North Sea remained major theatres of the continuing war between Spain and the Dutch, but the English navy was given a small breathing space to take stock.

Buckingham's naval legacy is ambivalent. The commission set up under his direction in 1618 achieved a great deal in improving the material state of the navy by 1623. The 10 new ships built by its order were, on the whole, poorly designed and sailed badly, but nonetheless they were an important addition to the fleet. When this commission seemed to be exhausted, or to have succumbed to the prevailing administrative mores, Buckingham attempted to reinvigorate it by a new council at sea. He showed at least the sustained energy required to bring about significant change. His greatest success was actually to get a relatively powerful force to sea each year from 1624. Possibly his greatest mistake was to employ it in an offensive manner. Whilst it remained a threat, it was a force the Spaniards, Dutch and French had to take seriously. Its failures at Cadiz and La Rochelle exhausted it and exposed the underlying weakness. In 1625 Richelieu had stepped back from a confrontation with England over the Huguenots, fearing that his newly founded and tiny royal navy was no match for the English fleet. By 1627 he was sure that Charles had neither the money nor the material to hinder his plans to crush the Protestant stronghold in the west of France.[28]

Whatever his achievements, it is difficult to conclude other than that his strategy of involvement in a war with Spain did great damage to the navy by exacerbating the fundamental difficulty of mobilising and exercising naval power. The offensive strategy, based upon Elizabethan precedent, was beyond the power of the Crown in the early seventeenth century. The owners of private warships and transports could be compelled to provide vessels, but the success of the Tudor war against Spain had been based upon being able to persuade them that sailing with an expedition was a great opportunity. Buckingham could do the former, but not the latter. In the absence of this incentive only worthwhile payment by the Crown would suffice, but without parliamentary support Buckingham could not do this either.

The result was disaster. Ships were slow to arrive at rendezvous points, with a consequent delay to operations, consumption of victuals, wear and tear and a decline in the general health of the seamen. The crews were, very often, not paid. When on service during the two expeditions of 1625 and 1627 the seamen and the masters of the merchant vessels, in particular, performed badly.[29] In 1628 there was a strong suspicion that deliberate delays were being created to avoid putting to sea. On returning from service, the ships brought disease to the ports and no services were available for the sick and dying seamen. The combined impact of these failings fed a growing unrest among seamen and shipyard workers. There were mutinies at Portsmouth and Chatham in 1627 and at Portsmouth and Plymouth in 1628. There were demonstrations in London by seamen and shipwrights in 1627 and 1628. In 1629 Mervyn, the commander of the King's ships in the Channel, noted that 'Foul winter weather, naked bodies, and empty bellies make the men voice the King's service worse than a galley slavery'.[30]

The navy lacked the money and the administrative structure to resolve these problems. Expedients such as the threat of draconian punishments could not have a lasting impact upon seamen who were desperately pessimistic about life and limb in the service. The Ordnance Office, which had provided all the ordnance for the Cadiz expedition rather than relying upon the armaments of private warships, had found its resources exhausted by the effort. The apparatus for the provision of victuals and naval stores was nowhere near being centralised or organised. Attention was being turned towards these problems before Buckingham was assassinated, but little could be done until the immediate pressures of an offensive war had been removed.

The old idea that this was a period of English maritime decline has been dismissed by modern scholars. The seamen were as capable as and even more experienced than their predecessors. Their ships were technically better. It was, however, a period of absolute and relative decline in English sea-power. The administrative structure of the navy could not cope with the changes in the maritime community in England, or with a political crisis that deprived it of funds. Whilst Spain, France and Holland were building up their state warships, the English navy was trying, and generally failing, to face these domestic challenges and to come to terms with the tasks that Charles and Buckingham were setting it.

It is going too far to suggest that Buckingham's strategy was a key factor in the fall of the House of Stuart,[31] but his use of the navy did contribute to widening the gulf between the maritime community and the Stuart navy. Also the experiences of 1625 to 1628 added fuel to the political fire and played an important part in the desertion of the navy from the Stuart cause in 1642.

1628–1642: The English Navy and Ship Money

The peace that followed 1630 gave the Crown the opportunity to tackle the issues raised by the war. Unlike his father, Charles I was interested in his ships, and his views were going to be stamped upon policy. Other factors also contributed to a greater sense of direction than that which had existed at the conclusion of the last war with Spain in 1604. It was now much clearer that the Crown could not rely upon the merchant marine as a primary source of naval reinforcement in times of crisis. Theory and practice on the Continent also pointed to a greater need to centralise the resources for making war. The balance between the royal forces and those of the merchant marine had to be shifted significantly in favour of the former, but concentrating naval power in a larger number of royal vessels had several important implications.[32] Not only did such a shift entail major additional expenditure on construction and maintenance, but it also imposed significantly increased operational problems. A royal navy could never hope to be as numerous as a fleet of armed private merchantmen and whilst the main tactical demand was to close upon the enemy *en masse* to board, it was by no means self-evident that disciplined management of a relatively small number of royal ships would overcome numbers. The relative power of *mêlée* and line of battle under professional officers was only worked out by experience in action in the second half of the century.

Such a shift also threw into sharp relief the issues surrounding the officering of warships. There had always been tension between the gentlemen or nobles put aboard ships as representatives of the Crown to command in battle and the seamen officers who sailed and navigated their vessels. Neither was dispensable but the former lacked sea experience and the latter lacked the social status and code of ethics to command in war. The expansion of the Crown's fleet, whose sole *raison d'être* was to fight, intensified the tensions between the 'gentlemen' and the 'tarpaulins'.

This process of change was also hindered by the fact that other aspects of naval policy had not been clarified as a result of the war. The relative importance of concentrating resources upon the large man-of-war as opposed to the smaller warship capable of combating the privateers and pirates that infested British waters in the 1620s was not clear. Charles's preference, like that of his father, was for the stately warship. Enormous sums were expended between 1635 and 1637 on the first true English three-deck man-of-war, the *Sovereign of the Seas*, designed to carry between 90 and 100 guns. The large number of guns was indicative of an English ship habit of carrying a relatively great weight of ordnance for the size and burden of the vessel, compared to European practice.[33] During the 1630s this great ship never had the opportunity to prove its worth in action, thereby creating considerable debate about the policy which consumed so many valuable resources for an unproven principle, when smaller vessels were needed for the immediate defence of the coasts. The attempt to provide vessels for such a defence, in the Whelps, was a failure.

The juxtaposition of two possible policies, building large to reflect state power or building small to preserve the merchant marine upon which state sea-power is founded, simplifies the matter too much. The maritime situation in northern European waters was very uncertain. During the 1620s and 1630s shipwrights established firmer theoretical underpinnings for the construction of warships, in terms of length to breadth ratios and the weight of materials in construction or ordnance.[34] For all nations, the large man-of-war was the ship that promised the greatest security at sea. The French and Spanish royal navies were building increasing numbers of these warships. Louis XIII had 39 warships at his command along the Atlantic coast by 1636. In 1637 Philip IV's chief minister, Olivares, had plans to keep the English from interfering in the war with the Dutch by maintaining a vast fleet of 100 large vessels from Flanders to Cadiz. Likewise, the Dutch shipyards were turning out these vessels. Charles wanted to restore England's old claim to the sovereignty of the British seas and for this he judged a royal fleet of large men-of-war to be essential. Without vessels of equal power it would be impossible for England to challenge the actions of her maritime neighbours at sea.[35]

On the other hand, without small ships it was impossible to prevent the depredations of pirates, privateers, fishing fleets and smugglers.

Whilst Charles might plausibly have argued that it was not the duty of his navy to protect individual merchantmen, he could have some hopes that the deficiency of small ships might be made good by the merchant community, whose vessels were better suited to such operations and whose interests were so clearly served by them. In the event there was little merchant willingness to fill the gap. It is not surprising, therefore, that although the desire to shift the balance of the fleet towards a professional royal standing force was evident in naval policy by 1630, it was a slow and painful process.

The process of restoring English claims to sovereignty of the seas required money first and foremost. In 1629 Charles's failure to obtain funds on a satisfactory basis provoked him to decide to do without Parliament. In the absence of parliamentary subsidy the principal device to secure funds for the fleet was to be Ship Money. Ship Money has been described by one historian as 'the most notorious and important financial device of the Personal Rule'.[36] Andrew Thrush has recently demonstrated how, despite a number of precedents dating back to the 1590s, Ship Money was significantly different from any precedent, and constituted an arbitrary form of taxation in the way that earlier projects did not.[37]

Maritime counties had had the duty of providing ships for the defence of the realm since the Middle Ages. The coastal towns provided vessels and maintained them to cooperate with royal forces, but remained the property of the citizens. Elizabeth had considered extending the obligation to inland towns of maritime counties in 1596 and to inland counties in 1603, but popular reaction in the first case, and her death in the second, aborted the plan. However, the obligation to provide money rather than ships had its attractions to both Crown and subjects. In 1617, the City of London preferred to pay money rather than maintain its own vessel. From the Crown's point of view, such a move extended the possibility of obtaining resources from regions which could not supply ships. This was the case in 1626 when Scotland, which could not provide the ships demanded of her, provided money to purchase them instead. These ships would be owned by the Crown and remain a continued charge upon Scottish levy payers. The policy of paying for the maintenance of the royal vessels continued during the late 1620s, when Yarmouth and Kings Lynn victualled royal ships protecting the east coast trade.[38]

The principle of demanding money for the support of royal ships, rather than the temporary employment of private ships, was therefore reasonably established by the mid 1630s. The specific nature of the tax was important for the Crown and the naval administrators. They hoped that it would be more acceptable to the nation if it could be seen that the money was utilised for maritime purposes rather than for the further aggrandisement of the court. Charles seems to have recognised the importance of this public perception and he laid particular emphasis on combating pirates in his public declarations, although the large men-of-war he raised were singularly ill-designed to counter that menace. Administrators also hoped that by having the money paid into an account separate from the Exchequer, not only would they make the public believe that the funds were being used for naval purposes, but that this would actually be the case.[39]

In the short term the plan succeeded. The first Ship Money warrants were issued for 1634–5, and almost all of this levy was collected. Over the next three years, £200,000 was demanded and largely collected. It was, however, in 1637 that the legitimacy of Ship Money was first effectively challenged with the prosecution of John Hampden for refusal to pay. Hampden was an MP long associated with the Puritan opposition to Charles. He rested his case, not upon the legal right of the Crown to demand the money, but upon the Crown's justification for doing so. Hampden was convicted by a majority of seven to five among the judges, which was enough to cast doubt upon the legitimacy of the tax.[40] Allied to many other doubts about the behaviour of the King, the Ship Money levy was for the political nation an irritant against which action could be taken. The yield for 1638 fell to about two-thirds of its total. In 1639 less than a quarter was collected. In 1640 the tax was failing to carry out its prime function. Charles's war in Scotland against his Covenanting subjects took first call on all revenues. In 1641 the King tried to trade its abolition for a parliamentary subsidy and in May 1641 it was finally abolished by Parliament.[41]

As a long-term mechanism for financing a navy Ship Money failed. It failed because Charles's fiscal policy as a whole was falling apart by the late 1630s in the face of renewed warfare. During the years of peace since 1630 Charles's financial position had been steadily, if slowly, improving, to reach 'the acme of productivity of the Stuart fiscal system'.[42] Charles had found that in peacetime he could rule without parliamentary subsidy. Funds were provided for the navy that Charles envisaged and despite the declining yield of Ship Money other revenues ensured that by 1639 there were funds for a limited war. It was nonetheless a fragile situation, destroyed by the disastrous campaigns in Scotland in 1639 and 1640 which absorbed all Charles's available revenues and galvanised political resentment against his policies so that the fiscal system without Parliament crumbled. Ship Money, as part of that system, crumbled with it.

Although a failure as a long-term method of naval finance, what had Ship Money achieved? There is a strong case for considering that this fiscal device was a major contribution in the movement towards a permanent royal or state navy. Ships were refitted to give them greater firepower. Ten ships were added to the navy list by a building programme from 1634 to 1640.[43] Of equal importance was that every year from 1635 to 1641 a squadron of royal ships was assembled for cruising in the Channel. Hired merchant vessels remained an important part of these squadrons, but they were never as great a proportion of the force as they had been in 1627. Officers and seamen were at last getting concentrated experience of being at sea in warships.

The impact of these squadrons on foreign powers was important, but less than might have been hoped. In 1635 France had joined with the Dutch in their war against Spain. It was not in English interests that any of these powers should achieve an overwhelming victory resulting in control of the coastline from Holland to France being in the hands of one state. The navy was therefore very much a tool of diplomacy aimed at preserving the balance of power. It seems that the first Ship Money fleet, under the Earl of Lindsey, was influential in keeping the French from joining Dutch vessels in the North Sea.[44]

The weakness of Spanish naval power was becoming apparent by 1636. Although Dunkirk privateers caused increasing damage to the Dutch fishing and carrying trade in these years, the difficulties facing Spain in convoying reinforcements and money through to their armies in Flanders were growing. It required a concentration of ship-building effort on warships in the Iberian peninsula which, combined with French attacks on the Biscay ports, caused great damage to their merchant ship-building capacity. Spain looked outside the peninsula for naval support, and England was prepared to provide it. A naval treaty had been signed with England in August 1634, which promised assistance to Dunkirk should it be required.[45]

Although the Spaniards held their own at sea during 1637 and 1638, the French inflicted a major defeat upon them at Guetaria in August 1638 when 21 large vessels, 3000 seamen and some of the most experienced officers available to the Spanish navy were lost. To secure the vital sea route to the Low Countries, Philip IV gathered what naval forces the monarchy could muster in 1639 for an ambitious plan to destroy the French squadrons in the Bay of Biscay, reinforce the army in Flanders, destroy the Dutch fleet blockading the Flanders ports and raise a rebellion in Normandy. The plan relied upon England to provide transports for the troops and a handful of warships. The contracts with English merchants were negotiated and settled between February and March 1639.[46]

Command of the armada was given to the Duke of Oquendo. It sailed from Corunna on 5 September 1639, comprising about 100 ships with 2000 cannon, 6000 sailors, 8000 troops for the vessels and a further 8500 soldiers for Flanders. By 15 September the force was in the Channel and a running battle developed as the Dutch squadron under Tromp gradually fell back up the Channel. Oquendo recognised that if his fleet passed Calais there was no safe anchorage to disembark his forces, so he anchored in the Downs. With English support Oquendo was able to disembark the Flanders reinforcements and transfer them to Dunkirk vessels for night crossings of the Channel. However, it was much more doubtful if the English fleet, under Sir John Pennington, would risk itself in defence of English sovereignty and the Spaniards if the Dutch attacked. Pennington's squadron of about 19 vessels was reinforced during September and October to approximately 30 ships. The Dutch, on the other hand, had about 130 ships in the area. Oquendo's ships were short of money for repairs and their crews were falling sick. On 21 October the Dutch attacked and scattered the weakened Spanish fleet. Pennington kept his vessels clear after satisfying honour by demanding that the attacking force observe the neutrality of English waters.[47]

Thus, as the Scottish war broke the fiscal system that had enabled Charles to build up his fleet, so events in Europe destroyed the prospect of the navy being able to hold the balance of power at sea. Nonetheless, the navy continued in being, manned and prepared for sea during 1640 and 1641. It was not the power that Charles had hoped to make it, but it was maturing as an organised force of the state. Among its ships were some of the newest and most powerful warships in northern waters, maintained on a permanent footing, officered by men who increasingly saw themselves as fighting seamen in the service of the state. The latest research on the Caroline navy, by Andrew Thrush, has shown that on the whole the administration responded effectively to the demands placed upon it and that the corruption of the administrators was not as pervasive as the complaints in the state papers or the insights into the navy given by the seaman, Sir William Monson, or the Commonwealth naval administrator, John Hollond, seem to suggest. Although officials exploited opportunities to enrich themselves, they were on occasion forced to dip into their own pockets to ensure the navy was able to pursue operations at sea.[48]

That the navy as a whole improved during Charles's reign seems unquestionable, but it remained an extremely fragile force and it lacked financial and organisational strength. During the first half of the seventeenth century, and particularly after 1634, the navy was becoming a standing state-owned force. That this was militarily justifiable was demonstrated during the wars of the 1620s, but the consequence was that the Crown was required to finance and control more and larger vessels.

Historians have quite reasonably concentrated their attentions upon the problem of finance, given the importance of Ship Money both to the navy and as a factor in the breach between King and Parliament. Less attention has been paid to the problem of controlling this expanding navy. The pressure of war and the work of the Commissioners in the 1620s seem to have reduced the scale of fraud and inefficiency. Yet this improvement was more apparent than real. The period of peace and relatively good funding after 1630 meant that administrative control was never severely tested. This hid the fact that in essence the administration of the navy had not changed since the failures of the period 1625 to 1630. The fundamental problem was that the navy had long outgrown contemporary means of controlling the activities of its servants or employees. The mechanisms available to large-scale enterprise in the early modern world – contract, close supervision or an emerging professional ethic – did not evolve evenly or quickly. The debate over the relative advantages of each is clear in John Hollond's *Two Discourses of the Navy*, written in 1638 and 1659, and they remained issues for naval administrators over 100 years later.[49]

While the English navy was a force balanced between a core of royal warships and a pool of private warships that could be taken up or dismissed at short notice, the problem of control was not serious. However, as the permanent standing force became more important the Crown's servants had to manage the long-term supply of diverse crafts, skills and materials. They were burdened by financial constraint, action at short notice, and rapid expansion or contraction. Seamen have always cursed the administrators, but during the seventeenth and eighteenth centuries the latter were facing problems of management unknown in any other field of work. In the 1630s peace and adequate financing reduced the tension. By 1640 neither of these conditions applied any longer, but when the Civil War broke out in 1642 it was Parliament and not the Crown that was to face and resolve, as best it could, these problems.

3

1642–1660: CIVIL WAR, THE REPUBLIC AND A STANDING NAVY

1642–1648: The Navy in the Civil War

One of the many surprising features of the English Civil War is the speed with which the navy allied itself with Parliament. There had been humiliations and disappointments, such as the Battle of the Downs, but there was no obvious cause for disloyalty. The peace after 1630 had allowed Charles to establish a respectable navy. It was capable of a partially effective blockade of Scotland in 1639 and 1640. Squadrons cruised against pirates in the Channel, and supported operations against the Irish rebellion which broke out in November 1641. These operations had stretched Charles's navy to the utmost, but they had not resulted in the disastrous loss of life and misery experienced during the more ambitious expeditions of the 1620s.

In November 1640 Charles recalled Parliament in an attempt to raise money for the Scottish war. The needs of the navy had to be addressed if a fleet was to put to sea in 1641. Parliament set to work enthusiastically. A parliamentary committee prepared a bill for the manning of the fleet, or summer guard, for 1641. A joint committee of Commons and Lords met to consider the state of the kingdom's defences. A special Navy Committee was appointed to assist the Lord High Admiral, the Earl of Northumberland, to manage the revenues voted from Tonnage and Poundage and the naval expenditures.[1]

Northumberland had been Lord High Admiral since March 1638.

After Buckingham was assassinated in 1628 the powers of the Lord High Admiral had been in commission, headed by the Lord Treasurers, Portland and then Juxon. The success of Ship Money and the appointment of Northumberland might have been expected to change the emphasis of naval policy from economy to effective activity, and to an extent this was the case. However, in the longer term, Northumberland, like Ship Money, disappointed the King.

Northumberland was an experienced seaman, who had commanded the fleet at sea in 1636 and 1637. As Lord High Admiral Northumberland's closest professional relationships were with those officers connected to City merchant interests and Trinity House. These officers were like the seamen of the sixteenth century who would have served in either merchant or fighting ships when the distinction between the two was not clear. During the 1630s they were following a traditional career pattern, working their way towards commands. Perhaps the most senior of these officers in 1640 was William Rainsborough, who was appointed to command a small expedition against the Barbary Corsairs at Sallee in 1637. This expedition was one of the occasions which demonstrated the growing social conflict between this group of officers and an increasing number of gentlemen, who entered royal service directly under the patronage of the King. All except one of Rainsborough's captains, George Carteret, were seamen from the Wapping community. So stark was Carteret's isolation in this company that he maintained a secret correspondence with Sir John Pennington, a fellow gentleman seaman.[2] As the veterans of Elizabeth's navy, such as Sir Robert Mansell, Sir William Monson and Sir Richard Hawkins, passed out of service during James's reign they were being replaced by a body of officers who were more socially divided than their predecessors. The Ship Money fleets were organised to represent much more explicitly than before the King's sovereignty at sea. Command was placed more firmly in the hands of those socially capable of representing the King's dignity – the gentlemen seamen. With the return of Parliament, the growing strength of the gentlemen seamen was aborted. Parliament quickly showed an interest in the appointment of officers. In November 1641 Robert Slyngsbie, a gentlemen seaman with distant connections to the Earl of Strafford, was rejected by Parliament as a captain on the Irish guard.

In January 1642, after his abortive attempt to arrest five members of Parliament, Charles left London to set up court in York. Northumberland remained as Lord High Admiral, and the administration of the navy, under the four Principal Officers, continued in London. In March the summer guard of 18 royal and 24 merchant ships had to be organised. Charles wanted the veteran gentleman officer, Sir John Pennington, as commander and nominated the captains for the royal ships. Parliament rejected Pennington and three of the officers since it wanted a staunch Puritan and colleague of Northumberland's, the Earl of Warwick, as Admiral, but did accept another gentleman officer, George Carteret, as Vice-Admiral. Charles was so affronted at the rejections that he refused to allow Carteret to serve.[3]

Northumberland, who had acquiesced to Parliament's demands, recognised the growing rift between the King and Parliament, and declared himself too ill to serve further. Under pressure from Parliament he nominated Warwick to act in his stead, with another Trinity House officer, William Batten, to be his Vice-Admiral. The eighteen captains of the royal ships were divided evenly between seamen and gentlemen officers. The nine who can be described, broadly, as being gentlemen captains, gained their experience of command in the Ship Money fleets, whilst at least eight of the other nine were seamen who had experience in merchant and royal vessels. Of this latter group, five were experiencing their first command of royal vessels in 1642.[4]

In April Charles failed in his attempt to take Hull, but secured Newcastle as a port. In June, ships under Warwick's orders were cruising the North Sea in search of vessels carrying arms or munitions to the King. The *Providence*, bringing arms from Holland, was chased into the Humber and captured, although not before the arms had been secured by the Royalists.[5] Parliament's use of the navy compelled Charles to react. He revoked Northumberland's patent as Lord High Admiral, thereby nullifying Warwick's authority, and ordered Sir John Pennington, who was with the King at York, to go to the fleet anchorage at the Downs. Pennington was to bring the fleet north to Bridlington Bay. The plan failed when, on 2 July, Warwick returned to the fleet before Pennington arrived, and heard of his dismissal by the King's messenger who had preceded Pennington. Warwick called a council of captains which endorsed his command. Five captains, all gentlemen, refused to attend Warwick's council. One, Burgley, then surrendered, but the other four stood out from the main body of the fleet. Once Warwick received confirmation of his authority from Parliament, he summoned the recalcitrants to surrender. Two did so, whilst the last two vessels were taken over by their crews.[6]

This might have been a simple case of indecision and inaction losing the day, as the royalist historian Clarendon believed. Perhaps a more vigorous officer than Pennington might have secured the fleet for the King, but what is clear is that by 1642 the fleet, like the political nation, was divided. There had been no sudden revolution in the fleet. Professional tension had been rising during the late 1630s and the close relationship between the seamen officers, Trinity House, the Thames maritime community, the City merchants and Parliament gave that resentment a political focus.

The common seamen's role in the defection of the fleet to Parliament is critical, but their attitudes are, unfortunately, very difficult to determine. In 1948 the eminent naval historian Michael Lewis confidently asserted that the seamen were 'quite innocent of what we should now call ideological views'. As the methodology employed in discovering history 'from the bottom' has become more sophisticated, historians are now less sure of this. The opinions of artisans and the poor have become the focus of intense debate. However, in the case of seamen and the maritime community generally, this re-examination is still very much in its early stages and has concentrated upon later periods. Some important pioneering work has been done, but the historian of the Civil War is still left with impressions largely drawn from official records, in which seamen appear as supplicants, victims or villains.[7]

With this caveat in mind, it seems that the common seamen largely shared the loyalties of the seamen officers, and responded to bonds of leadership based upon a common heritage in the maritime community of merchants, shopkeepers, artisans, shipowners, masters and sailors. In January 1642 seamen demonstrated in London in support of the Five Members. Behind this action and their behaviour at the Downs, may also have lain years of resentment against the Crown's navy, resulting from delayed pay, poor victuals and clothes. Whatever its cause there was strong support among the seamen for Parliament. Once Parliament had secured the main body of the fleet and the support of the seamen, the navy remained solidly behind parliamentary leadership throughout the Civil War, and its allegiance only changed as the officer corps gradually evolved a divergent political view.

As well as the ships, Parliament also secured the administrative structure that kept the ships at sea. The Principal Officers who managed the navy's administration were officers of the Crown, and on 7 July 1642 Charles ordered them not to obey any instruction that came from Warwick. Parliament ordered them to obey Warwick, and after some weeks of standoff Parliament used a request from Warwick to supply cables to the fleet to issue an order from both Houses for the Principal Officers. They decided to obey, removing the last major means of control exercised by the King over the state's navy. Two weeks after this event an ordinance was passed, dismissing the Principal Officers and replacing them by a Commission of twelve, which was to remain unchanged as the effective administrative support for the navy until 1660. The last vestiges of royal control over the navy disappeared when the officers of dockyards agreed to obey the instructions of the commission.[8]

Throughout the Civil War the administration and command of the navy remained very stable. On land the crises of the war demanded military reorganisation, and eventually the creation of the New Model Army. At sea, Parliament's general security was so sound that little change was demanded. Financial matters were handled by the Navy Committee of Parliament, which lasted until the Long Parliament was dissolved in 1653. The direction of the fleet continued to lie in the hands of the Lord High Admiral, or a commission exercising his powers. In 1642 Parliament placed the powers in the hands of a joint commission of Lords and Commons, but at the end of 1643 Warwick was reinstated as Lord High Admiral, until he was compelled to resign his post under the Self-Denying Ordinance in 1645. The powers of Admiralty remained in commission until 1648, when Warwick resumed the post to deal with the mutiny in the Downs. In 1649 the powers were taken over by the Council of State as part of the function of this executive organ of the new republic. In the meantime, the day-to-day administration of the navy continued in the hands of the navy commissioners until 1660 and, in essence, even thereafter.[9]

On the whole, therefore, this was hardly a naval revolution, except at the very highest level of the state, where Parliament and then the

Council of State replaced the monarch. The relationship between the officers and men of the fleet remained unchanged. The mechanics of controlling the fleet, through the Lord High Admiral or Commission and the navy commissioners, were well established by precedent. Different men were holding the important posts, be they officers on warships or MPs on commissions, but the organisation of the navy remained largely intact. However, this continuity may hide a more significant change brought about by Parliament's control of the fleet. Although Parliament was dominated by landed gentlemen, the representation of the merchant community expanded, and with it its influence on the state. Their attitudes, assumptions and ambitions may have differed little from the country gentry, but their interest and experience in maritime affairs were put at the disposal of the fleet. When the office of Lord High Admiral was put into commission in October 1642 the commissioners were strongly linked with merchant or colonising activity. In December 1642 three more merchants were added to the committee. A similar increased representation of men experienced in overseas trade can be traced in Parliament's Navy Committee and the Committee of Merchants for Regulating the Navy and Customs in 1649.[10]

The contribution of the navy to Parliament's victory by 1648 is yet another area of controversy. The King's cause was undoubtedly lost in battle on land, and it is commonly accepted among naval historians that the navy 'held the ring', in as much as they insulated the war from large-scale foreign intervention.[11] Whether this was critical, as is believed by some, is much more open to question. How far the navy tilted the military balance in favour of Parliament is difficult to establish. Dutch and French assistance to Charles was forthcoming in limited quantities, and it is impossible to be certain how much more would have been provided in the absence of the parliamentary fleet, given the commitments of these states to a war against the Spaniards in Flanders.

However, in one respect the navy was crucial. Both King and Parliament, but particularly the latter, depended upon customs revenues and mercantile credit for ready cash. In the long term, financing the war depended upon the efficient exploitation of landed wealth. However, gathering these tax receipts was a laborious and long process, and in the meantime the day-to-day transactions of both sides depended on credit and other sources of ready cash. In London the credit was made available by merchants, but the credit of these men depended in turn on the profitability of their trade investments. Warwick recognised that the protection of trade, which underwrote both customs receipts and commercial credit, must be one of his principal objectives.[12]

Both sides were initially cautious in their treatment of English and neutral merchant vessels. Only gradually did they extend and strengthen their orders regarding contraband and privateering. However, as the campaign against commerce grew, it was Parliament that reaped the balance of advantage. Despite the growth of royalist privateers and smugglers, the navy kept open the Thames, helped to capture or preserve major ports such as Hull, Portsmouth, Plymouth and with them an important source of revenue. The importance of trade to the parliamentary cause was such that its protection by convoy and cruising became a principal function of the fleet for the first time in its history.[13]

Beyond this strategic role, the navy played a tactical role in the war.[14] Almost the first function Parliament's navy was required to carry out was to secure ports under attack by royalist forces. In April 1642 the important magazine at Hull was relieved by ships. In August Portsmouth was retaken from the Royalists by a landing at Southsea, after its governor had defected to the King. Plymouth was relieved from the sea in 1642 and 1643 and the Isle of Wight was secured. The navy was also used to blockade the enemy. Newcastle, the King's principal port in the north, was under the eyes of parliamentary sea captains from the middle of 1642. Parliament's vessels patrolled the Bristol Channel, providing succour for their supporters in Wales and preventing reinforcements for the King coming from Ireland.

All these activities stretched the navy to capacity in the first full year of the war and, as if to demonstrate that the royalist cause was not dependent upon foreign assistance, 1643 proved to be a bad year for Parliament's armies. Sir Ralph Hopton's forces in the West Country cleared Cornwall, Devon and Somerset for the King. Although Plymouth held on, Exeter, whose approaches from the sea lay under guns ranged along the banks of the river Exe, could not be relieved. Worse was to follow. Bristol, the major port in the West Country, fell to a royalist assault on 26 July 1643. In practice all the shipping plying trade from that port suddenly became royalist. During the summer the Royalists took the war into South Wales, threatening the ports from which the parliamentary navy's operations in the Bristol Channel were based. Dartmouth, another major harbour, fell late in the year.

In the north, the Duke of Newcastle's royalist forces drove the parliamentary forces from Durham and much of Yorkshire, threatening Hull. In October the first elements of the Duke of Ormonde's army from Ireland began arriving at Minehead. The year ended with much more of the nation's shipping in royalist hands, expanding the numbers of privateers and revenues available to the King. The task of Parliament's navy was now much harder. With less of the nation's shipping to call upon, and particularly having lost Devon, the home of its best deep sea mariners, it had to protect the fragile parliamentary position in the west. The peace in Ireland had released a number of Irish privateers to prey upon vessels from parliamentary-controlled ports. In the east small royalist privateers operating from Holland, Flanders and France threatened the south coast and East Anglian trades and fisheries.

The change in fortunes in the war in 1644 owed little to the navy directly, although it was present in providing tactical support in convoys and transports. The Covenanter invasion of the north in January 1644 threw the Royalists on the defensive. The navy was active off the north-east coast all summer as the campaign unfurled. Seven parliamentary ships lay off Newcastle as the Scots began their long siege of the town, which lasted until it surrendered in October. The campaign reached its climax on 2 July when at Marston Moor the royalist forces in Yorkshire and the north were shattered. The navy had played a part in keeping the sea route for supplies open to Hull, which was the main magazine for the parliamentary forces operating in Yorkshire.

In the south the royalist advance on London was halted by the Battle of Cheriton. The navy continued to provide important support to the garrisons holding out on the coast in the rear of the royalist advance. Plymouth and Lyme, the last parliamentary stronghold in Dorset, continued to hold out with the help of reinforcements brought in by Warwick's fleet.

In Wales, the vigorous assaults of Captain Richard Swanley's Irish guard temporarily recovered the harbour of Milford for parliamentary patrols and created a temporary blockade of Bristol. However, without facilities to refit at Bristol, Swanley was eventually forced to retire to the south coast. Later in the year he was back in the Irish Channel, to take advantage of the renewed war in Ireland and to blockade Dublin.

The role of the navy changed little in 1645. Although royalist privateers posed a threat to east coast shipping, Parliament's navy and loyal privateers were able to contain their depredations. The main focus of naval activity was in Ireland and Wales as parliamentary forces strengthened their positions on the coast. Meanwhile, the decisive action was fought well away from the navy's sphere of control – at Naseby in Northamptonshire.

During the following year, the parliamentary armies recovered much of the lost ground in the West Country. The recovery of Exeter and Dartmouth finally brought an end to the main threat to shipping in the Channel. The King's cause was all but lost and he fled from Oxford to Newark, where he was taken into the care of the Covenanter forces and thence transferred to Newcastle. Fearing that Charles might try to escape to Europe, Sir William Batten was ordered to lie off the town with three men-of-war. His task was to prevent Charles's flight and to assist the commissioners sent by Parliament to negotiate the handover of the King to them. In January 1647, Parliament and the Scots completed their negotiations and Charles was brought south, eventually to Hampton Court.

The years of the Civil War had seen an evolution in the political leadership within Parliament. The original leadership under men such as Pym was increasingly challenged by more radical Independents. These Independents were not a homogeneous group, but MPs with a wide variety of religious and social views, united by their common rejection of a single, established state church. Their power had grown since 1645 and was associated particularly with the New Model Army.[15] The presence of the King at Hampton Court seemed to herald a possible end to the war, which the less radical Presbyterian majority in Parliament, and the Presbyterian-dominated City of London, wanted to encourage.

During 1647 the political crisis in London grew. In August the army's demands for a dissolution of Parliament and their accusations

of treason against some members of Parliament had led to disturb-
ances in London. Fairfax marched the army into London, causing six
MPs to flee the city. The growing strength of the Independents
worried Sir William Batten, a firm Presbyterian, who suggested to the
Earl of Lauderdale that he would bring 22 ships over to the King if he
would establish Presbyterianism. Although this correspondence was
not discovered, Batten was suspected of being in league with the
Presbyterians and of allowing the six members to escape. Despite his
popularity in the fleet, he was called to appear before a committee of
both Houses where he was ordered to resign his commission as
Vice-Admiral or face unspecified charges. He was replaced by
Colonel Thomas Rainsborough, the son of the officer who had
commanded the 1637 Sallee expedition. Rainsborough was a
seaman, but his service in the army and independent republicanism
made him suspect to the moderates and gave him a power base on
land which he did not wish to leave. For the last three months of 1647,
whilst Fairfax and Cromwell tried to bring Rainsborough back into
the main consensus, the navy was without a commander, which
became the context for the great mutiny of the fleet in 1648.[16]

By the beginning of 1648 the clash between the Independents, led
and sustained by the army, and the Presbyterians had come to a head.
In November 1647, the King had escaped his captivity at Hampton
Court and sought refuge on the Isle of Wight. Here, although still a
prisoner, he continued his negotiations with the Scots and eventually
accepted Presbyterianism as part of the price of a Scottish invasion of
England in his support. In December of 1647 Rainsborough had
finally made his peace with the generals of the army, and prepared to
take the fleet to sea in support of the campaign against the Royalists in
Wales. Whilst these preparations were under way, royalist sympa-
thisers generated riots in Norwich and petitions in Surrey and Kent.
They went in among the sailors and took control of Sandwich and
Walmer castles, during which time six warships at Deal mutinied. In
the following days, three from Harwich and three others stationed in
the North Sea joined the revolt, two others refused to serve and four
more were in a mutinous state – 18 out of a total of 39 in the summer
guard. Nine vessels eventually left English waters and put themselves
under the Prince of Wales in Holland. A tenth joined the rebels in
July.[17]

The cause of this revolt, as sudden as that which deprived the King of the fleet in 1642, is not entirely clear but Presbyterian strength within the maritime community seems to have played a major part. The navy had been on service since 1642, and the continuity of the officer corps led by moderate puritans such as Warwick and Batten had built up a strong *esprit de corps*. Recently this continuity had been shattered. The dismissal of Batten had been extremely unpopular in the fleet. Rainsborough and other newly appointed officers were not popular nor were they in touch with the feelings of the seamen. The result was that they were taken by surprise and unable to resist the mutiny. Mixed with this tension of command in the fleet were specific issues of policy and conditions. Money was short in 1648 and pay lagged significantly behind that of merchant vessels. However, the seamen's petitions also clearly show a dislike of the radical policies of the army. Mention is made of supporting a personal treaty with the King to end the war. When the fleet had to be fitted out to pursue the mutineers to Holland, Trinity House, the seat of Presbyterianism in maritime London, refused to assist the manning of it.[18]

The merchants and Parliament seem to have been aware of these feelings. There was a petition of merchants to restore Batten to the rank of Vice-Admiral. Parliament had already restored Warwick to his old rank of Lord High Admiral. This move, together with the fact that the revolt in the fleet was not essentially pro-royalist, gradually brought the situation back under control.

The revolt on land was quickly put down by Fairfax, whilst Warwick pacified seamen at Portsmouth. The rebellious ships taken under royalist command failed to capitalise upon the initial surprise. The seamen had little love of the royalist cause, especially when their officers were replaced by royalist appointees, and Batten, who had joined the revolt, ended up at loggerheads with the Royalists over tactics. By late August Batten had been replaced in command by Prince Rupert and after an abortive raid up the Thames, the little fleet retired to Helvoetsluys in Holland. For the rest of the year Warwick blockaded them in that port, capturing one, driving one aground and accepting two back into Parliament's fleet. On 2 November 1648 Warwick retired to winter quarters, allowing Rupert to escape to Ireland, but the revolt had been contained and Parliament retained control of the vast bulk of the English state's fleet.[19]

1648–1660: The Navy of the Republic and the First Dutch War

The events of 1648 had demonstrated that the security of London, and with it the south-east of England, could depend upon the fleet. Blockade and seaborne support to rebels were as dangerous as foreign invasion to an unstable regime. However, the loyalty of the seamen could not be taken for granted. Charles's attempt to revive the Civil War had been crushed at Preston in August, whilst the final royalist stronghold in southern England, Colchester, surrendered in the same month. The Kentish Rebellion had been quelled, the fleet had been secured and the half-hearted royalist blockade of the Thames had been broken, but the resolution of the political contest between the Independents, supported by the army, and the Presbyterians, among whom numbered some prominent sea officers, including Warwick, did not bode well. On 6 December 1648, the purge of the House of Commons by Colonel Pride left a Rump dominated by the Independents.[20]

The execution of the King followed on 30 January 1649 and in his place a Council of State of 41 assumed supreme executive authority. The new Commonwealth faced a hostile Europe and a limited but destructive royalist capability at sea under Prince Rupert. The Council could depend upon the army, but it was far from clear that it could be so sure of the navy. Yet under the Commonwealth, the importance of trade, colonies and sea-power were to be raised to a height unknown before. State power and sea-power were intertwined as they had not been under the Stuarts. The use of sea-power to destroy the last royalist resistance in Barbados, Virginia, the Scillies, the Channel Islands and at sea complemented its use as a diplomatic tool, both to secure recognition of the English Republic and to advance the economic interests of the London merchants. The very closeness of the relationship between state-building and commercial expansion has led to yet another area of intense controversy between historians.[21] What is undeniable is the success with which the Commonwealth pursued its policy of securing and expanding the fleet, and directing it towards policy objectives. The eventual cost was to be crippling, but in the 11 years between 1649 and 1660 the shape, organisation and function of the modern Royal Navy was consolidated.

The expansion of the fleet occurred at the same time as the Council of State took measures to ensure its political loyalty. The Lord Admiral, Warwick, had been left in command of the fleet until the execution of the King, after which he was replaced by three Generals-at-Sea, Colonel Edward Popham, Major-General Richard Deane and Major-General Robert Blake. In theory this arrangement made the overall command of the fleet the collective responsibility of officers and ensured a greater loyalty to the Council, but in practice the operational demands of the period meant that the three acted largely independently of each other. The Admiralty powers that Warwick had exercised were placed in the hands of a committee of three, nominated from the Council of State.

Even before Warwick was replaced, a parliamentary Committee of Merchants was established to examine the administration of the navy. It reported in favour of purging the Navy Committee, Trinity House and the Customs.[22] The loyalty of the officer corps and seamen was more difficult to ensure, but the expansion of the fleet assisted in the first instance.

	N° of ships	Average displacement (tons)	French ships	Dutch ships
1640	43	883	53	–
1645	53	736	38	–
1650	72	680	32	62
1655	133	676	23	101
1660	131	671	26	97

Source: Glete, J., Navies and Nations, I, 128, 130; II, 639.

During the Civil War the size of the fleet had been fairly static. The state's ships were supplemented in the traditional manner, by the hire of private warships. Consequently, the officer corps was fairly static, opportunities for advancement occurring only through death, invalidity or desertion. However, between 1648 and 1651 Parliament's navy began a major expansion. These new vessels had to be officered, and the Generals-at-Sea and captains played a large part in their selection. Although social status was still considered desirable for senior command, a number of factors played a part in causing the further expansion of the seamen officers or 'tarpaulins'. The pool of socially desirable officers who were also politically acceptable was limited, and with rewards and social status being higher in the army, the navy's ability to attract large numbers of the gentry was limited. The Civil War had seen an expansion of the number of tarpaulin officers, and they were in a position to recommend officers from a similar background, who were experienced seamen, ideal for the mundane and dangerous duties of convoys and cruising. These officers, with their roots in the Thameside maritime community, were also well placed to encourage seamen into the service. Bernard Capp has pointed out that 'the interregnum navy probably came as near to providing a career open to talent as was possible in that age'.[23] A further factor may have been the influence of the merchant community. The years of expansions, between 1649 and 1653, coincided with the time when the independent merchants of the City, who dominated the American and interloping trades to the Far East, reached the peak of their influence both in City government and in national administration. Capp noted the striking number of officers who had served their time in merchant vessels trading to the Americas. The result was that officers appointed under the Rump were often experienced seamen, whose religious and political reliability was attested by their patrons in the service and merchant community.[24]

After Cromwell's *coup* in 1653, there was a slow but significant restoration to power of the traditional merchant elite in the City and national administration. The success of the Commonwealth in securing the loyalty of the sea officers is apparent when compared with the navy's lack of enthusiasm for the Protectorate. Far too little is known about the seamen to provide any firm conclusions about the adherence of these men to either the Commonwealth or the Protectorate. Parliament had played its hand well in 1642 by ensuring that the loyalty of the seamen was rewarded by an increase in wages. A further increase in wages occurred in 1649 and another in 1653. Other changes, related to discipline, better provision for the sick and wounded, victuals and prize money may have closed the gap between living standards on merchant vessels and on the state's ships.[25] Apart from an apparent improvement in living conditions, the seamen's loyalty may have continued to be conditioned by their loyalty to the officers with whom they served. The tarpaulins came from seafaring families, and Bernard Capp has provided evidence that these officers shared the attitudes and concerns of the seamen. The community of feeling may be evidenced by the paternalistic concern over pay, victuals and clothing, by a common religious radicalism, by the relatively lenient sentences of courts martial and the rarity of mutiny and disobedience. During the Commonwealth only one ship, the *Hart*, defected to the Royalists, and that was recaptured shortly afterwards.[26]

The Council of State could not be entirely sure of the navy, but events between 1649 and 1653 did a great deal to confirm the fleet as a loyal and important organ of the state. The first role of the fleet was to stamp out the last embers of the royalist military resistance to the Commonwealth. The substantial resistance lay in Ireland and Scotland. Cromwell's campaigns during 1650 and 1651 were supported by naval forces which ferried troops and supplies to the theatres of operations. Royalist forces still held on overseas, in the Scillies, Jersey, Barbados and Virginia. From 1650 to 1653 naval forces were sent out to reduce these outposts to obedience.[27]

Whilst this was being undertaken, the small royalist navy under the command of Prince Rupert continued to threaten trade and communications. Warwick's blockade of the Dutch coast had ended at the close of 1648, allowing Rupert to sail off to Ireland. Blake, Deane and Popham blockaded him in Kinsale until Blake was finally driven off station by the weather in October 1649. Rupert took the opportunity to get free again, this time putting in at Lisbon, where he was again blockaded and eventually forced to flee to the Mediterranean, once Blake's pressure had made his stay unwelcome to his Portuguese hosts. Forced to seek shelter so far from England, Rupert's little squadron lost its menace to the Commonwealth, finally disbanding in 1653.[28]

The Commonwealth's navy contributed significantly to the collapse of the royalist military presence outside the immediate reach of the army, but of equal importance was its use as a diplomatic tool. The navy had been used in this way since the sixteenth century, but the opportunities open to the Commonwealth for applying naval power to achieve its objectives were far greater than for its predecessors. These opportunities were partly created by the Commonwealth itself and partly by the particular political and military situation that existed in Europe.

The Civil War had fashioned an experienced navy and the decision to expand the navy had created what was by far the largest fleet of specialist warships in western European waters. In Europe, meanwhile, the Thirty Years War had finally ended in 1648, but France and Spain remained at war. Whilst the English fleet expanded during the 1650s the French and Spanish fleets went into decline. Only the Dutch managed to keep close to the English expansion, but even they were to find themselves at a disadvantage in action with the larger and heavier warships the English were building. War was to settle, temporarily, their maritime relationships, but so far as other countries were concerned there was little desire to try to provoke the invigorated English power, and potentially something to gain by courting it. In 1650 Spain recognised the English Republic in expectation of English help in reconquering Portugal. The Republic's relationship with France was fragile in the extreme. Since the 1630s French ambitions in the Low Countries had concerned England, whilst royalist sympathy in France produced a practical nuisance and potential threat to the new regime. However, English attacks on French shipping and the blockade of Dunkirk caused Mazarin to recognise the Republic in 1652. In the same year Portugal's recognition was obtained together with a trade treaty. Further maritime disputes with France during 1654 and 1655 led to increased activity by English warships on both the Atlantic and Mediterranean coasts of France. The disputes were eventually settled in October 1655 by a treaty in which Louis XIV agreed to expel Charles II from French soil.[29]

The most significant result of this resurgence of English naval power was the First Dutch War (1652–4). Relations with the Dutch had been strained since the early years of the seventeenth century. English trade had expanded significantly in the first half of the century, stimulated by English neutrality in the Thirty Years War and the fortuitous location of Dover astride the main trade artery that linked the warring powers. Disputes with the Dutch over the cloth trade, the Great Fishery off the British coasts, and the carrying trade had grown in the years since 1642. Added to these old differences were disputes related to the Civil War. Holland was a centre of royalist intrigue and propaganda. The activities of Dutch and French privateers were making life very difficult for English merchants, whilst the depression that followed the war led to increasing fears of Dutch domination of commerce. This last point was pressed particularly strongly by those merchants from the 'new' trades to America and the Far East, whose influence in administration and government had been so significantly increased by the Civil War.[30] For England the war was aimed at the destruction of Dutch trade, whose routes lay exposed in the Channel and North Sea. The English could afford to avoid a clash between the battle fleets, in order to concentrate on the destruction of the Dutch merchant and fishing fleets. For the Dutch the only real hope of protecting themselves lay in destroying the English warships.

The war was preceded by a confused *mêlée* in the Channel in May 1652 between a Dutch fleet under Martin Harpertszoon Tromp and an English force under General-at-Sea Robert Blake. This was the first really significant naval action the English had fought since 1588, and demonstrated the changes wrought by naval technology in the intervening years. Although less emphasis was placed upon the Great Ship as a medium of prestige as well as naval power, the Commonwealth had continued the Stuart policy of increasing the size of the navy's workhorses, the middling ships, and of providing them with a relatively large number of cannon. The particular need for relatively small, well-armed, manoeuvrable vessels had been recognised in the 1630s and had led to the building of the ten Whelps for Charles's navy. Although they had not been a success, owing to poor construction, the need did not diminish and in 1645 the Earl of Warwick financed the building of a narrow, single-deck ship carrying 26 cannon. The predecessor of the frigate, the *Constant Warwick*, performed well and Parliament authorised the building of more of this type of vessel in 1649, but larger and more heavily armed. By 1654 the type had retained its sleek lines but had evolved into two-deck ships carrying up to 60 cannon. The same tendency to growth was apparent in the middling ships, whose tonnage and firepower saw appreciable, if less spectacular, increases.[31]

The Dutch ships which met the English fleet in the Channel in May 1652 were relatively lighter and poorly armed, and although the Dutch fought a valiant action they were forced to retire northwards. In August, a Dutch squadron under Michel Adriaenzoon de Ruyter successfully contested command of the Channel, and was able to pass through the Western Approaches after an indecisive action fought against Vice-Admiral Sir George Ayscue's squadron off Portland. In September a Dutch fleet of 62 warships under Admiral de With attacked Blake's force of approximately equal numbers off the Downs, in an action known as the Battle of the Kentish Knock. The Dutch were again forced to retire towards their own coasts, but two months later Tromp defeated Blake off Dungeness. The defeat sent a shock through the senior command of the navy. Blame was laid upon the captains for indiscipline, so attention over the following months was devoted to reorganising and recovering discipline in the fleet.

As soon as practicable in 1653, Tromp again pressed through the Channel to escort a large convoy southwards. He picked up the northward bound trade of about 200 vessels and headed back into the Channel. On 18 February he encountered Blake's fleet off Portland and commenced a running battle for two days. Although battered, Tromp got his convoy through.

It was after this encounter, as the English fleet put into Stokes Bay to refit, that tactical orders 'nothing less than revolutionary'[32] were issued to the fleet. The fleet was ordered to engage the enemy in line ahead. When the cannon was first used at sea, it was principally a defensive weapon. The use of the broadside at close range had been slowly evolving as a defensive tactic at least since the 1540s. The development of an offensive tactic used to exploit the firepower of the increasing number of heavy cannon available to the sailing ship was slower to emerge, but the single line ahead, which presented a solid wall of cannon to an enemy, and which had proved successful in defence, was utilised, albeit in very limited way, for attack by the 1580s.[33] It was a tactic particularly suited to English ships which were armed with relatively large numbers of heavy cannon, and served by experienced sea-gunners. By the 1630s English seamen such as Nathanial Boteler were well aware of the advantage the solid build of English ships gave them in a stand-up artillery duel at sea. However, the disposition of the fleet into a single line of battle, rather than a massed formation by division in line abreast, designed to bear down on the enemy and break his order of sailing before relying upon individual ship actions to destroy him in detail, only slowly developed as an explicit tactical doctrine.[34]

The precise reason for this doctrine becoming formalised in the 1650s remains conjectural. It has been claimed that General George Monck was responsible for it, or that it owed its origin to the employment of soldiers who had experience of the power of artillery as senior commanders afloat. There is a great deal to support Sir Julian Corbett's suggestion that the concept had already been given form by the exigencies of action. The instructions dated 29 March 1653 do not seem to demand that the captains fight in a single line of battle, but that they approach the enemy in line of division. As there could be a number of divisions in a fleet, this does not suggest that it was the intentions of the Generals-at-Sea to cause the entire fleet to fight as a single unit – the classic eighteenth-century line-of-battle. This was an attempt to concentrate firepower, and was more formalised than attempts made on many occasions and by a number of maritime powers. However, it was only experience and even accidents in subsequent actions at the Battles of the Gabbard (2 June 1653) and Scheveningen (31 July 1653) that caused naval officers to employ the fleet in the single line of battle. There is little evidence of the deliberate use of line tactics in these battles. Like so much else in military and naval affairs, before the formation of staff colleges, the formalisation of doctrine occurs at the point when broad consensus on its value has been reached. For English seamen and soldiers, the experience of success and failure in the bloody pitched battles fought between large squadrons with cannon capable of shattering vessels was new. However, their experience in seamanship and in warfare generally gave them a good foundation from which to learn and build an informed consensual view.

Whatever the contribution of battle tactics, the results of these actions were important. After the Battle of the Gabbard, the Dutch were forced to retire to their own coast. The Battle of Scheveningen, in which Tromp was killed, confirmed English control of the North Sea. The English ships dared not venture into the treacherous sandbanks off the Dutch coast, but their objective of disrupting Dutch commerce was largely achieved.

The stalemate continued into 1654, but Cromwell, who had seized power in 1653, had less sympathy for the 'new' merchants' interests than he did for a Protestant alliance. He quickly brought the war to conclusion by the Treaty of Westminster, but the peace solved nothing. Although badly damaged, the Dutch carrying trade remained intact and easily able to respond to the renewed business opportunities. The potential for clashes in sensitive areas like the Baltic or the Far East remained unchanged. What had been demonstrated was that groups of the new, heavily armed warships, unencumbered by transports or vessels unsuited to northern waters, could manoeuvre and manage their artillery in confined waters more readily than their predecessors. The emergence of a clear tactical doctrine, however imperfectly applied, reflected the increasingly decisive role of the heavy cannon.

The success of the navy in the early years of the Republic led Cromwell to more ambitious uses of sea-power, but whether these schemes were the result of diplomatic calculation or the desperate need to justify the expense of the fleet is still a matter of debate. By 1655 the possibility of a Franco-Spanish reconciliation, aimed at attacking England, forced him to choose between an alliance with one and war with the other. He chose war with Spain. The fleet could be used to encourage the French to enter an alliance through threats to their commerce and colonies, but neither of these would have a decisive impact on the ability of France to make war. The Spaniards on the other hand were a much more attractive target.

The popular belief in the efficacy of sea-power in humbling Spain in 1603, and the hostility towards the leading military power behind the Counter-Reformation, far outweighed the now hushed voices of the City merchants whose trade to the Mediterranean, the Iberian peninsula and America was threatened by the war.[35]

Pressure on France brought her into alliance in October 1655, whilst the great project against Spain was the 'Western Design', the capture and occupation of Hispaniola. This was the first sustained attempt by the English state to establish its presence in the West Indies. The fleet of ships and men was assembled under generals Venables and Penn and left England in 1654. The expedition failed to secure its foothold on Hispaniola after its assault on the fortified city of Santo Domingo failed. Penn and Venables agreed to attempt the unprotected island of Jamaica. Against the veterans of the New Model Army the local Spaniards stood little chance and were driven into the mountainous interior. It did not seem much to show for the effort, but the English had established themselves in the central Caribbean.

Apart from a few raids upon the Spanish Main, there was little to be done but hold on to the island.[36]

The conquest was not what Cromwell had hoped, nor was the blockade of the Spanish coast by first Blake and then Stokes, but there were some successes. Stayner captured part of a small treasure fleet off the Spanish coast in September 1656. In 1657, he and Blake appeared before Santa Cruz, in the Canaries. The *Flota*, or Treasure fleet, from Mexico lay in the bay, but by the time Blake mounted his daring assault on the fleet most of the treasure had been unloaded and secured inland. Nevertheless, the Spanish vessels were all destroyed and the Spanish Crown was denied the silver which was vital to finance the war into 1658.[37] Troops were sent to assist the French in an attack upon the Low Countries, where with the assistance of naval guns, Mardyke and Dunkirk were assaulted and captured in June 1658.

When Cromwell died in September 1658, the war had reached stalemate. It had achieved, temporarily, its primary objective of securing the Protectorate by dividing the two powers most likely to oppose the militant Protestant republic. The naval force developed by the Republic had also enabled Cromwell to put a squadron in the Baltic to ensure that the vital naval stores, tar, masts and hemp gained free passage through the Sound without interference from the Danes or the Dutch. Another squadron was in the Mediterranean protecting Levant Company vessels from Barbary pirates and Spaniards. But the cost was enormous. Money for the fleet and the army was extremely short and the prospect of continuing credit was not bright as the merchant community began to feel the increasing burden on their trade. Between 1200 and 2000 English merchant vessels fell prey to Spanish privateers in these years and into the gap sprang the Dutch.[38]

The balance of advantage or loss in these years is still contested by historians, but what is clear is that the navy underwent major development as an organised military force. For the first time the state's ships were ranging across most of the waters of Europe and the North Atlantic, in pursuit of defined policy objectives of the state. This should not be overstated. It was to be many decades before the navy had an adequate infrastructure to sustain itself for long in distant parts, particularly in the Americas, but so long as it was adequately financed, its reach and power had increased greatly.[39] The reason for

this development has been ascribed to a more determined government than the Stuart monarchs and to the willingness of Parliament to
fund the expansion.[40] These were both major contributions but to
them must be added the fact that the navy was able to adjust itself in an
incremental manner to the demands placed upon it over the period
1649–60. The expansion and utilisation of the navy were driven by
the needs of the Republic, but were not forced, as in the 1620s, by
external pressures to an unsustainable point. The internal strength of
the navy was adequate at each stage to absorb the demands and
evolve. Only in the late 1650s did finance again fail to sustain the
development.

It is perhaps this period that was most crucial for the evolution of
the Royal Navy and its relationship with English society prior to the
nineteenth century. The ambiguities regarding what the navy was,
what it was for and how it should be developed achieved a high degree
of resolution. The exact nature of this resolution is, once again, the
matter of dispute, but the incremental changes during the Civil War
and particularly the Interregnum, changed the navy for good.

The most obvious development was the role which the navy was
playing in English foreign policy. Both Tudor and Stuart monarchs
had used the fleet to achieve foreign policy objectives, but neither the
power of the fleet nor the interests of England's neighbours, with the
important exception of Spain, was able to make sea-power a decisive
weapon. Both these conditions had altered by 1660. Western European economies were increasingly relying upon overseas trade as a
source of bullion.[41] The land and agriculture remained the main
source of wealth, but trade was the source of liquidity, vital to mobilise
the fixed resources of society. The power of the English fleet was
fortuitously expanding, absolutely and relatively, in a period when the
economic benefits of world trade were impinging with increasing
force upon western European states and society. A navy would never
be as important as an army to the states of Europe, but along the
whole European littoral, no state could be indifferent to the activities
of hostile warships.

The exercise of the fleet in support of English foreign policy was
possible only because of the development of the navy itself. In 1642
the office of the Lord High Admiral was a major department of state,
but the underlying administrative infrastructure was minimal. By

1660 that infrastructure had been substantially strengthened. In 1657 the victualling of the fleet was put under the control of commissioners responsible to Parliament. Although this was abolished in 1660, the experience of the Dutch wars (1664–7 and 1672–4) stimulated the constitution of a separate Victualling Department in 1683. Debate within the administration as to the precise point at which administrators should leave victualling functions to contractors continued into the second half of the eighteenth century but thereafter the state maintained its specialist victualling department. The ability to supply enough food of adequate quality was a major prerequisite of naval power. Despite periodic crises and endemic complaints from seamen, the Victualling Department met the challenge of an expanding fleet and sphere of operations throughout the next 150 years. Given that the primitive preserving techniques remained largely unchanged, this represented a major triumph of naval administration. The supervisory work of the navy commissioners was made easier and more effective by the appointment of additional commissioners permanently residing in the ports. For the first time the naval administration in London had permanent, responsible administrators coordinating the functional requirements of the navy at the points where it was needed.

It was not just the administration that had evolved. Warship design had been consolidated around the frigate and the ship-of-the-line. Both the shape and the functions of these ships had been confirmed by events between 1642 and 1660 and the trend for growth in size and armament was also firmly established.

Issues related to the seagoing personnel of the navy were also firmly established in this period. The social balance between the gentlemen officers and the tarpaulins and the effect that it had upon the operational effectiveness of the navy is a recurrent issue in the navy's history. Although J. D. Davis has demonstrated that one cannot draw exclusive or sharp social distinctions, the differences were there and were never entirely eradicated.[42] From 1653 social status was re-emerging as an important prerequisite of high command, and at the same time more attention had to be paid to the development of professional expertise in young gentlemen officers. The problems of training, promotion and status were apparent in the 1630s, but it was the expansion of the fleet and its role in policy during the 1650s that established them as major and continuing concerns for England's navy.

As in the entire history of the navy in the early modern period, the seamen themselves pose the greatest problem for historians, but even here it is possible to see the events of the Interregnum as being important to the subsequent history of the group. The growth of the fleet placed increasing demands upon the maritime community. The expansion of trade increased the pool of seamen, and the fact that the new, larger men-of-war could be manned up to a third by landsmen or apprentices meant that the pressure was not as heavy as it might have been. Nonetheless, if life was no harder or more hazardous than on merchantmen or privateers, the difficulties over payment, low wages and longer voyages made service in the state's navy a greater nuisance than it once was. Pressing, which had proved necessary since the sixteenth century, would become an increasingly important social and political factor within the merchant and maritime community.

The Interregnum also saw the clarification of the role of the navy in the life of the state and society. The development of the fleet as a diplomatic tool has already been commented upon. By the Restoration, it was also clear that a primary role of the state's navy was the defence of commerce. The navy had long been seen as important in the protection of commerce, but apart from a few voices, attention focused upon the protection of coastal trade and fishing. The need for defending commerce had been slowly growing since the early seventeenth century as the numbers of small, independent merchant traders grew.[43] They did not have the resources of the monopoly companies, which were expected to defend their own investments, but neither had they the political strength to demand protection. The Civil War had seen these independent merchants assuming greater political significance locally and nationally, which was allied to Parliament's reliance upon credit generated in the City of London. The defence of trade was critical to Parliament which by 1650 had accepted that defence of the mercantile interest was essential to the development of the state. The First Dutch War (1652–4) was largely the result of growing English pressure, both economic and military, upon Dutch maritime industries. Arguments about the symbiosis between the navy and trade had been common since the sixteenth century, but from the 1650s the navy was committed, ever more closely, to the protection of trade as a principal role.

Whilst the politically educated were becoming increasingly aware of the beneficial role of the navy, they were becoming more concerned about the army. Fears of a standing army were not new in England, but the experience of living with the New Model Army frightened gentry, merchants and radicals alike. The Interregnum provided the foundations of an antipathy to the army that permeated the entire English world. It was a political antipathy based on infringement of liberty, taxation and the threat to social order that far outweighed any supposed benefit of security or influence in foreign policy. Both the army and the navy had become powerful standing forces, but as a result of the 1650s only the navy was to emerge as politically accep-table. This level of political acceptability gave the navy the role of primary defender of national sovereignty and interests, and deter-mined what was politically practicable in the realm of foreign policy until the twentieth century. The explicit link between security and economic growth based upon a maritime strength became firmly established in English political thinking during this period.[44]

Although there was no 'revolution' in the sense of a fundamentally new doctrine or world view displacing an earlier one, there was by 1660 much less ambiguity remaining over what the navy's position was. It was a state-owned and -maintained standing force. The merchant fleet would continue to provide privateers and small auxil-iary vessels but the divorce between the state's military fleet and the merchant marine was now clearly established. Nor was there much doubt about what it was for – it was the principal bulwark in defence and the main offensive weapon of the state. In view of this, the future was somewhat clearer to seamen and administrators than it had been in 1642. The size of the fleet, the size of the vessels and the weight of the broadsides were all increasing. The importance of the fleet in the defence of the state and trade was established in most minds and clearly demonstrated in the events leading to the Restoration itself.

After Cromwell's death relations between Parliament and the army deteriorated rapidly. The restoration of the Rump Parliament in May 1659, after the collapse of Richard Cromwell's ineffectual regime, did not improve matters. Relations between the army and the navy were also under growing strain, as the financial strength of the regime crumbled under the pressure of military demands. By April 1659 the naval storehouses were empty and there was no credit available for more. The payment of wages to seamen had become erratic as the scarce money was directed towards the pay of the soldiers. The senior officers of the navy, particularly Edward Mountagu, came under increasing suspicion from the army officers.

In the mounting crisis, senior army officers led by generals Lambert, Desborough and Fleetwood carried out a coup, evicting the Rump Parliament and establishing a Committee of Safety. The action split the army and commanded little support in the country at large or in the City. Vice-Admiral John Lawson, with a squadron at the Downs, was sufficiently encouraged to sail northward to blockade the Thames. With the City trade and coal supplies cut off, and General Monck's army moving south, the 'Grandees' restored the Rump. Lawson and Monck joined the Council of State, and although those members of Parliament who had been purged since 1648 were restored no long-term political solution seemed near at hand.[45]

By this time Mountagu had decided that the only alternative to chaos or army rule was a restoration, and he began working within the fleet to help bring this about. By early May he had engineered a core of reliable officers to bring the King back to England. The key role was played by the army, particularly General Monck, but the navy's ability to isolate London had created a political stalemate from which a royal restoration looked a practicable solution.

To suggest that the English Republic played a critical part in the evolution of the navy is not to suggest that somehow its political and administrative leaders were more prescient or capable than their Stuart predecessors and successors. Some social and political features of the Republic, such as the opening of political, administrative and military leadership to the lower gentry, merchants and tarpaulins, probably played an important part in shaping the operational efficiency of the fleet. But more important was the fact that the navy developed in a measured manner, drawing strength from the economic, political and diplomatic conditions of Europe. The temporary relative decline of Spain, France and the United Provinces as competitors put the naval initiative into English hands. Parliament's financial organisation for war provided the navy with resources for expansion it had never experienced before. The political means and will to finance the fleet were greater than before 1642 and for many years after. The physical resources for naval expansion – seamen, shipyards, skilled artisans and shipwrights – capable of producing the larger men-of-war in quantity and quality, existed as a result of 50 years of gradual expansion of oceanic commerce. This commercial expansion was building upon and stimulating technical and navigational developments that made the handling and disposition of naval forces easier.

In some respects, the Interregnum navy developed in an unbalanced manner. While the investment in ships grew and the means of ensuring their immediate needs were satisfied, little attention was paid to developing the longer term supporting infrastructure for repair and support. Additional works were carried out at Chatham, Woolwich, Deptford, Dover and Harwich to meet the Dutch threat. Plymouth received some attention, and Portsmouth grew to become a major naval base. It should be remembered that the management of expenditure on large-scale fixed capital assets was a skill foreign to seventeenth-century men of business. Like so much else, once the need became apparent, learning the appropriate skills took time. Meanwhile, the ports remained cramped and poorly organised for their enlarged responsibilities.

In the long run, the military demands of the Protectorate outran the political will and the financial mechanisms to pay for them. Funding the navy caused a strain as early as 1653, but it was not until 1658 that political reaction broke the financial support. By that time, the navy had become firmly established within the political, economic and social fabric of English society. Its future would depend less upon establishing its role or shape, and much more upon resolving the political, financial, professional and policy issues implicit in maintaining that role.

4

1660–1713: CONSOLIDATION, CHALLENGES AND EXPANSION

1660–1664: The Restoration Navy

When Charles II arrived back in England in May 1660 he inherited what was probably the most powerful navy in Europe at that time. In numbers, his Royal Navy of about 88 large warships exceeded that of its nearest rival, the Dutch, by approximately 16 vessels. His ships were also, on the whole, larger and more heavily armed than Dutch vessels. Although the financial support for the navy had collapsed since 1658, Charles was not inheriting a derelict fleet. Of the 15 first and second rates, the largest vessels in the fleet, carrying between 80 and 100 cannon on three gun decks, 11 were survivors of his father's reign, but they had all been refitted. With the four additional ships built between 1655 and 1658, they remained some of the most powerful warships then afloat. The Commonwealth had carried out a vigorous building programme, including 45 'great frigates', mounting between 40 and 70 guns. They proved their value throughout the 1650s and 30 were still in service in 1660.

The Commonwealth had not just bequeathed powerful ships. The fleet had been in constant employment since the beginning of the Civil War. The record of fairly constant success at sea had created an experienced core of officers, seamen and administrators who knew how to handle those vessels. The involvement of merchants, soldiers, seamen and gentry in the formulation and execution of maritime policy had clarified the structure and function of the navy. It was never doubted that the navy's primary role was the defence of the state, but now the defence of trade outside coastal waters was seen as essential and practicable. Private merchant warships were gradually disappearing from the battle fleet and were increasingly redirected towards convoy protection and privateering. Only the state could afford to provide adequate numbers of the large, heavily armed warships that had proved decisive in the war against the Dutch and held other powers in awe during the 1650s.[1]

	N° of ships	Average displacement (tons)	French ships	Dutch ships
1660	131	671	26	97
1665	143	713	47	115
1670	104	804	120	129
1675	110	863	134	110
1680	133	992	135	93
1685	117	1154	132	95
1690	109	1137	131	74

Source: Glete, J., *Navies and Nations*, II, 550–1, 575, 639.

These features singled out the English navy in 1660. The Dutch, prevented by the shallow waters of their estuaries and coast from building the large three-deckers, and hindered by disputes between the different provinces of the United Netherlands, seemed incapable of matching either the size or the strategic control of the English. The French navy had all but ceased to exist as the Crown lost control of coastal provinces in the civil wars (the Frondes, 1648–49 and 1650–3). Even when domestic peace was restored, the war with Spain continued to preoccupy France until the Peace of the Pyrenees in 1659. Likewise the Spanish navy suffered from this war and the civil wars that convulsed the peninsula until 1664.[2]

Charles seemed to possess great advantages at the beginning of his reign, made all the more favourable by the political acceptability of the navy and his own personal interest in it. Yet the traditional view of naval historians was that the period between 1660 and 1688 was disappointing. There are a number of reasons for this. The most obvious is the comparison with the apparent performance of the navy in this period with the years preceding and following. As late as the mid eighteenth century, writers compared the naval achievements of their own age unfavourably with the great successes of Elizabeth and Cromwell. Contemporaries in the later seventeenth century made similar comparisons. The two wars fought against the Dutch (1664–7 and 1672–4) were clear failures compared with the war of 1652–4.

The feeling of failure and decline was exacerbated by the political disputes surrounding the navy in these years. Although the political history of the period has been extensively researched, the impact of the debates and disputes upon the development of the navy has not received much attention. A great deal of debate still surrounds the influence of Parliament upon foreign policy and strategy. Even less is known about how the navy was influenced as a profession and an organisation. Parliamentary interest in the conduct of naval affairs was well developed during the Republic and continued to grow in the next two centuries. The misadventures of the Dutch wars reverberated in Parliament and created an impression of anxiety and decline which owed more to domestic politics than military realities.[3]

Historians have had additional grounds for concluding that this was a period of decline. The failure of the fleet to prevent William of Orange's landing in November 1688 and its poor performance between 1688 and 1692 pointed to a navy incapable of carrying out its prime functions. Ironically, one of the most able administrators of the later Stuart period, Samuel Pepys, may have had something to do with the very poor image of the navy. His diaries and papers, taken so often at face value, portray him as a tireless fighter against corruption and ineptitude. His works are full of cases of both, detailing the weaknesses of the naval officers and, when he was out of office between 1679 and 1684, the incompetence of the Admiralty commission. Pepys was a capable administrator and, like John Hollond, highlighted the discrepancies between intended outcomes of policies and the actual outcomes or behaviours of the actors involved. But he, like his predecessor, was not an impartial witness and neither was his technique analytical.[4]

If the fighting record and the works of Samuel Pepys provided the empirical data required to demonstrate the poor standards of the navy, the political context was provided by the Stuart kings. Charles II has been seen as dissolute and misguided. James II misunderstood the domestic political status quo and lacked resolution. Together they seemed to preside over an incompetent foreign policy and the failure of naval power.

Recently, historians have challenged these conclusions. The works of Sari Hornstein and J.D. Davies have demonstrated the partiality of Pepys's opinions. Peter Le Fevre's work on the biographies of naval officers has set the political and professional activities of these men in a much clearer light. As this work progresses, it is clear that the achievement of the Restoration navy has been seriously underestimated.[5]

The strength of the new Royal Navy was founded upon the growing maritime culture and economy in Britain. During the 40 years following the Restoration, England was at the very forefront of important technological and social changes. English shipwrights had made improvements to hull design and chartmakers had popularised more accurate maps using the famous Mercator projection.[6] The growing popularity of science among the educated population also helped. Many of the technical changes of the sixteenth and seventeenth centuries had been pragmatic, incremental adjustments to received practice, implemented by practical craftsmen. However, by the mid seventeenth century theoretical sciences had taken a firm hold across western Europe. Indeed, much of the administrative history of Europe from this time on was concerned with what was possible, practical and optimal in balancing scientific principles with political realities. Royal patronage and the charter granted to the Royal Society in 1662 gave some impetus to this. In England, the navy was at the centre of these new ideas. Its value to the Crown, the great cost of ships and installations, and the importance of technology in building, maintaining and operating the ships, all ensured that scientific ideas would be applied to the service. The first Astronomer Royal, John Flamsteed, was appointed and the Royal Observatory founded in 1675, to improve navigation by the more accurate recording of astronomical movements. The purpose of the Royal Society was always to marry theoretical science with practical applications, including navigation and ballistics. Among its members was the naval administrator Samuel Pepys.[7]

Great tensions arose as new methods of thinking clashed with established practices, political necessities and social habits. This is quite clear from building policy to strategy. There was a slow growth in the theoretical literature related to ship design and construction. Royal and administrative sponsorship of shipwrights such as Sir Anthony Deane, who could articulate their craft in theoretical terms, increased. Shipwrights not so gifted felt the decline in patronage, although cases of their producing superior products by intuition or eye continued to occur.[8] The growing demand for expositions on shipbuilding and seamanship is further reflected in the growth of printed works on these subjects by the 1680s.

The belief in an optimum standardised design was not new, but in 1677, under the influence of Pepys and Deane, it was decided to have 20 third rates built to a single design specification. The Crown did not possess the facilities to build such large numbers and it was decided, reluctantly, to contract out the building of half of these vessels in private yards, under the supervision of Deane and the Surveyor, Sir John Tippetts. The result was a highly successful class of ships which, in the view of one authority on naval architecture, Frank Fox, 'must rank among the best-looking warships ever built'. Both the design and the system for building them had worked.[9]

The desire for reliable information upon which to standardise regulations and ensure predictable and effective results also lay behind the most celebrated problem of the later Stuart navy – the gentlemen officers' distrust of the administration. When Charles assumed control of the navy it was officered by a corps of men who owed their position to the Republic. They could not be dismissed *en bloc*, but it was vital that Charles integrated a solid body of officers who owed their loyalty unequivocally to the Stuarts. Although hard and fast distinctions should not be drawn, this latter group was generally connected to the court rather than being sailors whose origins lay in the maritime community. Only gradually, as the opportunity arose, did these gentlemen begin to assume a dominant position in the officer corps, but in the process their competence in seamanship had to be assured. Some of the measures adopted aroused little controversy. As a means of ensuring a training in seacrafts, the *Volunteer per order* system was introduced in 1661, by which a young gentleman who intended a career at sea would be attached to a captain as a *King's Letter Boy*, to receive the rudiments of training. In 1662 the process by which boys might enter as officers' servants was formalised as a seven-year apprenticeship. The testing, or confirmation, of skills and knowledge was also introduced although not in a competitive manner. Aspirant officers had to obtain certificates of good conduct from their superiors before they could be entered on the Admiralty list for promotion. In 1677 an oral examination before a board of senior captains was introduced for the post of lieutenant. Although there were always exceptions to these rules, and many flaws in their execution, the regulations provided a framework by which the gentlemen officers could eventually assume professional equality with their tarpaulin colleagues.[10]

Other regulations, stemming from the same desire to ensure efficient professional behaviour, were more controversial. In 1663 the Lord High Admiral, the Duke of York, promulgated a series of regulations for the navy which, like the articles of war of 1661, owed much to the disciplinary codes developed under the Commonwealth. The regulations detailed the records the captain and his officers must keep and the returns required from them. This intrusion into the internal running of the vessel was resented by many captains, both tarpaulins and gentlemen, but particularly by the latter, as it challenged the social assumption that the officer was responsible directly to the monarch rather than to the administrator in London. An important aspect of the regulations was the attack upon unofficial means of supplementing officers' incomes. Only when pay and allowances were increased in the 1680s did the policy meet with some success, but the animosities created by these clashes continued into the 1690s.[11] Far too little work has been done so far to chart with confidence the evolution of the relationship between two sets of emerging 'professionals' – the sea officers and the civil servants. However, from the work already carried out it is clear that the period 1660 to 1714 was crucial in shaping the eventual *modus vivendi* of the eighteenth century.

The need for standardised behaviour was equally required in the administration of the navy. The Stuart monarchs were committed to a navy that would continue to defend the realm and project their foreign policy ambitions. To this end, the navy had to grow. It had to grow in terms of ships to meet the expanding naval forces of France and the Netherlands. Furthermore, the ships themselves had to grow as the technical possibilities of larger vessels became known. To service this expansion the yards and ports which had been relatively neglected under the Commonwealth had to grow as well. To meet this demand the process of contracting and provisioning had to be standardised. The state became the direct employer of increasing numbers of artificers, for whom supervision, employment patterns and norms had to be established. This direct labour force posed a problem of management unknown in other large-scale industries.[12] Other relationships had also to be worked out, particularly with contractors of raw materials. Reliable suppliers of large quantities of materials had to be found. The contracting system took time to establish, and differed between materials, but was generally effective throughout the eighteenth century.

The navy also needed to be sure of the actions of its own administrators, and in 1662 the Duke of York's instructions made explicit the responsibilities of the Principal Officers of the Navy Board. As the work load increased, administrative changes were required. The need for constant supervision in the dockyards had led to the resident commissioner becoming a permanent feature of the navy. The horrific casualties caused by enemy action and disease in the Second Dutch War led to the creation, albeit temporarily, of a Board of Sick and Wounded: an expedient that achieved a degree of permanence in 1701. However, the most significant administrative development was the establishment of the Victualling Board in 1683. Victualling had been a consistent problem since the sixteenth century and the experience of the Third Dutch War had shown that it remained unsolved. As in other aspects of the naval administration, the establishment of a department was an imitation of the body that served the Commonwealth between 1654 and 1660.[13] The existence of a group of men responsible for the provision of adequate, good victuals did not immediately ensure that such food reached the fleet, but over the long term, principally because money became more readily available, this board was able to ensure that British squadrons could operate at ever greater distances from the British Isles with adequate supplies of food.

The final area in which predictability was sought was in manning the fleet. Here, the conflict between the maritime community and the navy was most acute and the limitations on what was administratively practicable most evident. The press and embargoes were the traditional means of bringing the fleet up to strength in times of war. Both these expedients were disliked by the mariners and merchants.

Seamen found themselves with lower earnings, less reliable payment and long, unplanned voyages. Merchants found their vessels held up and their crews reduced. Yet the alternatives were politically unacceptable. Parliament would not sanction higher wages, fearing the burden on the public purse. Nor would it accept conscription. The idea of a register of seamen which listed them for call-up was in use in France. The concept had been discussed as early as the 1630s, but by the end of the seventeenth century such a formal mechanism of compulsion was considered to be inimical to the liberties of Englishmen. In practice, such a device was unnecessary. Throughout the period the expansion of the shipping industry provided an adequate pool from which the navy could draw in times of emergency, although never as quickly as it would have wished.[14]

In the field of strategy, the navy's role expanded. Strategy and diplomacy were still conducted in the terms of fundamental religious or dynastic interests, but mercantilist policies, aimed at increasing the wealth of the state by inflows of bullion through favourable trade balances, were significant strategic tools. The Navigation Acts of 1651, 1662, 1663 and particularly 1696, were a recognition that English shipping and trade formed the crucial 'sinews of power' in any struggle, be it commercial or ideological.[15]

All these developments were wrought by changing attitudes to the administration of the state's affairs. Pepys, who represents one of the major proponents of this new approach, carefully listed the failures of others to reach the standards he was expecting. However, in doing so he distorted the achievements that were made. He argued for standards that were desirable but which required changes in attitude that took decades to achieve. The failings that he noted were often exaggerated or coloured by personal feelings and animosities. What Pepys also ignored was that the problems were not unique to the English navy, and that in many cases England came closer to resolving them than her competitors. The French navy was riven by the distrust between the sea officers and the administrators and between the gentlemen officers, the 'reds', and the tarpaulins, the 'blues'. For economic and geographical reasons, the Dutch were never able to meet the demands of the changing maritime technology.[16]

The achievements of the Restoration navy are put into greater relief by taking account of the other changes which it was having to accommodate. A major change was the relative rise of France and the recovery of the Netherlands. The renaissance of the French navy is associated with Jean Baptiste Colbert. France lacked a large and dynamic maritime trading tradition but Colbert was determined to create one under the protection of a royal fleet. In some respects this had advantages. The blank sheet with which Colbert was faced enabled him to decide what was required and create the navy accordingly, rather than having to rely upon the entrenched interests and inappropriately positioned fixed capital resources. Colbert was able to buy the vessels he wanted from the Netherlands, whilst expanding the installations at Brest, La Rochelle and Rochefort. He brought in skilled artificers from the Netherlands and arranged administrative systems for the supply of vital raw materials to the expanded dockyards. This was a remarkable achievement, which saw the fleet expand from 25 warships in 1661 to 81 ten years later. Although the increase was less dramatic thereafter, the numbers of French warships continued to rise so that by 1688 France had a fleet of ships-of-the-line greater than that of England.[17]

Likewise, the Dutch navy was undergoing reconstruction in the early 1660s, centred around more heavily armed two-deckers, capable of giving a better account of themselves against the English three-deckers. The Commonwealth navy had expanded into a vacuum during the 1650s. This vacuum was being filled by competitors and neither France nor the Netherlands would be in such awe of the English as they had been before the Restoration.[18]

The second major problem facing the navy after 1660 was its position in the new political settlement. The factional politics of the Stuart court naturally embroiled the navy. However Charles might wish to balance the interests of gentlemen and tarpaulins at sea, the exigencies of court politics ensured that jealousies and animosities went to sea. In the Second Dutch War there was a faction just waiting for any bad news in order to condemn the command of the Duke of York. The disappointing results of the 1665 campaign provided the opportunity for those who hated the influence of the Earl of Sandwich to raise a cry against him. The joint command in 1666 by Prince Rupert and the Earl of Albemarle was intended to diminish the jealousies, but the loss of the Four Days Battle in June only heightened them and added poison that continued until the end of the war. The same divisions between senior officers and between the sea officers and the administration were evident in the Third Dutch War. Although, as J.D. Davies has pointed out, there was probably more to unite the officers than to divide them, the public nature of the quarrels may have done much to convince contemporaries and historians that the navy had lost its way.[19]

One final change was taking place in this period which was to have a growing influence on the navy. This was the increasing importance of the wider world to the navy. The period 1660 to 1688 saw a major expansion of overseas trade, principally in the re-export of colonial produce, such as tobacco and sugar, and East India goods. For the moment, London was the centre of this trade, which was tightening the bonds of mutual reliance between England, the West Indies and America. This was not of immediate concern to the navy. Despite the establishment of the Hudson Bay Company and the Royal African Company, much of the trade was carried out by independent merchants, who lacked the political power of the older chartered companies. Furthermore, the threat to Atlantic trade was more spasmodic and limited compared to that posed to the dominant Mediterranean trades. Political and economic considerations therefore kept naval attention focused on the Mediterranean, but by the 1690s the Americas could no longer be ignored. English relations with the Baltic powers were not so good that the possibilities of an alternative source of naval stores could be ignored. The threat posed to English colonies in the Caribbean and North America required greater naval attention. The expansion of trade with the Americas brought the navy into increasing contact with colonial society, both as the enforcer of the Navigation Laws and as a drain upon colonial manpower for the ships.[20]

It is against this background that the performance of the later Stuart navy must be viewed. To meet the challenge required time, peace and, last but not least, money. None of these were available in the early years of the Restoration. The greater the crises and the less money there is, the more time is required to implement effective change, but within five years England was embroiled in another Dutch war. Money, which had dried up in the 1650s, had become more available as a receptive, if careful, Parliament was initially willing to support the Crown's foreign policy and dignity. Charles I had maintained a respectable fleet quite adequately for a number of years with the assistance of Ship Money. Such expedients were not available to his sons, and the support of Parliament was proportionately more important. Parliament, unfortunately for Charles, was neither generous nor unconditional in its support of his foreign policy and war was quickly to drain any surplus the King was able to accrue. So much change, both internal and overseas, was taking place that it is little wonder that the navy's performance appears lacklustre and incompetent.

1664–1667: The Second Dutch War

In 1660 the navy debt stood at £1,250,000, and an annual charge to maintain the fleet in peacetime was £400,000. There was little Charles could do in the immediate term but to retrench as far as possible. However, the following years saw increasing pressure for action from the City, the Commons and a powerful coalition at court headed by James, Duke of York. Their motives included political and commercial hostility to the Dutch, but war provided the opportunity for the Stuart court to stamp its identity upon the navy. War came in 1665 partly as a result of a private expedition mounted by the Royal African Company against Dutch ships and forts on the Guinea coast and partly through an English blockade of the Channel and attacks on Dutch trade in the Mediterranean.[21]

As in the First Dutch War, both sides were anxious for a clash of the main fleets, the result of which would be dominance of the Channel and North Sea for the victor. The English fleet, under the Duke of York, possessed the initiative from the start of the campaign, and won a significant victory at the Battle of Lowestoft on 3 June. The victory was not followed up and York left the fleet under the Earl of Sandwich. Sandwich sent a detachment under Sir Thomas Teddeman to destroy or capture the Dutch merchantmen sheltering in Bergen. This was to be done in conjunction with the Danish Crown, which had given its secret agreement on condition of a share in the plunder. In the event the assault was resisted by the Danes and it ended as a fiasco, which seriously damaged Sandwich's reputation at home.

Despite parliamentary grants to support the war the debt was rising. For the 1666 campaign Prince Rupert and Albemarle were given joint command as a means of reducing the factional squabbles that had divided the officer corps during the previous campaign. The two commanders divided their forces so that Rupert could sail south to intercept a French squadron that was rumoured to be coming north from Brest. The Dutch fleet, this time commanded by one of the great naval officers of the century, de Ruyter, came out to try to blockade the English fleet in the Thames, but arrived too late to achieve this. On 1 June, Albemarle sighted de Ruyter's fleet off the North Foreland, and inspired by his success in the First War and the victory off Lowestoft, immediately bore down upon the Dutch. The fleets remained engaged until 4 June, and despite Rupert finally joining the battle the losses sustained by the English forced them to put back into the Thames, allowing the Dutch to blockade its mouth.

On 25 July Rupert and Albemarle defeated de Ruyter at the Battle of St James's Day. De Ruyter was forced back on his own coasts to repair, once again opening up the Thames. A raid to destroy naval stores on the islands of Vlie and Schelling, north of the Texel, was rewarded with the discovery and destruction of over 150 Dutch merchantmen sheltering in the shallows. 'Holmes' Bonfire' created excitement in England but it proved impossible to maintain the fleet off the Dutch coast, and the year ended with both fleets preparing for the next encounter in the spring.

By now credit for the war was all but exhausted. The fighting had not yielded the quick destruction of Dutch sea forces and English trade was suffering from Dutch warships in the Channel. There was little prospect of the money being made available to fit out the fleet and Charles was compelled to lay up his ships in the Thames and Medway and hope that privateers would sweep up Dutch trade. The result was the most humiliating reverse in the Royal Navy's history. In June, de Ruyter's fleet appeared in the Thames. Forces were landed at Sheerness, which was burned. Dutch ships sailed up the Medway to burn and take off some of England's largest vessels, including the 86-gun *Royal Charles*, which was displayed as a trophy in Rotterdam for a number of years thereafter.

With little hope of a counter-stroke, Charles concluded a peace at the Treaty of Breda on 31 July 1667. The Dutch were conceded trading rights in English possessions, but the English retained their one major conquest of the war – New Amsterdam, renamed New York. The agony over the disaster in the Medway raised quarrels and accusations to new heights. There were serious errors of judgement, from which much political capital was made, but the English fleet fought its actions in good order, using the line of battle very effectively at Lowestoft and the St James's Day battle. The strategic objective, the destruction of the Dutch fleet, seemed sound but in the 1660s the English did not have the decisive advantage in the quality of ships that they possessed in the 1650s, neither did they have the resources to conduct a long war. Although English naval power remained impressive, conditions had changed significantly since the 1650s. Charles could not afford long wars even when Parliament and the City were generally supportive of his objectives. Success had to come quickly. The longer the enemy avoided a decisive battle, the more the prospect of victory diminished. The Dutch no longer had to win, they just had to avoid defeat. This was precisely what happened when Charles engaged in the Third Dutch War.

1672–1674: The Third Dutch War

The origins of this war lay in Charles's secret Treaty of Dover, signed in June 1670, by which he allied himself to France against the Netherlands.[22] This was the highpoint of his personal foreign policy. Charles gambled on French armies quickly overwhelming the Dutch. English forces would support the French by an invasion of Dutch coastal provinces. Speedy success might have convinced Englishmen to support a campaign that cut the Dutch down to size and relieved English trade of a tiresome competitor. It was, despite the apparent superiority of Louis' armies, a strategy fraught with danger. Although there was a long-standing hostility to the Dutch in England, there was no love of an alliance with Louis XIV. Louis' military power and aggressive behaviour towards Spain in 1667–8 had been an important factor in bringing England and the Netherlands to peace and causing them to join together with Sweden in a defensive Triple Alliance.

The war opened in February 1672, with an order to attack Dutch trade. In March an unsuccessful attempt to seize a returning Dutch Mediterranean convoy provided the spark. English strategy was the same as in the previous wars – to destroy the Dutch battle fleet so as to close the Dutch coast to trade. The only real change was that on this occasion an army was to be landed to create a diversion for Louis' invading armies. Dutch strategy, however, evolved very differently from that of previous wars. Initially, de Ruyter tried either to pin the English fleet back on its own coast or to destroy it. Later, during 1673, the French invasion compelled the Dutch to strip their fleet of manpower for the landward defences. De Ruyter's task was to avoid battle, preserve his fleet and pose a potential threat to an English landing on the coast. This version of the 'fleet in being' strategy successfully thwarted English plans. It was a strategy that was to be hotly debated in England when her fleet was forced on to the defensive in the war against France in 1690.

The war commenced with the Duke of York again in command of the fleet. De Ruyter avoided battle until James put back into Sole Bay on the Suffolk coast to provision and water. De Ruyter then put across and caught him at a disadvantage on 28 May. The damage was enough to delay James sailing for the Dutch coast. Victualling problems dogged the fleet throughout the summer and on 10 September the landing was called off for the year.

By the end of 1672, the French advance on land forced de Ruyter to preserve his fleet for the exigencies of a crisis on land. In May 1673 an attempt to blockade the English in the Thames failed and de Ruyter retired to the Scheldt to await the arrival of the combined Anglo-French fleets under Prince Rupert. The fleets met at the First Battle of Schoonevelt off the east channel of the Scheldt on 28 May. De Ruyter fought a defensive action. A similar action was fought on 4 June, after which Rupert withdrew to the Thames to refit, hoping that his absence would tempt de Ruyter out into the open sea.

During these actions the English and French fleets had not cooperated well, but Rupert sailed on 19 July to position himself off the Texel in order to blockade Dutch trade. De Ruyter sailed shortly after to open the way for an East India convoy. The Battle of the Texel on 11 August, in which the French fleet, which formed the rear of the allied line, failed to come up to support Rupert's centre, was another defensive victory for de Ruyter. The Allied fleet retired to the English coast, opening the way for Dutch trade. By this time, Charles had once again run out of money. The unease of an alliance with France, stimulated by a vigorous Dutch propaganda campaign and the almost complete failure of the maritime war, ended Charles's hopes of gaining anything from the war, and peace was concluded in February 1674 by the Treaty of Westminster.

The English navy was large, well supported by maritime industries and seafaring communities, and increasingly well organised, but it lacked the basic financial strength for full mobilisation over a long period. It had not been able to achieve a decisive result against the Dutch. In 1672–3, the enemy avoided a decisive engagement. The line of battle was a tactic devised as a defensive measure but it was also well suited to a battle in which two adversaries were intent on offensive action. It was not ideal in a situation where one party wished to avoid action. Very seldom throughout the whole period of the line-of-battle sailing warships was a decisive naval action to be fought, unless both sides were intent on a close range firefight, or a means of breaking the line was found.

1674–1688: The Navy and the Wider World

This was the last occasion on which the Stuart monarchs tried to maintain their fleet on a war footing for a long period. The fleet was mobilised in 1678 during a war scare with France, and finally in 1688 to resist the invasion of William of Orange, but difficulties with Parliament, and later James's concentration upon his army, made the prospect of long-term mobilisation impracticable. However, the relative peace between 1674 and 1688 enabled the navy to absorb many of the changes imposed upon it during the 1660s.

By 1688 the Royal Navy had emerged as an organisation with a growing significance in British society. It was carrying out its function of defence of the realm. Its administrative procedures had became more reliable, and its officer corps evolved a professional ethos. Ships could remain abroad longer and the naval officer could be respected as a representative of the Crown in distant parts. The navy was called upon, increasingly, to act as a diplomatic lever and to ensure the protection of British interests overseas. Of course, the navy did not do this in isolation, but was part of an expanding network of professional and honorary diplomatic contacts across Europe.

The region where the navy's influence was most evident between 1674 and 1688 was in the western Mediterranean. Squadrons were maintained off the Barbary coast to prevent the depredations of the North African corsairs. Sir John Narborough negotiated a peace with Tripoli in 1676 and his successor, Arthur Herbert, concluded a peace with Algiers in 1682. During this period an effective system of convoys and patrols protected English vessels from attack, providing a great stimulus to English shipping in the region. Occasionally, the presence of one or more warships also acted as protection to English merchants resident in places such as Lisbon, Seville or Cadiz.[23] It is not possible to measure with any certainty the impact this protection had upon English commerce, but during this period both the relative and absolute position of England in trade with countries in the western Mediterranean remained healthy.

The North African port of Tangier had been received by Charles II, along with Bombay, as part of the dowry of Catherine of Braganza. It was once thought that Tangier was critical to England's position in the Mediterranean, but this view is no longer accepted. Whilst England was at peace with the major Mediterranean powers she could draw support from almost any port along the coastline. For example, Cadiz and Gibraltar were used to support action against the Barbary states. However, if the strategic significance of Tangier is now largely discounted, its political importance for the Royal Navy is not. Service in the Mediterranean was the first long-term overseas appointment in the navy, and the first opportunity for the development of a cohesive corps of officers, bound by shared experience and the patronage of a relatively independent senior officer. The officer who most profited from this independence was Arthur Herbert. Herbert built around him a network of officers who looked to his patronage. With his distant command and his claim to experience, Herbert was able to challenge the Admiralty as an alternative centre for policy. This was not welcome to an Admiralty struggling to impose a discipline upon the officers, but must have seemed attractive to sea officers irritated by what they saw as the intrusions of clerks and landsmen.[24]

The importance of this was apparent in 1688. Herbert carried the letter to William of Orange which invited him to take the throne. His defection, followed shortly by that of another senior naval officer,

Edward Russell, played a part in undermining the naval officers' loyalty. Many other factors were at work. Although there were few Roman Catholic officers in the fleet, the appointment of some Catholics in 1687 and the conversion of Sir Roger Strickland, the commander-in-chief, caused unease. There was also a disinclination to fight the Dutch again. The behaviour of the fleet during October and November has been the subject of a number of examinations. The failure of the navy to prevent William's landing was a necessary, but not a sufficient, cause of William's victory. The most recent analyses differ in their conclusions. It is argued by J.L. Anderson that the winds prevented the interception of the Dutch fleet until William was too firmly established ashore. While accepting that the winds could account for the failure to intercept the Dutch, J.D. Davies has argued that an attack as late as 5 November was possible and could have been decisive. Both accept the existence of an Orangist conspiracy within the ranks of naval officers, but neither is inclined to give it the exceptional weight it carried in earlier histories.[25]

1689–1697: The Navy in the Nine Years War

The Glorious Revolution, which had placed William III on the throne, has traditionally been viewed as a major turning point in British history. So far as the navy was concerned, this had less to do with the changing dynasty or political philosophy and much more to do with the two wars, the Nine Years War (1689–97) and the War of Spanish Succession (1702–13), which together dominated international relations for 24 years. The change in dynasty itself brought far fewer changes than the revolution of 1642. There was no change in the basic assumptions concerning organisation, purpose or control. Some of the personnel, most notably Pepys, left office, to be replaced by adherents to the Orangist cause but, unlike 1642, there was no profound impact on the type of skills brought to the administration. The Admiralty was put into commission, but there was a strong precedent for this and it implied no major change in proceedings. Roman Catholic officers and Stuart loyalists were purged from the officer corps, but three-quarters of the officers remained in post. There was no change in the locus of authority or the direction of policy. The monarch remained the executive head of the navy and the prime need in 1688 was to continue the retrenchment that had been the hallmark of policy up to the mobilisation of the summer of 1688.[26]

However, the wars which were a consequence of the Revolution stimulated some major developments in the navy. It had not fought a major campaign since 1673, and apart from the mobilisations of 1668, 1678 and 1688, the navy had been allowed to develop its internal structure in an atmosphere of peace and penury. From May 1689 England was faced with a major war. France was a powerful land and sea power. French land forces had carried most campaigns they had fought by numbers and professionalism. The French fleet, which had not performed well in conjunction with the English in 1673, had gone on to give a very creditable performance against the Spanish and Dutch in the Mediterranean between 1674 and 1678, and had done significant damage to both those powers' merchant fleets plying across the Atlantic. In the Dutch wars, the prevailing westerly winds had given England the advantage, but the French Atlantic ports of Brest and Rochefort lay well to windward of the main English bases of Portsmouth and Chatham. The prospect of a French descent in support of James II on the West Country, Ireland or Scotland was a very real threat.

	N° of ships	Average displacement (tons)	French ships	Dutch ships
1690	109	1137	131	74
1695	159	1081	156	116
1700	177	1113	146	113
1705	188	1058	143	108
1710	180	1116	122	119
1715	182	1126	76	95

Source: Glete, J., *Navies and Nations*, II, 551, 576–7, 639–40.

The war did not get off to a good start. The navy was unprepared for the conflict and allowed a French fleet under Lieutenant-General Château-Renault to take James to Ireland in March 1689. Arthur Herbert (later Earl of Torrington) finally caught up with the French fleet in Bantry Bay on 1 May, but he was unable to inflict decisive damage on the French warships or to get at their convoy of transports.

Once the French fleet got back to Brest little further action took place that year, apart from the steady growth of privateers taking advantage of any opportunity to prey upon enemy merchantmen. The French Toulon squadron, under Lieutenant-General Tourville, managed to link up with Château-Renault's fleet at Brest, but did not come to a confrontation with Torrington.[27]

In 1690 Tourville managed to get out to sea before the Anglo-Dutch fleet was ready. Torrington eventually faced Tourville with a fleet of 56 against the French 70. Although he wanted to avoid battle he was ordered to attack the French and the battle was joined off Beachy Head on 30 June 1690. Torrington was defeated and he decided to retire to the Thames to pose a threat should the French attempt to invade the east coast. This strategy of holding the 'fleet in being' to deter invaders was hardly new, but it was a great contrast to the aggressive thinking that dominated the Dutch wars. Torrington was condemned by his political enemies, arrested, and replaced by his rival Edward Russell. Although acquitted by court martial he never served again. Historians and naval strategists have continually debated the virtues and vices of this policy. It remains one of the perennial issues of naval strategy and Torrington's name will always be associated with it.[28]

Apart from a raid on Teignmouth, the French did nothing with their superiority in the Channel and 1691 passed in a series of small actions against merchantmen and in support of the war in Ireland. The major confrontation which both fleets sought finally occurred on 19 May 1692 off Cape Barfleur. Tourville's smaller force was defeated by the Anglo-Dutch fleets under Russell. The defeated French vessels sought refuge in the bay of La Hogue in Normandy, where the allies again caught and burned a number of them. Having lost 15 warships France replaced them within a year but she lacked the financial resources in the middle of a great land war to match the challenge of the expanding allied navies.[29]

By 1695 France had reorganised her naval strategy for a concentrated assault upon allied commerce by individual privateers and royal vessels – the *guerre de course*. This decisive shift in naval policy has provided another point of debate among naval strategists into the twentieth century. Historians are still divided on the issue. They broadly agree that the policy served French needs, but disagree on the importance of surrendering the challenge to the allied battle fleets. Allied trade and credit were seriously damaged during the mid 1690s but the campaign also drained the slender resources of the French maritime community. The allies had to mount a major effort to protect their trade but they were also free to use naval forces in other ways. Coastal raids upon France diverted enemy resources from the battlefields of Flanders. William's crucial decision in 1694 to maintain a powerful squadron in the Mediterranean crippled French maritime power in those waters. When the war ended in 1697 the balance of advantage lay marginally with the allies, whose mercantile marine had emerged from the war slightly less damaged than their French counterparts, and who also had a pronounced advantage in being able to cover their maritime operations by squadrons of warships superior to those of the French.[30]

For England, the war had brought about a decisive shift in her naval commitment. To meet the challenge from France the focus of naval activity moved from the Channel, where France had no bases for her large men-of-war, to the Western Approaches. To support operations, Plymouth was developed as a major naval base. From this point until the emergence of the threat from Germany in the 1890s, British naval installations developed along the south coast, whilst the old establishments on the east coast – Chatham, Sheerness, Harwich – went into gradual decline. Blockade of the French Atlantic ports became a primary function of the fleet.[31]

1702–1713: The Navy in the War of Spanish Succession

The War of Spanish Succession (1702–13) followed much the same course as its predecessor. Allied trade suffered from French privateers, whilst French seaports suffered the steady attrition of the capture of their vessels. With the threat of invasion less immediate, a large part of the Anglo-Dutch fleet was employed in the Mediterranean. It was here that the only major fleet confrontation was fought off Malaga (13 August 1704) between the allied fleet under Sir George Rooke and the Toulon squadron, under the Comte de Toulouse. Although provoking criticism in England, the battle was a decisive victory in that the French were prevented from relieving Gibraltar and the

Mediterranean continued under allied maritime control. On occasions French squadrons were sent out, for example to support a Jacobite rising in Scotland in 1708. However, allied maritime superiority effectively covered these threats, with enough spare capacity to undertake major operations in the Mediterranean and North America, which were real strategic alternatives to the main confrontation with France on the battlefields of the Low Countries.[32]

During the course of these wars there had been a major expansion of the British fleet. The wars consolidated a number of features that were apparent in the Stuart navy, as well as presenting new challenges and providing solutions to problems that had dogged the navy for decades. The most evident consolidation of a previous trend was the professionalisation of both the officer corps and the administration. Some of the key features of professionalisation had been resolved in the second half of the seventeenth century. The body of knowledge and skills that set its members apart from amateurs had been identified. The formal responsibilities and powers of its members had been defined. Other features were imperfectly developed. One of these was the idea of a permanent membership of the professional body. For this to exist, officers had to be retained in peace as well as war. Steps had been taken since the 1660s. Flag officers were granted half-pay in peacetime in 1668. The captains of first and second rate ships were given the same privilege in 1674. This was extended to commanders of squadrons and the masters of first and second rates in 1675. Lieutenants and masters could also obtain a retainer by serving as volunteers on ships from 1676. In 1693 half-pay was granted to all commissioned officers, and although this was severely restricted after 1700 – to 50 captains, 100 lieutenants and 30 masters – the principle of a corps of officers equal except in seniority of service was carried forward.[33] It was a step in establishing a unified corps, but it was not a great advance and, together with the lack of a pensions strategy, it left some ambiguity about the commitment the officers had to the Crown when not on service.

The administration was also given the opportunity to define its role more clearly. Resentment among officers at the demands of the administration was still evident in the early years of the war, but over the course of the conflicts the parameters of responsibility were established. A comparison of Navy Board papers between the 1690s and the years 1710 to 1714 shows that procedures had largely been accepted. Naval officers would continue to blame the administrators for the poor performance of their vessels, and disputes over authority, particularly in ports, would reoccur, but blatant disregard of the procedures diminished.[34]

It would not be true to suggest that all the problems of two emerging professions co-existing within a complex government department had been resolved. Indeed, too little research has been done on this subject for the historian to be sure of what those problems were, but it would be fair to suggest that, as far as we know, the long period of generally successful war at sea established a stable relationship between administrators and sea officers that lasted at least until the 1830s, when changes to naval administration, to general administrative theory and practice, and to the navy itself, as a result of the slow emergence of steam power, wrought major shifts within the service.[35] One consequence of this stronger relationship between administrators and seamen may have been a diminishing role for the Admiralty. With the strategic direction of the navy in the hands of the monarch and administrative control vested in the Navy Board, the role of the Lord Admiral, or the commissioners of the Admiralty, became increasingly ambiguous.

Another important relationship consolidated during this period was with the London maritime community. The period between 1660 and 1689 had witnessed a great expansion in overseas trade, particularly in the re-export of colonial produce and East Indies goods. This economic expansion, which stimulated ship-building, ancillary industries, and the demand for craftsmen and seamen, made possible the expansion of the navy after 1689. Unlike France, which built a world-class navy on a very narrow base of maritime resources, England's oceanic mercantile expansion provided what was one of the largest and probably the most diversified maritime economies in the world. However, this expansion did not eliminate tension. Just as in 1666–7 and 1672–3, naval demands continued to generate tensions with the maritime community. During the wars, projects were suggested to resolve these tensions, but in almost all areas little was achieved. Although after 1692 English policy-makers could not be entirely confident that their naval defences were impregnable, there were no maritime crises to make them question well-established principles and practices.[36]

Ship-building was one of the areas of tension. Shipwrights in the state's yards often continued a private business, sometimes utilising the same yards for the purpose. This confused state of affairs had been frowned upon by administrators for decades. Apart from embezzlement of the state's stores, experience of private builders suggested that the state could not be certain of the quality, cost or even dimensions of the vessels built by them. After 1660 there was an attempt made to build all naval vessels in royal yards, but this proved impossible since the yards had not been expanded in line with the growth of the size or number of ships in the navy. The royal yards were desperately needed for the building of the biggest men-of-war and the cleaning and repair of vessels. In 1677 the Admiralty reluctantly agreed to contract out the building of a larger percentage of the new third and fourth rates, and in 1691 the same expedient was necessary. The results were not satisfactory compared to those of the 1677 programme, partly because the design and building specifications were not as good, neither was the contracting relationship as flexible with William's new and inexperienced Navy Board.[37]

The difficulties in building and design were compounded by the changing naval war after 1692. The French decision to pursue a privateering war switched the focus away from the line-of-battle ships to smaller, faster vessels to combat well-armed French privateers. This became the subject of intense debate among constructors such as Sir Anthony Deane and Joseph Daniel. The result was a confused building programme, subject to experiment, disappointment and confusion about the role and provision of the smaller fighting ships of the fleet.

The contracting system was well established and, except for timber, the markets were sufficiently large and flexible to supply the navy's needs. However, the boards found themselves dealing with a relatively small number of contractors, and in the case of sailmaking only one. Few merchants could enter these markets. The quantities required were all large by contemporary standards and payment was slow. This gave the contractors the opportunity to combine in order to force up prices. The tension between the boards and their suppliers was to continue intermittently throughout the eighteenth century.[38]

The final point of tension with the maritime community was over manning the fleet. The difficulties of this in the opening years of the war led to the Register Act of 1696. This provided for a voluntary register of seamen along the same lines as the compulsory French *Maritime classes*. Resented from its inception, the act was repealed in 1710, having failed to produce a reliable list of seamen for orderly and fair conscription. The administration was forced to fall back upon the old expedients, such as embargoes and the press. Additional measures were taken to support these, such as the issuing in 1704 of exemptions from being pressed for landsmen who had served two years, and a relaxation of the Navigation Laws in 1708 to enable merchantmen to take on more foreign seamen. Without a radical solution or the supply of seamen growing at a significantly faster rate than the demands of the Royal Navy, the problem was insoluble. On the whole, the expansion of the maritime community kept pace with naval demands during the eighteenth century, but the margin was never comfortable for either the merchant or naval fleets. The idea of a register was revived in pamphlets in the 1720s and 1740s, and even proposed in Parliament in 1740, but never commanded great support. It was not until the 1780s that non-compulsory, non-governmental alternatives to the press seemed to be becoming practicable.[39]

The wars also saw the Royal Navy operating for extended periods in distant waters. The navy was no stranger to the Caribbean, Mediterranean or Baltic, but the scale of operations in these waters increased dramatically. The relative superiority of the Anglo-Dutch fleet in home waters released ships for operations further afield. The war of 1702–13 concerned the future of the Spanish Empire in Europe and America, making operations off the coast of Spanish territory an important aspect of the war. The economic importance of Mediterranean and American trades in financing the war, and the fact that the emphasis of French naval effort was in these regions, put an imperative upon operations in these areas which they had not had previously.[40]

During the wars of this period the navy established a base in the Mediterranean. The plan for such a facility can be dated back at least to 1678 but it was not until 1708, with the capture of Minorca, that the navy had obtained a base of its own. The capture of Gibraltar in 1704 also provided Britain with a base at the entrance to that sea. One further consequence of these extended operations in the Mediterranean was the necessity of the naval commander acting as the representative of the monarch at meetings with foreign princes. Sir George Rooke, Sir John Leake and Sir Cloudsley Shovell all exercised an authority and independence of command enjoyed by few officers before 1688, but which was to become an significant feature of the squadron commander's role in the eighteenth century.[41]

In the Americas, naval activity had not been intense during the seventeenth century. This had less to do with the importance of the region than with the fact that contemporary states lacked the mechanisms to maintain military and naval forces there at realistic cost. While no state upset the balance of power there, the colonists could be left to fight their wars unaided. This began to change during the Franco-Dutch war of 1672–8, but the difficulties of campaigning at such distances encouraged the powers to negotiate a treaty of neutrality for the Americas in 1686. In the desperate situation in which William III found himself in the 1690s there was no chance that he would respect this neutrality, and for almost every year of the war squadrons were sent out to the West Indies to help defend the Spanish colonies and annoy the French. During the War of Spanish Succession British expeditions were turned against Spain and France, and by 1711 the military and naval infrastructure was adequate to allow Britain to mount an amphibious assault upon Quebec. These were, however, operations at the end of an extremely fragile line of communication back to Europe, and it was to be a further 40 years before the means of effective warfare in America became realised.[42]

1689–1713: The Emergence of an Oceanic Naval Power

Politically, diplomatically and structurally, the wars of 1689–1713 had an important impact upon the Royal Navy. From 1642 Parliament had maintained an interest in the navy. Although the Restoration had broken a link between Parliament and naval policy, the expense of the fleet and the quarrels between naval officers had ensured that it had the potential to be an item on the parliamentary agenda. Parliament could have an influence on policy. The failure to grant money for the fleet in 1674 had caused Charles to abandon the war against the Dutch, but votes after the peace helped him maintain a credible naval policy. Between 1675 and 1677 debates were influential in the building programme that emerged at the end of the decade.[43]

In the decades after 1689 Parliament became both better informed about the navy and more concerned in its well-being. This was not simply because the navy had become a greater charge on the taxpayer, nor was it because of a new political philosophy ushered in by the Glorious Revolution. The end of the Licensing Act in 1694 greatly reduced censorship of printed discussion about government policy. The change in the naval administration also meant that men knowledgeable in this technical and alien sea service were on opposition benches and capable of producing a more informed debate. The strengthened position of the merchant lobby in Parliament increased interest, whilst the utilisation of war strategy as a point of division between Whig and Tory put party animus and intensity into debates concerning the navy and affairs at sea. By 1714 the navy was fair game in the political arena.

The last decades of the seventeenth century had witnessed the consolidation of a system of European diplomacy. Contacts between states were becoming more formal and regular, and in this the sea was playing a part. Although the sea divided nations, the improvements in navigation and commerce were making the seas a great medium for bringing nations together in trade. Almost any state which had a coastline was finding the significance of its maritime interests increasing. The precise impact of maritime pressure on these nations is still a matter of debate. Jeremy Black has trenchantly argued that English historians have overestimated its impact on states, whose primary interests remained dynastic and territorial. England, which did not possess a large professional army, never carried the diplomatic weight with her neighbours that she hoped to do.[44] Nevertheless, English monarchs and ministers believed that the fleet was an important diplomatic lever. English warships were mobilised as deterrents in the Baltic during the 1650s and in 1699 and in the years that followed 1715. The Barbary cruises, the mobilisation of 1678, the sending of the fleet to the Mediterranean in 1694 and 1704, the naval support to Portugal in 1703, all had a diplomatic purpose. Although in many cases the attempts were misguided and unrealistic, there were enough apparent successes to preserve the notion that the fleet had an important, and in some cases decisive, role to play in Britain's foreign policy.

William III's accession to the throne had been stimulated by his desire to bring British resources to the aid of the Netherlands against France. He could not abandon a military campaign in the Low Countries, and British troops were rapidly despatched to support the Dutch forces. Whig support for William and the Protestant Succession was quickly identified with support for the war in Flanders. Tories, who saw in this the sacrifice of English interests to the Dutch, articulated a 'Blue Water' policy of fighting France at sea, England's natural element. The reopening of war with France in 1702 saw the despatch of another army to Flanders. The Duke of Marlborough assumed command of an allied army there that was to drain French military power between 1704 and 1710. However, from 1689 the structure of the English fleet gradually changed. The powerful battle fleet in the Channel was maintained, but greater numbers of 70-gun ships, better suited for sustained operations in distant waters, were added to the fleet. This development was not matched by the French and was another important step towards making 'Blue Water' strategy an attractive option.[45]

When the war ended in 1713 the ambiguity surrounding the strategic role of Britain's armed forces had not been resolved. The political debate over strategy raged during the war and remained a point of dispute for politicians during the eighteenth century and beyond. Until 1939 there was still a division among strategic thinkers about the 'British Way of Warfare'. It remains a highly contentious historical issue. At the time, politicians had to make sense of the options that were available to them. The end of the Grand Alliance with Holland, Austria and other states, the exhaustion of France, the elevation of Habsburg Austria, the continuing tensions in the Mediterranean and the Baltic, had broken down the diplomatic consensus of previous years. Political dogma instructed but did not inform. British policy-makers had to come to terms with the limitations of their military force. It was a slow and painful process but it resulted in what Daniel Baugh has characterised as a British concept of victory, which aimed not directly to defeat the enemy but to secure a satisfactory result, leaving the nation stronger at the end of the war than it had been at the beginning. Britain's insular position, which made military success on the Continent so difficult, protected her and enabled her to concentrate on maritime conquest and the enlargement of commerce.[46] Baugh's thesis goes to the very heart of our understanding of British strategic policy in the modern world, and is sure to stimulate great debate and further research. In 1713, without allies, Britain's principal diplomatic and military lever was again her navy, but its role was to fluctuate dramatically in the uncertain diplomatic and political environment of the period post-1713.[47]

The final change that impacted upon the navy in these years was financial. When Charles II had gone to war, his financial resources required him to win quickly. In 1689, William III plunged England into a war with France which could not be quick. France was not highly susceptible to defeat at sea, and the English army sent to Flanders was unlikely to be decisive. In the event the war seemed to be driving England towards catastrophe.

The losses in trade were compounding a crisis brought about by what D.W. Jones has termed the 'Double Forward Commitment' – a war by land and sea. The cost was crippling at over £1 million a year by 1696. The strategy, imposed by William's urgent needs, was the first conflict in modern times that seriously destabilised the English economy. Trade collapsed as bullion flows out of the country depressed demand. The war had damaged England's European and Irish markets, and French privateers were wreaking damage on England's vital colonial and Mediterranean trades. The shipping industry had been disrupted by government demands for transports. By 1696 loss of confidence had precipitated a monetary crisis. Government action gradually restored an uneasy balance, of which the most important factor was the supporting of the Bank of England, which had been established in 1694 to underwrite government debt. The government was able to secure its credit to continue the war until peace was made in 1697.[48]

It is very doubtful if these measures would have been sufficient when war resumed in 1702, if other economic changes had not taken place between 1697 and 1702. The willingness to increase tax levels, a boom in the Portugal trade, the grain trade and the woollen trades, and the restructuring of the East India trade all played a part in stabilising the City capital market. When war came, the Bank of England was a valuable agent in handling government debt. Although the war hampered trade, the markets were protected by the fleet and credit remained stable. A system was now in place to enable the government to finance its expenditure within a solid credit market. So long as the fleet protected trade credit remained intact.

The wars of 1689–97 and 1702–13 had not produced the dramatic battles of the Dutch wars. Apart from Bantry Bay (1689), Beachy Head (1690), Barfleur (1692) and Malaga (1704), there were few clashes of battle fleets. The reason was that the Anglo-Dutch battle fleets had defeated the French challenge by the end of 1692. Little was demanded in terms of fleet tactics or ship handling. The principal challenge came from the privateers. The great success of the French privateers demonstrates that command of the sea could not be secured simply by a dominant battle fleet. However, this dominance did give the British state a significant degree of security from large-scale invasion which in turn gave the British naval administration time and space to come to terms with their problems of victualling, storing, building and designing a battle fleet with oceanic capabilities. The sheer scale of the allied dominance in fleet movements, as opposed to raiding activities, provided the stability for the navy to develop to meet an expanded role in the new, less predictable environment of the 1720s.

5

1713–1815: The Establishment of Oceanic Supremacy

Unlike the seventeenth century, the period 1713 to 1815 is rich in naval studies and literature. Biographies, novels, scholarly and popular studies of ships, administration, tactics and strategy are plentiful. In the popular imagination it is the classic age of the Royal Navy, culminating in the charisma of Nelson, victory at Trafalgar, and Britain's continued domination of the seas for the next 100 years.[1]

During the eighteenth century there was a growing consciousness of the importance of the navy in defending a distinctly British social and political system. Histories of the navy began to appear and were regularly reprinted. An ideology which despised the standing army and linked naval power, economic progress and liberty came to dominate political discourse. As tastes changed, the navy became increasingly sentimentalised in the popular nineteenth-century imagery of the Nelson cult and the 'Jolly Jack Tar'.[2] By the 1890s the navy was at the very centre of political debate. The imperial drive of the time was underpinned by a quasi-Darwinian philosophy, which saw nations as biological organisms bound by scientific laws, competing for survival. The navy was essential to expansion. It was assumed that there were some immutable scientific principles that determined the successful application of naval power. What better way to identify these principles than to study the history of the Royal Navy? The American Captain Alfred Thayer Mahan most effectively encapsulated the apparent lessons of the age of sail in a scholarly study intended for a popular audience in 1890, called *The Influence of Sea Power Upon History, 1660–1783*. However, Mahan's work was one of many that appeared in the years between 1870 and 1914, and although the navalist movement had limited political appeal, it produced a mass of material ranging from the crudely sentimental to the highest standards of intellectual endeavour.[3] Some of the best of this material formed the basis of later twentieth-century studies of maritime strategic doctrine, and at the centre of it all is the eighteenth-century navy.

The volume of work on the eighteenth century makes it impossible to do more than touch upon the most salient features of the navy's development during the period. The extent of change was less than during the preceding and succeeding centuries but was, nonetheless, important. Most organisational and operational features of the navy were in place by 1713 and remained little changed until the 1830s. The formal relationships between the Admiralty and its subordinate boards (Navy Board and Victualling Board), the monarch, Cabinet and naval officers were well established. Ship design, building and maintenance proceeded according to well-known principles. The navy's relationships with the maritime community – the merchant marine, seamen, dockyard workers and contractors – were fairly stable throughout the period. The main features of the Royal Navy's strategy and tactics changed little. The shift to the west, with the concentration of naval forces at Portsmouth and Plymouth, had been effected between 1690 and 1713. The strategy of blockade had been worked out and was altered little until the advent of steam power and high explosives made a rethink vital.[4] The line of battle remained the principal tactical formation. Strategically, the navy continued to be the basis of independent offensive and defensive action. Although the size and function of the army was hotly debated in Parliament there was no doubt about the need to maintain a navy capable of defeating its nearest rivals.

The changes that took place focused upon the more efficient functioning of existing practices, strategies and structures. Improvements were made in the dockyards, to signalling and victualling. Over the course of the century these changes enabled the Royal Navy to keep more of its ships at sea for longer in more distant parts of the world or in more dangerous waters. Naval dockyards in Britain were expanded and working practices improved. Victualling improved in quality and reliability. Fresh vegetables and citrus fruits reduced the incidence of scurvy, and greater attention to hygiene generally improved the health of seamen. Gradually, a more detailed coastal knowledge enabled the navy's blockade of enemy coasts to be conducted more effectively. The development of facilities in America and the Caribbean enabled the fleet to conduct more effective operations in those waters. Improved signalling, greater experience and confidence gradually enabled commanders between the 1770s and 1805 to use their line of battle flexibly to break the enemy's line and make decisive encounters at sea more practicable. In the same period, changes in the internal organisation of ships' crews, and changes in naval cannon, gave British vessels an increased advantage in ship-to-ship combat.

Most of these changes have been thoroughly researched. One of the first serious works in the field of eighteenth-century naval administration, by Daniel Baugh, covered the period 1714–39. The standard he set has been followed by historians covering later periods. The internal management of warships and the lives of their crews have been dealt with by Michael Lewis, who focused upon the period 1793–1815, and, more recently, in an excellent study of the mid-century navy by Nicholas Rodger. The tactical changes have been researched and recounted in modern biographies of the admirals Edward Hawke and George Rodney, besides more general works.[5]

During this period the navy was sustained by growing financial and physical resources in Britain. The expansion of oceanic trades from the 1660s created a base of wealth, skilled manpower and a powerful maritime infrastructure. Growth slowed during the first half of the eighteenth century, creating a fear that France would eventually overhaul Britain in world trade, but the decisive victories of the Seven Years War (1756–63), accelerating growth based on textile production from the 1780s and the devastation of European industries during the French Revolutionary and Napoleonic wars (1792–1815) ensured British domination of world trade and shipping until the last decades of the nineteenth century. Yet this long-term perspective hides a series of crises that faced the British state and the navy. These crises raise important questions about the role of the navy in British foreign policy, the economy and society. The first of these has been the subject of extensive research and argument, but the latter two remain largely unexplored.

1713–1739: Diplomacy and the Boundaries of Naval Power

The contribution of the Royal Navy to the War of Spanish Succession was rather ambiguous. The war had ended in exhaustion and stalemate. Sea-power had not proved decisive. France had been contained on the battlefields of Europe by the combined armies of the Grand Alliance. The Spanish Empire was divided. Spain's Italian lands were handed over to the Austrian Habsburgs. The Anglo-Dutch fleet had dominated the waters on both sides of the Atlantic and in the Mediterranean, but had not managed to prevent France from installing and maintaining the Bourbon claimant to the Spanish throne in Madrid. Nor had it been able to split Spain's American empire from the new Bourbon King of Spain's inheritance.

However, attitudes to sea-power had been absorbed into the political rhetoric of the time. In 1704, the High Tories, who opposed the moderate Tory–Whig ministry headed by Godolphin and Marlborough, saw the capture of Gibraltar and Admiral George Rooke's victory at Malaga as a perfect foil to the Duke of Marlborough's victory at Blenheim. When Marlborough's campaigns in Flanders became bogged down, discontented Whigs and Tories championed alternative 'Blue Water' strategies in the Mediterranean (1707–8) and later Canada (1711). When the Tories came to power in 1710, there was a marked run down of activities in Flanders and eventually a peace without reference to Britain's allies.

Although the accession of George I (1714–27) ushered in almost 70 years of Whig government, the significance of sea-power and the navy had not been lost on the Whig ministers. Britain had ended the war with the largest navy in the world. It was firmly part of the fabric of British society, commanding the support of all sections of the political nation. Britain's material gains from the war – Gibraltar, Minorca, Newfoundland, Nova Scotia – had all been won by amphibious action and added to the navy's power in the Mediterranean and America. King George loved his British army and his electorate of Hanover, but the British public loved neither, which posed the King's ministers a problem. Hanover had to be defended, but the army could never be expanded to confront other European powers without allies. On the other hand, the navy exceeded all its rivals, and symbolised British interests and the fruits of the peace of 1713. It was militarily plausible and politically attractive to concentrate upon naval force as Britain's major diplomatic lever. It was also entirely consistent with Stuart and Orangist policy, though seriously complicated by the added dimension of Hanover.

	N° of ships	Average displacement (tons)	French ships	Spanish ships
1715	182	1126	76	26
1720	155	1122	33	29
1725	153	1165	46	29
1730	154	1228	48	53
1735	154	1240	55	61
1740	154	1264	59	59
1745	207	1137	73	41
1750	220	1255	68	29

Source: Glete, J., *Navies and Nations*, II, 551–2, 577–8, 629.

British and Hanoverian interests were not entirely at odds. Both powers were uneasy about Swedish and Russian ambitions in the Baltic. From the 1650s North America was considered as a supplier of timber and pitch for ships, but the Baltic remained the navy's principal source. Fleets were sent to protect British trade between 1715 and 1718, 1719, 1721, 1725, 1726 and 1727. These operations indicated that deep-draught warships were little use against the galleys used by Sweden and Russia in the shallow Baltic waters.[6]

If the experiences in the Baltic were not encouraging, operations in the Mediterranean and Caribbean promised greater things. Philip V of Spain and his wife, Elizabeth Farnese, were determined to regain the Italian lands surrendered to Austria by the Treaty of Utrecht. The movement of armies by sea was a vital part of Mediterranean warfare and, gradually, the Spanish navy was rebuilt to make this possible. In 1717 Spain launched an attack upon Sardinia and in June 1718 Spanish forces landed on Sicily. After the strain of the War of Spanish Succession, France, Britain, Austria and Holland desperately wanted a period of peace. Between 1716 and 1718 they united to form a defensive alliance and took action against Spain. In July 1718 a fleet under Sir George Byng caught the Spanish fleet off Cape Passaro in Sicily, routing it as it fled southward. The British covered the Austrian occupation of Sicily, and a French army invaded Spain, forcing Philip to abandon his plans.[7]

In 1725, Spain and Austria finally settled their disputes over Italy in return for mutual support against Britain. Spain wanted to regain Gibraltar and Minorca; Austria was determined to expand her own maritime commerce through the Ostend Company and Antwerp. Again with the support of France, as well as Prussia and Holland, British squadrons were sent out to maintain a supply line to Gibraltar, blockade Cadiz, and prevent the annual treasure fleet to Mexico, the *Flota*, from sailing. Another squadron, under Vice-Admiral Francis Hosier, was sent to blockade Porto Bello in modern Panama, to prevent the return of the Peruvian treasure fleet, the *Galleones*. Although the standoff lasted for two years the lack of silver from America eventually broke the Austro-Spanish alliance.[8]

Over this period, the English government may have learned some vital lessons about the limitations of naval power, particularly in relation to the Baltic. These lessons included the important fact that the threat of naval power could be more terrifying than its use. However, for a large section of opinion, the successes of the 1720s only confirmed the power of the British fleet.[9] Hosier's passive blockade of Porto Bello had led to terrible losses from disease, including the death of Hosier himself. It was believed that vigorous naval action could have brought success at a lower price than blockade. This view was reinforced by successful naval action against Spanish coastguards who harried British merchantmen in the Caribbean in 1730–1. The despatch of a squadron to Lisbon in support of Portugal during a dispute with Spain in 1736 also ended successfully. The impression was established that British naval power could be a decisive diplomatic weapon.

Although there is some truth in this, there is no agreement on how much. Jeremy Black has shown that the fundamental factor underlying the successful employment of naval power between 1716 and 1731 was the alliance with France, which secured home waters, permitted the British fleet to range freely across the oceans and provided Britain with a first-rate land force to put pressure upon her enemies.[10] Likewise Spain, unlike Russia, was peculiarly vulnerable to British sea-power. Spain depended upon American silver for her fiscal solvency and could not hope to achieve her Italian ambitions without secure sea communications between Italy and Spain. The end of the French alliance in 1731 and the employment of the fleet against powers without vulnerable maritime connections greatly diminished British diplomatic power, but whether this reliance on the navy precluded Britain from participating in European affairs as a first-rate power during the eighteenth century is an important and continuing debate.

1739–1748: War, Crisis and the Development of Naval Power

In the years that followed 1714 the navy had been kept at a fairly constant strength, numbering about 120 warships. Likewise, the infrastructure of port facilities remained intact. However, France and Spain had been slowly but surely rebuilding their naval strength. Observers in Britain were not blind to this and were even more concerned by the dramatic growth of French maritime commerce, which provided both a physical and a financial base for the growing strength of the French fleet. It remains a point of debate as to how far Walpole's ministry was culpable in this erosion of British naval superiority. Whatever the realities of Britain's position, there was a widespread belief in the 1730s that the navy could end a prolonged conflict with Spain over merchants' access to the markets of Spanish America.

By 1739 diplomacy had been exhausted and the time seemed right to impose a solution by force.[11] A French alliance with Spain acted as a deterrent to action, but eventually it was calculated that France would not intervene and a major expedition was sent to the West Indies to seize Spanish territories and bring Spain to terms. France reacted by sending both the Toulon and Brest squadrons to support Spain, and although they had a negligible direct impact on the fate of the expedition, the threat of unpredictable French forces at sea contributed to Britain's inability to achieve anything of significance against Spain between 1740 and 1743. Spanish trade was driven to neutral flags, but invasion of Spain was impossible without a large army. Sea-power alone had proved to be of limited value as an offensive weapon, even against a power as exposed as Spain.

Before this situation had been reached the Anglo-Spanish war had been subsumed into the wider War of Austrian Succession (1740–8). Britain was bound by treaty to support the Habsburg succession to the Holy Roman Empire, so when the Emperor Charles VI died in October 1740, Britain, Hanover and the United Provinces declared their support for his daughter Maria Theresa and her husband, the Archduke Francis. However, Prussia, France and Spain were determined to profit from a disputed succession and supported the rival claim of the Wittelsbach Elector of Bavaria, Charles Albert. In December 1740 Prussian troops invaded Silesia and during 1741 Franco-Spanish forces assembled in Bavaria to invade Lower Austria. George II realised that neither the small armies of Britain and Hanover nor the large British navy could defend Hanover, let alone turn back the tide, and therefore he unilaterally declared Britain and Hanover neutral in the conflict.

A major Austrian recovery at the end of 1741 persuaded George to commit himself to the conflict and a *Pragmatic Army* of British, Dutch and Hanoverian troops assembled in Flanders to divert French forces from Germany and Italy. The campaigns in the Rhineland and the Low Countries were generally indecisive, but by 1745 the balance of advantage undoubtedly lay with the French, who were advancing on to Dutch soil.

During this time the Royal Navy had found itself forced on to the defensive. Although larger than either the French or Spanish fleets, it could not be strong everywhere. From 1740 its primary task was to prevent the French and Spanish fleets from uniting, but keeping them apart proved impossible as intelligence was slow and inaccurate and the weather drove blockading squadrons off station. In December 1741, Vice-Admiral Richard Haddock was unable to prevent the Spanish Cartagena and Cadiz squadrons escorting an invasion force to Italy and uniting with the French Toulon squadron. The strain of keeping adequate squadrons at sea in the Channel, the Mediterranean, and the Caribbean was intense. Shortages of stores, manpower and victuals were experienced everywhere, and the ships suffered the wear and tear of long periods at sea. By the beginning of

1744 the Royal Navy was facing a major crisis. Vice-Admiral Thomas Mathews, commanding the Mediterranean squadron of about 28 men-of-war, tried to support the Austrian and Piedmontese campaign in Italy against the Franco-Spanish armies, whilst watching an equal number of French and Spanish ships-of-the-line anchored in Toulon. He could not do both effectively. On the Atlantic coast, 17 French line-of-battle ships, under Lieutenant-General de Roquefeuil at Brest, were ready to sail. Their objective was to cover the crossing of troop transports gathering in the Channel ports for an invasion of England. Meanwhile, in British ports and coastal waters there remained some 21 comparable warships, in various states of readiness.

By 27 January 1744 the Brest fleet was standing towards England. The Admiral of the Fleet, Sir John Norris, was immediately ordered to sea with as many ships as he could muster. Despite confusion of intelligence and the difficulties of gathering the fleet, Norris got to the Downs just before the main body of the Brest squadron arrived. Norris heard of the arrival of the French off Dungeness and on 22 February weighed anchor to attack. At that point gales set in which lasted for four days, scattering de Roquefeuil's fleet back down the Channel and shattering the transports in the Channel ports. Norris's squadron was also badly damaged but the immediate invasion threat was over.

In the Mediterranean, the Franco-Spanish squadrons emerged from Toulon to seek battle with Mathews and clear the way for Franco-Spanish reinforcements to go to Italy by sea. Mathews came out from his anchorage to meet the enemy but although both sides sought battle, both fleets also contained elements that did not press an attack with vigour. The action off Toulon on 22 February 1744 was indecisive and greeted in England with disappointment, which eventually turned to anger as the recriminations between Mathews and his second-in-command, Richard Lestock, became public knowledge.[12]

The war at sea and on land did not go well throughout 1744 and 1745. The defeat of the allied army at Fontenoy on 11 May 1745 and the landing in Scotland of Charles Edward Stuart, the Young Pretender's son, on 23 July, ended any hope of military victory against France or Spain in the near future. The navy, which had failed public expectations since 1739, was at least now prepared to mount a formidable challenge to any French attempt to invade England in support of the Scottish rising. The precise role of the navy in defeating the rebellion is still a point of controversy. Naval historians have seen the fleet as being decisive, but recently some historians have cast doubt upon this. It is argued that the French were not deterred by the presence of a large squadron in the Downs, and their failure to invade England was occasioned by the retreat of the Jacobites from Derby in early December 1745. Whether the Royal Navy was or might have been a decisive factor in the preservation of the House of Hanover is impossible to tell, but the fleet did make a very positive contribution to the defeat of the Stuart cause. The fleet convoyed the British army and Dutch troops back to England during the summer and autumn of 1745. It convoyed troops, stores and victuals up to Berwick, Edinburgh and Aberdeen, ensuring that the Duke of Cumberland's army was adequately supplied on its winter march north to meet and decisively defeat the Jacobite army at Culloden on 16 April 1746. The navy has been criticised for failing to prevent small numbers of French reinforcements reaching the Jacobites, but such close blockade was beyond the capacity of an eighteenth-century navy to mount in the short winter days and tempestuous weather of the North Sea.[13]

The last years of the War of Austrian Succession saw the allies unable to regain the initiative in western Europe. The French army consolidated its position on Dutch soil with the capture of Bergen-op-Zoom in September 1747. In Italy the French-Spanish position was much less secure, thanks in part to the assistance of the Royal Navy to the Austro-Sardinian forces. On the whole, however, almost until the end of the war the navy could not claim to have fulfilled the great, and perhaps unrealistic, hopes of the public. But during 1747 the navy did manage to give the public some cause for rejoicing amid the torrent of disappointment. On 4 May 1747 Vice-Admiral George Anson's squadron of 15 vessels caught a small French squadron which was escorting ships outward bound for the East Indies and Canada off Cape Finisterre in Spain. Many of the transports were captured. On 14 October, Rear-Admiral Edward Hawke's squadron of 14 met a French force of 9 warships covering a convoy 300 miles off Finisterre. Five of the French warships were captured along with 40 of the merchantmen, which fled towards the Caribbean. In combat, the

Royal Navy had proved itself still capable of inflicting defeat upon the enemy.[14]

When the war was ended by the Treaty of Aix-la-Chapelle on 18 October 1748, the navy's performance had not lived up to the hopes of 1739. Yet, politically, the navy's role as the principal means of defending British interests was more entrenched than ever. This had less to do with the battle fleet at sea than other aspects of the war. The failure of the land campaign in Flanders had undermined any idea that Britain could realistically expect to contain French ambitions on the European mainland. This was all the more apparent as Britain's allies, the United Provinces and Austria, seemed unable or unwilling to contribute to an adequate combined army. This may have been the result of incompetent diplomacy but, nonetheless, a land commitment to defend Hanover and the Flanders coastline looked increasingly problematic.

Although the supporters of a maritime or 'Blue Water' strategy could not point to decisive results, they had received some major boosts during the 1740s. One of these boosts was plainly political. In the parliamentary manoeuvring that followed the resignation of Sir Robert Walpole in February 1742, malcontent Whigs used divisions over war policy to strengthen their parliamentary position and thus their prospects of bargaining their way into a share of government. The most prominent, although by no means the only exponent of this tactic, was William Pitt. Pitt's very prominent declarations linking maritime war with British, as opposed to Hanoverian, interests lay at the base of his political strength. In February 1746 Pitt obtained a post in government to join like-minded men, followers of the Duke of Bedford, who had become First Lord of the Admiralty in 1744.[15]

The views of Pitt and Bedford were not allowed to dominate strategy in the wake of the rebellion and the imminent collapse of the Dutch, but they were given added strength by some events at sea. The battle fleet had not achieved what was hoped, but privateers from Britain and America had notable success. Although the number of prizes taken in this war was about half that seized during the War of Spanish Succession, the privateers were venturing further afield, disrupting the Bourbon powers' oceanic commerce with some spectacular and well publicised results. The other event was the capture of the fortified French town of Louisbourg (June 1745) on Cape Breton

Island, which guarded the entrance of the St Lawrence and the approach to Quebec. The town was captured by an army of New Englanders, assisted by a naval force under Commodore Peter Warren, who had come up from the Caribbean for the purpose. Bedford championed a major attack on Quebec, which actually assembled in the summer of 1746, only to be delayed by bad weather until it was too late to arrive off North America before ice closed the St Lawrence. The expedition was diverted to make some raids upon the French coast. A French attempt to recapture Louisbourg in 1746 was ravaged by disease and achieved nothing. Louisbourg was surrendered at the end of the war in exchange for the captured Dutch provinces, but its successful capture reinforced the perceived importance of such conquests to British interests in America, the vulnerability of the French colonies and their diplomatic value.[16]

1748–1763: Primacy at Sea and a Global Capacity

In the years of peace that followed 1748, financial economies dramatically reduced the size of the navy, but it did not go into an organisational slumber. Its importance was recognised, and men remained in power who were convinced of its potential, particularly the Earl of Sandwich, who took over the Admiralty from his political ally the Duke of Bedford in 1748. With him at the Admiralty was Admiral George Anson. Anson is one of the great heroes of naval tradition, a navigator, proven leader at sea, successful commander in battle and long-serving administrator and adviser to government. However, he left few personal papers and his precise role in the development of the navy in this period is unclear. The years 1748–51 are critical to an explanation of why the navy came to dominate the oceans of the world by 1763, yet they remain relatively under-researched. Attention has focused upon the Seven Years War itself or upon Anson personally, both aspects which are vital to a proper understanding of the victories but inadequate in themselves. More needs to be done to establish what changes took place and how significant they were in the context of the war that unfolded from 1755.

	N° of ships	Average displacement (tons)	French ships	Spanish ships
1750	220	1255	68	29
1755	216	1280	98	77
1760	301	1245	95	89
1765	266	1418	103	78
1770	235	1488	127	95
1775	227	1485	117	115

Source: Glete, J., *Navies and Nations*, II, 552–3, 578, 629–30.

What is clear is that some things did change. The Admiralty, particularly, not only recovered its organisational stability after the upheavals of 1739–44, but achieved a much more visible leadership in naval affairs. The Lords Commissioners of the Admiralty exercised the powers of the Lord High Admiral when this office was put into commission, as it was in 1628–38, 1645–8, 1652–60, 1673–1702, and from 1709 onwards. However, apart from being the formal channel through which the King's orders ran to all naval personnel, their function was very unclear. The Navy Board carried out the practical management of the navy, but from 1744 the Admiralty Commissioners began to assert their power over the Board. There was a very acrimonious dispute with the Navy Board over ship design during 1746–7, which ended with the Admiralty having the final word in the matter. In 1749 Sandwich conducted a major examination of the dockyards' labour practices and ordered significant changes. However, much more work needs to be done to establish the causes, impact and extent of these changes in naval administration.[17] The officer corps was tied more closely to the navy and given a clearer corporate identity by the adoption of uniform in 1748, the development of a pension system and the extension of half-pay whilst not in service. When the war came in May 1756, it arrived with plenty of warning. The Admiralty was able to complete its assertion of control over the navy during 1755 and oversaw the expansion of the fleet in a measured manner, so that although there were still crises and mistakes, the navy was prepared for the new conflict.

The Seven Years War has been the focus of a great deal of historical attention, much of it related to the performance of William Pitt as the great war minister. In recent decades, Pitt's reputation has been put into a much more realistic perspective, but if Pitt is no longer seen as the omnipotent organiser of victory over France and Spain, it raises questions about why the Royal Navy was able to carry Britain forward to such spectacular victories on land and sea during these years.[18] On the eve of war Britain did have a numerical advantage in warships fit for sea, but the early years of the conflict soon showed that this advantage was not decisive.

Anglo-French conflict had been brewing since 1748 in North America, and broke into violence in the Ohio valley during 1754. Both sides decided to reinforce their colonists and expeditions were sent out during 1755. It was during this period that the war in the backwoods spilled over into a conflict at sea, when Vice-Admiral Edward Boscawen intercepted a French convoy of troops bound for Canada. He managed to capture two French warships, but could not prevent the convoy reaching its destination, provoking Lord Chancellor Hardwicke's famous phrase that he had done too much to prevent war and too little to win it.[19]

The drift to war continued into 1756. Britain lacked allies to divert French land forces, and the majority of mobilised naval forces were held ready in home waters. This led to one of the great *causes célèbres* of the war. The decision to keep forces at home left the commander in the Mediterranean, Vice-Admiral John Byng, with less ships than he anticipated when faced by the Toulon squadron escorting an invasion army to Minorca. His failure to beat them and the loss of the island had political repercussions which led to his execution – the only admiral ever to be shot for cowardice.[20] The political impact of defeat at Minorca and in North America led to the fall of the ministry and its replacement by one headed by the Duke of Devonshire and William Pitt, whose outspoken championing of a maritime war in British interests left little room for doubt that the emphasis would be placed upon a naval war. This ministry fell in June 1757 to be replaced by one headed by the Duke of Newcastle and William Pitt. Attention would be paid to securing Hanover but the weight of the British contribution would continue to be based upon sea-power.

The first fruits of this strategy were not promising. Reinforcements were sent to America to attack Louisbourg but the assault was postponed. Pitt believed that raids upon the French coast would divert troops from an attack on Hanover and destroy French naval installations, but the force sent to attack Rochefort did not even land.[21] Despite these disappointments, the continued application of this strategy during 1758 saw the gradual reduction of France's ability to compete in a colonial and maritime war. The Royal Navy was beginning to receive the new ships ordered from 1755, particularly the smaller frigates, ideally suited to pursuit of blockade runners. This blockade of French ports made the reinforcement of Canada and the French West Indies difficult, whilst British regulars were crossing the Atlantic in larger numbers to link up with increasing numbers of Americans under arms. The French colonies lacked the manpower to match this build-up, although strenuous efforts were made to recruit Indian allies to offset this disadvantage. The French held their own in the Hudson valley, but Louisbourg finally fell to the Anglo-American forces in September 1758.[22]

The blockade of the French coast was reinforced by large numbers of privateers which gravely damaged French shipping. It was increasingly difficult to use coastal waters to bring supplies and merchandise to the dockyards and ports.[23] Not only was the French navy deprived of vital stores, but the capital used to finance it was draining away. Unlike Britain, which relied upon the large London capital market to buy the public debt funded by tax revenues, France relied upon the private credit of financiers. These financiers depended on the profitability of their own investments to raise credit. As French overseas trade felt the pinch of British attacks, so the credit of the financiers dried up. Although both states relied upon overseas trade for the liquid assets to finance the war, the French fiscal system was far more vulnerable. Pitt gave the House of Commons confidence to vote tax revenues to underwrite public loans. These loans were possible as income continued to be generated from overseas trade. In France there were neither the tax revenues nor the income from trade to resource an effective credit system.[24]

As the war progressed, French prospects diminished. Unlike the previous war, Spain and Holland were resolutely neutral. This denied France the assistance of the Spanish navy and removed the British fear of the occupation of the Dutch coastal provinces. 1759 saw the culmination of these pressures upon France. The steady build-up of British resources in America led to the fall of Quebec in September. A

British expedition captured Guadaloupe in the West Indies, weakening the defensive power of the French Sugar Islands. The blockade was tightened further as means were developed of revictualling at sea and providing adequate watering facilities at Torbay. French attempts to get reinforcements to America were too little, too late. With the campaign in western Germany stalemated, there was little the French could do but hope to bring the war to a conclusion by a direct invasion of the British Isles. The plan, which had caused crises in 1744 and 1745, was defeated by the overwhelming power of the British squadrons covering the French ports. The Toulon squadron, coming to reinforce the Atlantic squadrons, was defeated at Lagos, off Portugal. These latter forces were scattered by gales and the boldness of Admiral Hawke's pursuit of them into Quiberon Bay in October 1759. By September the credit capacity of the financiers of the navy, Beaujon and Goosens, began to crumble and on 14 November they went bankrupt. From this point on an effective naval strategy was impracticable.[25]

The rest of the war was a consolidation of this success. British money and small numbers of troops helped sustain the war in Germany. Montreal fell in 1760 and Martinique and some smaller islands fell early in 1762. A belated Spanish entry into the war, caused by the scale of the British victory, only added to the conquests, as Cuba fell with the capture of Havana and the Philippines with the conquest of Manila during 1762. When the Peace of Paris was signed on 10 February 1763, Britain, alone among the combatants in a war that had raged across Europe, could claim to have emerged with an outstanding victory. Although the West Indian islands were returned to France, Canada and India were left in her hands. Far more than in any previous war, the public were made aware that the navy had secured a clear victory. It was made possible by the maritime community's ability to provide the human and physical resources for an unprecedented expansion of the Royal Navy. Pitt's great contribution was to convince Parliament and people that the war at sea was crucial, profitable and winnable. However, part of his legacy was the belief that all conflicts might be resolved like this. The lessons of the 1720s had to be relearned in the next sixty years.

1763–1783: Naval Primacy, Strain and Recovery

The victory in the Seven Years War has been written about extensively, but a great deal of research is still needed to understand both its causes and the effects. Recently, historians such as John Brewer and Paul Kennedy have drawn attention to the economic foundations of the victory. Others, like Nicholas Rodger, have shown how the administration, officers and men of the Royal Navy were becoming much more professional in their conduct as the century progressed.[26] There is little doubt that both in finances and in performance Britain presented a clear contrast with her enemies. However, more research needs to be done, particularly in understanding the expansion of the Atlantic world, which put resources from both Atlantic coasts at the disposal of the navy. In this war, unlike its predecessors, the Royal Navy was truly capable of acting as an oceanic force. Integrating the resources of America, the Caribbean, and to a lesser extent of India, into the naval fabric was an important feature of success. It brought with it difficulties concerning social attitudes and administrative mechanisms which some historians have begun researching, but the issues have yet to be fully explored.[27] Likewise, the effects of the war on the navy are in need of further study. Important work has been done by Michael Roberts, Nicholas Tracy, Hamish Scott, Jeremy Black and Neil Stout on various aspects of naval policy following 1763.[28] As a result of their labours a great deal is known about the policy-makers' attitudes to the navy, but a full understanding of how the navy came to terms with the peace and the public's expectation of it requires additional research.

Since the sixteenth century the navy had been seen as the principal military force of the state. Events throughout the seventeenth and eighteenth centuries had confirmed its position. The link between trade, prosperity and naval power had been explicitly made for decades before Pitt used it so effectively in his rise to power. By 1763 this 'Blue Water' policy had proved itself and it became an article of faith to many, but it is in need of further analysis.[29] For some historians, most notably Eric Williams, the surpluses generated by slave-produced sugar supported the credit system upon which the state and navy depended and they financed the Industrial Revolution.

If this were so, the navy's role in protecting these islands and their trade would be crucial to Britain's economic development. Few historians are today willing to make such an explicit link between overseas trade and industrialisation, but the navy's role in Britain's economic development is an aspect of its history that is only now receiving the attention it deserves.[30]

The period between 1763 and 1783 is probably one of the most intriguing in the history of the navy. Barely 20 years after the greatest victory Britain had ever achieved over European enemies, she suffered a humiliating defeat at the hands of her rebellious American subjects in alliance with France, Spain and the Netherlands. Unlike the years of peace, 1763–75, the period of the War of American Independence (1775–83) has received extensive attention from historians.[31] There is little doubt that the war in America was not only lost on land, but it was lost at sea as well. The British army in America found itself unable to control the countryside from which it could draw its supplies. The result was that 'Every biscuit, man and bullet required by the British forces in America had to be transported across three thousand miles of ocean'.[32] This gigantic maritime effort had to be protected by the navy. It was equally imperative that the Americans were cut off from stores and cash generated by their trade and diplomatic relations with France and Spain. In 1778 France entered the war against Britain, followed by Spain in 1779 and Holland in 1780. From this point, it became critical to have adequate naval forces in home waters and the Caribbean to defend Britain and the important West Indies trade.

	N° of ships	Average displacement (tons)	French ships	Spanish ships
1775	227	1485	117	115
1780	286	1300	162	125
1785	306	1461	155	135
1790	312	1513	179	125

Source: Glete, J., *Navies and Nations*, II, 553, 578–9, 630.

In the end, Britain failed in all these aspects of the war. The army's failures – the indecisive New York campaign in 1776, the disastrous

Saratoga campaign of 1777, and the indecisions of 1778–81 – were primarily responsible for eventual defeat, but the naval failures played their part. The navy failed to prevent the large American maritime community from feeding the rebellion. The limited naval commitment to American waters allowed American privateers, merchantmen and the small American navy to wreak havoc upon British trade on both sides of the Atlantic. Supplies got through to the Americans while, by 1780, shortages of stores shipped to the British army were having a critical impact upon land operations.[33]

Once France and Spain had entered the war, substantial naval power was ranged against the Royal Navy. During 1779 the British Isles were faced with an invasion, prevented only by delays, sickness and lack of provisions in the Franco-Spanish fleet. French forces carried out a protracted and partly successful campaign in the West Indies from 1778. In September 1781, Admiral Thomas Graves's failure to dislodge the French squadron under De Grasse from the mouth of the Chesapeake River brought about the surrender of the British army in Yorktown – the defeat that finally broke the willingness of the British public to continue the war.

Traditionally, historians have seen Bourbon intervention as the decisive factor in Britain's defeat. Unable to divert the attention of France and Spain by sponsoring campaigns in Europe, as she had done in every war since 1689, she was eventually ground down by enemy naval activity which kept the rebellion alive. Currently, this view is very much a matter of controversy. Daniel Baugh has shown that by 1782 Britain had won the war at sea, but the victory came too late. The fundamental cause of the defeat was the failure to mobilise adequate naval and mercantile resources at the time when they were required.[34] The government was partly culpable, wishing to minimise expenditure on the navy while conducting extensive land operations in America. Inexperience of such large trans-Atlantic shipments was also an important factor.

The Treaty of Versailles was agreed in November 1782, bringing to an end a war that was an undoubted defeat. The 13 American colonies were recognised as the independent United States of America. Minorca, Britain's principal base in the Mediterranean since 1708, was ceded to Spain, along with West Florida. France regained Caribbean and African trading posts, which stimulated her

Atlantic commerce in the last decades of the century, as well as providing her some consolation for the 1750s. For the army the war was a disaster, but the Royal Navy had also been badly hit by the war. Much more than the army, the officers of the Royal Navy were split by the war. During the eighteenth century the two services had been gradually evolving as professions along slightly different lines. In the preceding century, the tension between the need for officers to have the social standing to warrant holding the King's commission at sea, and the technical skills of seamanship derived from a lifetime of service afloat, had been gradually resolved under the enthusiastic sponsorship of the Stuart kings. By 1688, when the first of a series of monarchs who had less regard for their navy than their army ascended the throne, the navy possessed the stature and maturity to recruit, train and develop officers who met both professional and social demands. The army had never had this tension. It had always been the preserve of the aristocracy, whose social ethos embodied the martial skills on land. The court was the centre of the army's existence, the more so under monarchs like William III, George I and George II who considered themselves soldiers. Since the 1640s the vital influences on the navy had been more varied. The Crown was important, but when the monarch's interest diminished there were informed and vocal parliamentary and mercantile interests who filled the gap. The Admiralty possessed a large amount of political patronage in the port towns. Posts in the Admiralty and its subordinate boards were also significant political prizes. This aspect of professional development is badly in need of serious research, but it would be unsurprising if party political considerations played a more significant part in the appointment of naval officers than of army officers.

The officer corps, associated with political party, reflected the national political divisions which were exacerbated by the war in America. This culminated in 1779, in the courts martial of the commander of the Channel Fleet, Admiral Augustus Keppel, and his third in command, Vice-Admiral Hugh Palliser. Palliser was a follower of the government party of Lord North, whilst Admiral Keppel was a supporter of Lord Rockingham's opposition party. The officers accused each other of inadequate support at the indecisive Battle of Ushant on 27 July 1778.[35] Both were acquitted, and it was fortunate that the entry of France and Spain into the war gradually helped to focus loyalties. The end of the war in 1783 removed the cause of the division.

What is remarkable is that despite the division and disappointment, the Royal Navy emerged from the war into what Paul Webb has characterised as 'almost a golden age of public and parliamentary support'.[36] The work of Webb, Daniel Baugh, David Syrett and Nicholas Rodger has demonstrated that the navy ended the war with improved ships, tactics, internal management, administration and public standing.

The navy had been able to build on the solid foundations of experience. The wars of 1739–48 and 1756–63 had bred a generation of seamen and administrators who knew their work and had confidence in their service. Officers like the admirals Richard Howe, George Rodney, Richard Byron, Augustus Keppel and Edward Hughes, although not uniformly successful, had substantial experience of naval action. In London, the Navy Board was headed by Sir Charles Middleton, an experienced naval officer and a gifted administrator. The First Lord of the Admiralty between 1771 and 1782 was the Earl of Sandwich, who had been First Lord from 1748 to 1751. His political and administrative acumen, against a Cabinet that was broadly hostile to the rapid mobilisation of the navy, was important in enabling the navy to absorb new developments and expand to meet the Bourbon challenge.[37]

The developments were technical and organisational. The carronade, a short-barrelled gun firing a heavy shot, was an important addition to the navy's firepower. The development of new firing mechanisms also improved naval gunnery. Ships were coppersheathed, a process whereby thin copper sheets nailed to the bottoms of vessels hindered the growth of barnacles and weed that slowed the ships down, thus reducing the amount of time which had to be spent in cleaning or repairing them. The internal organisation of the ships' companies was changed by Rodney, which improved the use of manpower. Rodney also took great care of the health of the men, stimulating successful experiments in sanitation and diet. By the end of the war there was a marked contrast between the efficiency and condition of British warships and those of France.[38]

The administration also worked effectively. By the end of the war major improvements had taken place with regard to hiring and

managing trans-Atlantic supply operations. The ship-building programme to meet the demands of the war swung into action too late,
but by 1782 the British had re-established a naval dominance over the
combined fleets of France, Spain and the Netherlands. France and
Spain had exhausted their naval resources by the end of 1781, but the
Royal Navy was well positioned to continue the war, with over five
times as much timber in stock in 1781 than there had been in 1770.[39]

Dominance was partly assured by out-building the enemy, but also
by the victories that the British navy was able to achieve. In January
1780 Vice-Admiral Rodney caught a smaller Spanish squadron off
Cadiz and, in what is known as the Midnight Battle, destroyed one
and captured six of them. The victory effectively broke the siege of
Gibraltar. Vice-Admiral Thomas Hood fought an important action in
January 1782 to outmanoeuvre the French fleet off St Kitts in the
Caribbean. On 12 April 1782 Rodney's fleet met the French under
De Grasse off the Saintes, between Guadaloupe and Dominica. Here,
Rodney's squadron successfully broke through the French line of
battle, disrupting their order and enabling him to concentrate his
firepower on small numbers of his enemies. Five French line-of-battle
ships were taken, including De Grasse's flagship, the *Ville de Paris*. The
line of battle which had evolved as a defensive measure since the
sixteenth century had posed a constant problem to naval commanders
seeking a decisive victory. The rigidity of the line prevented a fleet
from coming to grips with an enemy who was determined not to fight
at close quarters. It is unclear why the means of breaking the line
became apparent at this point, and from the time of this battle the
authorship of the plan has been disputed.[40] It remains another of the
current mysteries of naval history, but once the breakthrough was
made it provided a model to copy, and it was repeated and refined
during the wars with France between 1793 and 1815.

1783–1815: Preservation and Supremacy at Sea

The victories of the fleet were the one ray of hope in the otherwise
dismal situation surrounding the end of the American war. America
and Minorca might be lost, but the West Indies and Gibraltar, not to
mention the British Isles, had been saved. In the soul-searching

caused by the war, the navy remained largely untouched. The Commission on Public Accounts of 1782 had little to suggest and the Admiralty was able to ignore the recommendations of the more powerful Commission on Fees in Public Office in 1788. Opposition and government agreed on the importance of maintaining the navy. As with other periods of peace, too little research has, so far, been carried out to understand fully how the nation and navy viewed and used each other, but while the navy seemed to be contributing to a recovery of British diplomatic and economic power in the later 1780s, money was provided, ships were built and repaired.

	N° of ships	Average displacement (tons)	French ships	Spanish ships
1790	312	1513	179	125
1795	311	1644	162	133
1800	328	1663	110	113
1805	329	1735	87	74
1810	398	1691	84	–
1815	350	1740	92	–

Source: Glete, J., *Navies and Nations*, II, 553–4, 580, 631.

On the eve of the war with France in February 1793, the Royal Navy had never been so powerfully entrenched in British national life. The 1780s had seen a major revival in trade, adding to the pool of maritime resources upon which the navy drew. The navy itself stood at 425 vessels, greater than at any peace period.[41] It possessed an officer corps who, despite the failure of the sea war for America, could look back upon a series of victories and could rely upon a strong sense of corporate identity, forged by the retention in service of so many of their numbers from 1775. During the next war, victory reinforced self-confidence and paved the way for the explicit social shaping of this corporate, professional identity in the nineteenth century.[42]

The wars of 1793 to 1815 have been seen as the apogee of the old sailing navy. However, overwhelming victory, which left it by far the paramount oceanic naval power, brought with it a sense of lack of purpose in the years that followed. The diminished naval threat to homeland, commerce and colonies saw a decay in both the sea service and its shore-based administration. Domestic influences replaced international naval competition as the key factors in the navy's evolution. The powerful influence of Benthamite ideas of public administration saw the Navy Board's complex day-to-day functions absorbed by the Admiralty, to the detriment of both the Admiralty and the efficiency of the navy. The money which had kept the navy intact during the 1780s began to diminish. The re-emergence of a naval threat by the 1860s was associated with the new technologies of steam, iron and high explosives. To face the challenge, the navy had to change. The process was slow, painful and uneven, but one of the results was a reawakened, and even exaggerated, public reverence for 'Nelson's Navy'.

The contribution of the navy to the defeat of France and Britain's subsequent economic domination of world trade was important, but tends to be obscured by the image of Nelson. It was a navy that was at a high peak of effectiveness and efficiency, which was faced by enemies indifferently prepared. After the War of American Independence, the French navy was large and powerful. During the 1780s financial crises in France greatly weakened the navy and the revolution severely shook the officer corps. By 1793 the disastrous consequences of a land war against Austria and Prussia had precipitated another revolution, a major financial crisis and seething revolt in the western and southern provinces. The navy was still intact but not well prepared for an immediate or long campaign.

The Royal Navy's contribution was, in many ways, the classic contribution of sea-power, as understood by the strategic thinkers of the nineteenth and twentieth centuries. The navy succeeded in preventing any serious invasion of Britain, and eventually defeated all attempts to overwhelm her colonies. To transport armies across seas required control of a limited area of sea for a substantial time. From 1793 many plans were laid and preparations made to invade the British Isles. Only on two occasions were the French able to make effective landings. In 1797 a poorly disciplined force of about 1200 raided Fishguard in Wales, only to surrender to the militia. In August 1798, 1150 French troops landed in the west of Ireland to support the Revolt there, but were forced to surrender shortly afterwards. Further attempts to put troops into Ireland were thwarted by the navy.[43]

The tactics used to contain enemy sea-power remained largely unchanged. The blockade of Brest and Toulon by cruising squadrons was supplemented as time passed by small in-shore squadrons, which could inflict damage and extend the blockade to the smaller ports. Although the sea forces available to France were numerically large, they were seldom concentrated or individually equal to the experienced British forces. In individual ship-to-ship actions the enemy fought bravely and scored numerous successes, but they failed to make an impression on British sea-power. Blockade remained an imperfect strategy and blockading squadrons were frequently driven off station by wind and weather. When the French came out in strength they often escaped the blockading forces, but on the occasions on which they ran into the Royal Navy they suffered badly. On 1 June 1794, Admiral Lord Howe encountered Lieutenant-General Villaret-Joyeuse's fleet of 25 ships-of-the-line, escorting about 200 French merchant vessels. Howe engaged with his fleet of a similar number, capturing six of them and sinking one. The convoy escaped, but the capacity of the French to challenge Britain at sea was badly damaged.[44]

Throughout the rest of 1794–5 Britain was able to contain French fleet activities. The dangers increased dramatically at the end of 1795, when the Dutch capitulation to France added 12 Dutch ships-of-the-line to French strength in the North Sea. In July 1796 a treaty with Spain gave France the assistance of over 70 warships, many recently built in Spanish and Cuban yards. These accessions to French strength upset the balance in the Mediterranean, forcing Britain to withdraw her squadron from that sea at the end of the year. However, Britain's advantage was largely restored when Admiral Sir John Jervis's force of 15 ships-of-the-line met 27 Spanish line-of-battle ships under Admiral Jose Cordoba on 14 January 1797 off Cape St Vincent. Jervis's squadron completely outfought the Spanish force, capturing four and blockading the rest in Cadiz. The Dutch suffered a similar fate, losing seven ships-of-the-line to Admiral Adam Duncan's squadron off Camperdown on 11 October 1797.[45] In May 1798 the French fleet, which had concentrated in the Mediterranean, managed to escape Nelson's ships outside Toulon to land an expeditionary force near Alexandria in Egypt. On 1 August Nelson caught up with the French, finding them at anchor in Aboukir Bay. Two French ships-of-the-line were destroyed, nine captured. Only two managed to escape the débâcle.[46] By the time Britain made peace with the French Consulate under Napoleon Bonaparte, with the Treaty of Amiens in May 1802, British squadrons dominated Atlantic and American waters. French forces sent overseas to Egypt or the West Indian colonies had either been cut off and forced to surrender or had held out, like those on Malta, with little hope of relief from home.

The outbreak of war again in 1803 did not immediately change matters, but by 1804 Napoleon had drawn up a complex and ambitious plan to invade Britain. This involved drawing the British home fleet off to the West Indies, thus opening the way for a limited period to land troops in England. The operation, involving the combined French and Spanish fleets, led to the Battle of Trafalgar on 21 October 1805, the most famous naval victory in British history. Of the 33 French and Spanish ships-of-the-line, 20 were at some time during the battle in British hands. Nelson had taken the tactic of breaking the enemy line of battle, which had been developing since 1782, to the point of sailing his fleet directly at right angles into the enemy line. The battle and the campaign have been the subject of many studies and much violent debate, but it is clear that the result of the battle was not quite that of popular imagination.[47] It did not end the threat of a French invasion of Britain. Over the next 10 years the French fleet was gradually rebuilt. To these vessels were added the ships of nations Napoleon had in his sphere of influence: Spain, Denmark and Holland. Britain had to continue her watch upon these ships, taking the chance whenever possible to destroy them. In 1807 Copenhagen was attacked to destroy or take off the Danish fleet. In 1809 a landing was made on the Dutch island of Walcheren, as the first stage of a planned advance up the Scheldt to destroy the naval arsenal at Antwerp. An attack was also launched on the Basque Roads to destroy the vessels there.[48]

Whilst the victory at Trafalgar was not as clear cut as is popularly imagined, neither was the threat that preceded it. Although Napoleon had intended to launch his army on England from its encampments around Boulogne as soon as the British fleet was out of the way, the declaration of war by Austria changed his priorities. By the time that Trafalgar was won, Napoleon and his *Grande Armée* were marching along the Danube to Vienna. Despite these points, whilst the ships available to Napoleon remained scattered across the world the Royal

Navy remained unchallenged in any ocean or sea. This dominance enabled the navy to make other vital contributions to the war.

Whilst Britain could ward off a direct attack by France, she had little hope of bringing down the Republic or Napoleon by herself. In the end it was the combined power of Russia, Prussia and Austria that broke the back of Napoleon's Empire on the battlefields of Russia and Germany during 1812–13. British credit and loan guarantees helped to sustain various states, and particularly France's most persistent enemy, Austria, from 1794 until victory was finally achieved. This credit depended upon the strength of the London financial market. London depended upon the profits of trade and the navy secured that trade. It has been commonly asserted that the decision of British ministries to pursue campaigns in the West Indies from 1794 until 1798 was a major mistake. France would not be decisively damaged by such colonial campaigns, whilst British troops died in their thousands from disease for very little gain. Recently, Michael Duffy has produced a major re-examination of these campaigns, concluding that the strategy was vital to secure the import receipts which underwrote British credit and boosted the maritime economy. Piers Mackesy has also shown that the sustained operations of the navy in the Mediterranean helped to secure the sources of raw cotton and markets for finished goods in southern Europe upon which the booming textile industry depended. These arguments are vitally important to our understanding of the British role in the defeat of Napoleon. Both Duffy and Mackesy have made significant contributions to the history of the war, but more needs to be done to deepen this understanding and develop a coherent picture of the maritime dimension of Britain's economic power in 1792–1815. Britain's naval domination had been secured by the twin strengths of deficit funding of the growing National Debt and the size and vitality of her maritime industries. The two were linked together but the relationship was changing over the eighteenth century and still needs to be more fully explored.[49]

The final contribution made by the navy was its support for the British army operating in Portugal and Spain between 1808 and 1814. While not a decisive theatre, the 'Spanish Ulcer' played a role in draining French military power and undermining Napoleon's domination of Europe. Almost everything to supply the British, Spanish and Portuguese armies had to be transported from Britain.[50] In the background, throughout the war, British warships were engaged across the oceans and seas in minor operations: landings in Italy, Sicily, Spain, Egypt, the West Indies, North America, South America, South Africa, the Indian ocean and subcontinent. They were also engaged in harassing enemy merchantmen, privateers and small warships. Many of these engagements were not as successful as popular memory of the Nelson Legend would believe. But, whatever the individual defeats, British naval forces were so numerically strong that their impact was not great upon the wider issue of the war at sea.

The war had produced a major fear of invasion. British maritime and financial resources proved adequate to meet the threat, but for a brief period the fear of invasion and internal revolution presented the navy with a great challenge. The fleet was forced to withdraw from the Mediterranean. Mutinies wreaked havoc in the fleet at the Nore and Spithead during 1797.[51] Shortages of seamen and dockyard artificers to work the unprecedentedly large number of warships posed major problems to the Navy Board but the pressure was too short-lived to bring about dramatic changes. By the end of 1797 the main crisis was contained. The mutinies had ended, the Spanish and Dutch were defeated. Although badly disrupted by the prejudices of Lord St Vincent as First Lord of the Admiralty in 1804, the Admiralty and the Navy Board weathered the administrative pressures of renewed war with France after 1803. By 1815 important improvements in efficiency in the dockyards had been achieved. Working practices, productive and managerial techniques and investment had all improved. In the Admiralty, the division of labour, clear lines of responsibility and office procedures enabled work to be carried out efficiently, but the easing of war pressures caused more radical demands for change to fade away.[52]

Many of the gains of the great war with France were soon to disappear, but the navy that Nelson had known was an organisation operating in tune with its environment. Despite deep internal conflict the formal administrative procedures of the Admiralty and Navy Board were adapted to meet the needs of the fleet. It possessed the political support it required for its financial and manpower needs. The strength of the British state and economy were behind it. It could draw upon a dynamic and expanding maritime community. The press gangs were unpopular, but they were recognised as necessary and tolerated by the nation at large. Although challenged by mutiny in 1797, the navy's social system came through the conflict largely unchanged. The officer corps was secure in its identity and stature. Much more needs to be known about both these features of the navy. The external environment had presented a longstanding threat and many scares but except for 1797 and 1805, not one that gravely threatened the navy's or the state's existence. Divided, the navies of France, Spain, Holland, Denmark and the United States posed only moderate danger. There was always the possibility they could unite, but it was never realised.

Conclusion

The Royal Navy's dominance of the world's seas lasted for another 45 years. Thereafter, the rise of French, German, American and Japanese navies gradually diminished and then eclipsed British supremacy. There can be no doubt that the rise and decline of the Royal Navy reflect the changing financial and maritime requirements of Britain. Yet such a bland conclusion ignores many important features of the navy's relationship with British society and state. The process of achieving such dominance was extremely complex. It was the result of making short- and long-term adjustments to meet the changing requirements of social expectations, the economy, the objectives of the state, competition from enemies, its own social and organisational systems, and technology. The navy has been of crucial importance to the political, cultural and economic evolution of Britain. Britons' perceptions of themselves have been shaped to a marked degree by an understanding of their geographical position and the role of the sea in the development of the islands. Yet so little is known. Until fairly recently, histories have tended to concentrate on brave people and daring deeds. Vital questions are only now being addressed. The navy was a force of such size and sophistication that it has the potential to tell us a great deal about pre-industrial attitudes to large-scale organisations. The equally important issue of how ordinary people's lives were interwoven with this vast department of state has been relatively neglected. The symbiosis between navy and maritime economy is still poorly understood. Finally, despite decades of exposition and research, new techniques and perspectives are still deepening our understanding of the navy in battle, which in turn is having an impact on our knowledge of how the navy has been used and abused in political and diplomatic discourse over the centuries. Thankfully, the sailing navy has left behind it vast quantities of documents and artifacts from which answers can be obtained. Although the world role of the Royal Navy continues to change and its immediate impact on the lives of the population continues to decline, there is unlikely ever to be a point when a naval perspective on British history will be unnecessary or irrelevant.

NOTES

(Place of publication is London, unless otherwise stated)

1   1509–1603: MARITIME RESOURCES, THE NAVY ROYAL AND NAVAL
POWER

1. This definition is derived from the work of Sir Julian Corbett, whose *Some Principles of Maritime Power* was published in 1911 and still commands a great deal of respect among naval strategists. For an excellent series of essays exploring the development and use of sea-power since the late nineteenth century, which owed much to interpreting the history of sea-power under sail, see Hattendorf, J.B. and Jordan, R.S., *Maritime Strategy and the Balance of Power: Britain and America in the Twentieth Century* (1989), especially pp. 83–161.

2. On the employment of galleys in Mediterranean warfare in the early modern period and their inappropriateness for war in Atlantic waters, see Guilmartin, J.F., *Gunpowder and Galleys: Changing Technology and Mediterranean Warfare at Sea in the Sixteenth Century* (Cambridge, 1974), pp. 57–71. However, the superiority of sail over oars in Atlantic waters was only slowly established during the sixteenth century. For a notable victory of a Castilian galley fleet over English sailing warships, see Sherbourne, J.W., 'The Battle of La Rochelle and the War at Sea, 1372–5', *Bulletin of the Institute of Historical Research*, XLII (1969), 17–29.

3. McGowan, A., *The Ship. Tiller and Whipstaff. The Development of the Sailing Ship, 1400–1700* (1981).

4. On the French attempt on London in 1217, see Cannon, H.L., 'The Battle of Sandwich and Eustace the Monk, 1217', *EHR*, XXVII (1912), 649–70; Stanford-Reid, W., 'Sea-power in the Anglo-Scottish War, 1296–1328', *MM*, XLVI (1960), 7–12; Allmand, C., *The Hundred Years*

War: England and France at War, c.1300–c.1450 (Cambridge, 1988), pp. 13–16; Runyan, T.J., 'The Organisation of Royal Fleets in Medieval England', in Runyan, T.J. (ed.), *Ships, Seafaring and Society: Essays in Maritime History* (Detroit, 1987), pp. 37–52.

5. Allmand, *Hundred Years War*, p. 89: Oppenheim, M., *A History of the Administration of the Royal Navy, 1509–1660* (1896; 1988 edn), p. 8; Ford, C.J., 'Piracy and Policy: The Crisis in the Channel, 1400–1403', *TRHS*, XXIX (1979), 63–77.

6. Allmand, *Hundred Years War*, pp. 89–90: Oppenheim, *Administration*, pp. 24–5; For Henry V's navy, see Rose, S., *The Navy of the Lancastrian Kings: Accounts and Inventories of William Soper, Keeper of the King's Ships, 1422–1427* (1982). A very useful introduction can be found in Loades, D., *The Tudor Navy. An Administrative, Political and Military History* (Aldershot, 1992), pp. 11–35.

7. Oppenheim, *Administration*, p. 28; Crowson, P.S., *Tudor Foreign Policy* (1973), p. 18.

8. The development of the cannon as a weapon at sea is still the subject of intense debate, to which maritime archaeology has made a great contribution in recent years. See Guilmartin, J.F., 'Early Modern Naval Ordnance', *International Journal of Nautical Archaeology and Underwater Exploration*, XVII (1988), 35–53; Konstam, R. A., 'Sixteenth Century Naval Tactics and Gunnery', *International Journal of Nautical Archaeology and Underwater Exploration*, XVII (1988), 17–23; Martin, C. and Parker, G., *The Spanish Armada* (1988), pp. 195–225.

9. On the military changes of the period, see Hale, J.R., *War and Society in Renaissance Europe, 1450–1620* (1985).

10. For Henry's campaigns, see Gunn, S. 'The French Wars of Henry VIII', in Black, J. (ed.), *The Origins of War in Early Modern Europe* (Edinburgh, 1987), pp. 25–51; Wernham, R.B., *Before the Armada: the Growth of English Foreign Policy, 1485–1588* (1966); Cruickshank, C., *Henry VIII and the Invasion of France* (Stroud, 1990); Goring, J., 'Social Change and Military Decline in Mid-Tudor England', *History*, LX (1970), 185–97.

11. Crowson, *Tudor Foreign Policy*, pp. 50–3.

12. Oppenheim, *Administration*, pp. 38–9, 42.

13. The principle of using a dry landing for repairs to and cleaning of the hull was not new, but the use of a dock enabled faster and safer working. For contrasting views on how far Henry VII's dock was an advance, see Oppenheim, *Administration*, pp. 39–40, and Loades, *The Tudor Navy*, pp. 41–2. This particular dock fell into disuse by the early seventeenth century and was filled in during 1623. Portsmouth did not get another dry dock until 1656, but others were built in the Thames and Medway yards. The fully developed dry dock was a major technical

improvement that gave England a distinct advantage over France and Spain in the turn-around of vessels in dock. See Merino, J.P., 'Graving Docks in France and Spain before 1800', *MM*, LXXI (1985), 35–57.

14. Narratives of John Cabot's voyages to Newfoundland and Labrador, in search of the western route to China, can be found in Williamson, J.A., *The Cabot Voyages and Bristol Discovery under Henry VII* (1962). For exploration in general, see Parry, J.H., *The Age of Reconnaissance* (1963). For the English contribution, see Williamson, J.A., *Maritime Enterprise, 1485–1558* (Oxford, 1913); Quinn, D.B., *England and the Discovery of America, 1487–1620* (1974). Quinn's bibliography contains an excellent guide to sources and secondary literature related to individual enterprises. See also Andrews, K.R., *Trade, Plunder and Settlement: Maritime Enterprise and the Genesis of the British Empire, 1480–1630* (Cambridge, 1984).

15. Oppenheim, *Administration*, p. 37. For a contrasting view, based upon the qualitative changes in Henry's navy and the attitude he is supposed to have engendered, see Lewis, M., *The History of the British Navy* (1957), pp. 29–31.

16. Glete, J., *Navies and Nations. Warships, Navies and State Building in Europe and America, 1500–1860*, 2 vols (Stockholm, 1993), I, 130; Rule, M., *The Mary Rose. The Excavation and Raising of Henry VIII's Flagship* (1982).

17. For a general history of Henry's foreign policy and military affairs, see Wernham, *Before the Armada*. For the naval side of the war of 1512–14, see Loades, *The Tudor Navy*, pp. 55–70. See also Spont, A., *Letters and Papers Relating to the War with France, 1512–1513* (1897).

18. Gunn, S., 'The Duke of Suffolk's March on Paris in 1523', *EHR*, CI (1986), 596–634.

19. For the war of 1544–6, see Wernham, *Before the Armada*; Loades, *The Tudor Navy*, pp. 96–7, 126–36.

20. Corbett, J.S., *Drake and the Tudor Navy*, 2 vols (1898; 1988 edn), I, 59.

21. Davis, C., 'The Administration of the Royal Navy under Henry VIII: The Origins of the Navy Board', *EHR*, LXXX (1965), 268–87. Loades, *The Tudor Navy*, pp. 77–84.

22. For the evolution of the administrative system, see Glasgow, T. 'Maturing of Naval Administration, 1556–1564' *MM*, LVI (1970), 3–26. Glasgow argues that the external pressures on the state – the loss of Scotland and the marriage of Queen Mary to Philip II of Spain – provided the stimuli to preserve and develop the navy to the point where its administration had enough expertise to be an active force in the shaping of the navy in the first years of Elizabeth's reign. This is contested by D. Loades, who argues that the navy and naval service had become firmly established in English military thinking by the death of Henry VIII. See Loades, *The Tudor Navy*, pp. 7, 102. For an interesting view on the difficulty of using naval forces for political ends, see

Alsop, J.D., 'A Regime at Sea: The Navy and the 1553 Suuccession Crisis', *Albion*, XXIV (1992), 577–90.

23. Clay, C.G.A., *Economic Expansion and Social Change: England, 1500–1700*, 2 vols (Cambridge, 1984), I, 109.

24. Davis, 'The Administration of the Royal Navy', 282–6; Glasgow, 'Maturing of Naval Administration' 14; Andrews, *Trade, Plunder and Settlement*, pp. 104–8,116–17. There is general agreement that the administration of the navy took on a formal structure and drew in personnel that reflected its needs, but there is less agreement on the critical features of that development. Compare the above with Loades, *The Tudor Navy*, and Pollitt, R., 'Rationality and Expedience in the Growth of Elizabethan Naval Administration', in Love, R.W., *Changing Interpretations and New Sources in Naval History* (New York, 1980), pp. 68–79.

25. Andrews, *Trade, Plunder and Settlement*, p. 105; Andrews, K.R., 'Caribbean Rivalry and the Anglo-Spanish Peace of 1604', *History*, LIX (1974), 1–17, especially 4–10. Loades argues that the linkage between the aristocracy and the sea was forged by 1547, largely as a result of Henry VIII's patronage of navigational sciences and the social acceptability of military service afloat. This is an important perspective, but as the problem of blending social status and technical competence is one that bedevilled the navy into the twentieth century, it is a subject worthy of much more research than has currently been carried out. See Loades, *The Tudor Navy*, p. 102.

26. Andrews, *Trade, Plunder and Settlement*, pp. 63–5, 102–5.

27. Glasgow, 'Maturing of Naval Administration', 12–13.

28. Pollitt, R.L., 'The Spanish Armada and the Mobilisation of English Resources, 1570–1585' in Cogar, W.B. (ed.), *New Interpretations in Naval History* (Annapolis, 1989), pp. 22–4.

29. Ibid., p. 21; Martin and Parker, *The Spanish Armada*, p. 52; Corbett, *Drake and the Tudor Navy*, pp. 348–58. On the controversy between the high-sided Great Ships and the newer galleon design, see Oppenheim M. (ed.), *The Naval Tracts of Sir William Monson in Six Books*, 5 vols, IV (1913), 91–5.

30. Andrews, *Trade, Plunder and Settlement*, pp. 24–5.

31. Ramsay, G.D., 'The Foreign Policy of Elizabeth I', in Haugh, C. (ed.), *The Reign of Elizabeth I* (1984), p. 155.

32. Corbett, *Drake and the Tudor Navy*, II, 10–11; Thomson, G.M., *Sir Francis Drake* (1972), pp. 166–7. On the Dutch raids into the Caribbean, see Sluiter, E., 'Dutch-Spanish Rivalry in the Caribbean Area, 1594–1609', *Hispanic American Historical Review*, XXVIII (1948), 165–96.

33. The precise impact of the English interlopers, and in particular Drake's raid of 1572–3, in the dislocation of the Seville trade is unclear, but the

disruption of this trade was a major factor in the collapse of credit for the Spanish Crown by 1576. See Elliott, J.H., *Imperial Spain, 1469–1716* (1963; 1970 edn), pp. 263–4. See also Davis, R., 'England and the Mediterranean, 1570–1670', in Fisher, F.J. (ed.), *Essays in the Economic and Social History of Tudor and Stuart England* (Cambridge, 1961), pp. 117–37. By the 1540s, cheap cast-iron cannon were being used in increasing numbers on sailing ships. This gradually eroded the offensive capacity of Mediterranean galleys, so that by the 1570s it was much safer for English ships to sail to Italy and the Levant. See Guilmartin, *Gunpowder and Galleys*, pp. 263, 273.

34. There are a large number of published documents on the Armada campaign, which are very accessible to the general reader. Laughton, J.K. (ed.), *State Papers relating to the Defeat of the Armada, Anno. 1588*, 2 vols (1894; reprinted 1988, Aldershot). The quincentenary in 1988 also stimulated a large number of new studies of the campaign. A good bibliography of these works can be found in *The Mariner's Mirror Bibliography for 1988* (Greenwich 1989). Of particular interest is Martin and Parker, *The Spanish Armada* and Fernandez-Armesto, F., *The Spanish Armada: The Experience of War in 1588* (Oxford, 1988). Both tackle the question of the rate of fire of the Spanish ships, the first based upon the archaeological evidence, and the latter using Spanish documentary sources. They come to different conclusions. See Martin and Parker, *The Spanish Armada*, pp. 201–12; Fernandez-Armesto, *Spanish Armada*, pp. 155–75. The following account is based upon Corbett's *Drake and the Tudor Navy*, which remains one of the fullest narratives of events 1587–8. It is, however, modified in details to take account of the conclusions presented in more recent works. The most recent concise account of the campaign is Loades, *The Tudor Navy*, pp. 244–53.

35. Corbett, *Drake and the Tudor Navy*, II, 133.

36. Martin and Parker, *The Spanish Armada*, pp. 165–6.

37. Ibid., pp. 195–202.

38. Parker, G., 'If the Armada had Landed', *History*, LXI (1976), 358–65.

39. Wernham, R.B., 'Elizabethan War Aims and Strategy', in Bindoff, S.T., Hurstfield, J. and Wilson, C.H. (eds), *Elizabethan Government and Society* (1961), pp. 340–68.

40. Andrews, 'Caribbean Rivalry and the Anglo-Spanish Peace of 1604', 6–7.

41. It is only in recent years that the importance of the burning of Cadiz has been properly noted. See Usherwood, S. and Usherwood, E., *The Counter-Armada, 1596: The Journal of the Mary Rose* (1983); Loades, *The Tudor Navy*, pp. 265–6.

42. For the 1589 campaign, see Wernham, R.B., *The Expedition of Sir John*

Norris and Sir Francis Drake to Spain and Portugal, 1589 (1989). For the 1590s see Loades, *The Tudor Navy*, pp. 259–68.

43. For the late sixteenth-century view of the importance of blockade, see Quinn, D.B. and Ryan, A.N., *England's Sea Empire, 1550–1642* (1983), pp. 111–16. For two differing views on the effectiveness of this policy, compare Andrews, 'Caribbean Rivalry and the Anglo-Spanish Peace of 1604' and Wernham, 'Elizabethan War Aims and Strategy'.

2 1603–1642: DECLINE AND RECOVERY

1. Lockyer, R., *The Early Stuarts. A Political History of England, 1603–1642* (1989), pp. 12–17. For the financial position on the death of Elizabeth, see Dietz, F.C., *English Public Finance, 1558–1641*, 2nd edn (1964), pp. 101–13.

2. Andrews, K.R., *Trade, Plunder and Settlement. Maritime Enterprise and the Genesis of the British Empire, 1450–1630* (Cambridge, 1984), pp. 280–7; 'Caribbean Rivalry and the Anglo-Spanish Peace of 1604', *History*, LIX (1974), 1–17.

3. Andrews, 'Caribbean Rivalry and the Anglo-Spanish Peace of 1604', 9–12.

4. McGowan, A. P., *The Jacobean Commissions of Enquiry, 1608 and 1618* (1971), passim.

5. Oppenheim, M. (ed.), *The Naval Tracts of Sir William Monson*, 5 vols (1892–1914), II, 237; III, 433–5; Hollond, J., *Two Discourses on the Navy*, ed. J.R. Tanner (1896), pp. 14–15.

6. Kennedy, P.M., *The Rise and Fall of British Naval Mastery* (1983), p. 38; Aylmer, G., 'Attempts at Administrative Reform, 1625–1640', *EHR*, LXXII (1957), 233.

7. A.P. McGowan's thesis is the most detailed examination of naval policy under the Duke of Buckingham: 'The Royal Navy under the First Duke of Buckingham, Lord High Admiral, 1618–28', unpublished PhD thesis, University of London, 1967. This has now been supplemented by Young, M.B., *Servility and Service: the Life and Work of Sir John Coke* (Woodbridge, 1986), pp. 15–31, 48–86, 186–203; Thrush, A., 'The Navy under Charles I, 1625–1640', unpublished PhD thesis, University of London, 1991; Andrews, K.R., *Ships, Money and Politics. Seafaring and Naval Enterprise in the Reign of Charles I* (Cambridge, 1991); Hebb, D.D., 'The English Government and the Problem of Piracy, 1616–1642', unpublished PhD thesis, University of London, 1985. The issue of corruption in the navy is examined in Peck, L.L., *Court Patronage and Corruption in Early Stuart England* (1991), pp. 106–33. For a comparison of views, see Macaulay, T.B., *Critical and Historical Essays*, 2

vols (1907), I, 109; Fiennes, G., *Sea Power and Freedom* (n.d.), p. 121; Penn, C.D., *The Navy Under the Early Stuarts* (1921), preface; Kennedy, *The Rise and Fall*, pp. 38–40. For a contemporary view, see Perrin, W. (ed.), *Boteler's Dialogues* (1929), pp. 247–56.

8. Clay, C.G.A., *Economic Expansion and Social Change: England 1500–1700* (Cambridge, 1984), pp. 185–7; Andrews, *Ships, Money and Politics*, pp. 16–23.

9. Andrews, *Trade, Plunder and Settlement*, pp. 280–2.

10. Alcala-Zamora y Queipo de Lano, J., *España, Flandes y el Mar del Norte (1618–39): la Ultima Ofensiva Europea de los Austrias Madrileños* (Barcelona, 1975), p. 82. See also Oppenheim, *Sir William Monson*, IV, 90–5. On the Spanish reaction to the needs of naval war in north European waters, particularly the use of the frigate, see Stradling, R.A., *The Armada of Flanders* (Cambridge, 1992), pp. 22–8, 166–70. See also Thrush, A., 'In Pursuit of the Frigate', *Historical Research*, LXIV (1991), 29–45.

11. Glasgow, T., 'Maturing of Naval Administration, 1556–1564', *MM*, LXI (1970), 8.

12. Dietz, *English Public Finance*, p. 176; Lockyer, R., *Buckingham: The Life and Political Career of George Villiers, First Duke of Buckingham, 1592–1628* (1981; 1984 edn), p. 50; Oppenheim, *Sir William Monson*, IV (1913), pp. 174–5. On the 1619–21 Algiers expedition, see Hebb, *The English Government*, pp. 64–146.

13. Anderson, R.C., *List of English Men-of-War, 1509–1649* (1959), pp. 17–18.

14. Dietz, *English Public Finance*, p. 113.

15. Ibid., pp. 191, 111–12. The navy was not the biggest consumer of royal finances. The various expenses of the court far outweighed naval expenditures. Out of a total known expenditure in the years 1603–8 of £1,604,119, £193,000 was spent on the navy, or about 12 per cent. However, only fees and annuities paid by the Crown exceeded the navy as a single item.

16. Aylmer, 'Attempts at Administrative Reform', passim.

17. Oppenheim, M., *A History of the Administration of the Royal Navy, 1509–1660* (1896; 1988 edn), pp. 187–8: Kennedy, *The Rise and Fall*, p. 40.

18. Kenny, R.W., *Elizabeth's Admiral: The Political Career of Charles Howard, Earl of Nottingham, 1536–1624* (Baltimore, 1970), pp. 317–18; McGowan, *The Jacobean Commissions of Enquiry*, pp. xiii–xvii; Quinn, D.B. and Ryan, A.N., *England's Sea Empire* (1983), pp. 211–17; Peck, *Court Patronage*, pp. 118–20. For the professional backgrounds of the men appointed to the posts of Principal Officers, and comment upon changes, see also Johns, A.W., 'The Principal Officers of the Navy', *MM*, XIV (1928), 32–54.

19. Kenny, *Elizabeth's Admiral*, pp. 301–09, 321–31; McGowan, *The Jacobean Commissions of Enquiry*, p. xiv.
20. Lockyer, *The Early Stuarts*, pp. 49–50.
21. McGowan, *The Jacobean Commissions of Enquiry*, pp. xxvi–xxvii; Dietz, *English Public Finance*, p. 190.
22. Oppenheim, *Administration*, pp. 205–11.
23. For James's foreign policy in this period, see Adams, S., 'Foreign Policy and the Parliaments of 1621 and 1624', in Sharpe, K. (ed.), *Faction and Parliament* (Oxford, 1978); Adams, 'Spain or the Netherlands? The Dilemmas of Early Stuart Foreign Policy', in Tomlinson, H. (ed.), *Before the Civil War* (1983); Lockyer, *Buckingham*, pp. 105–11. For the rise of Dutch maritime power, see Israel, J., *The Dutch Republic and the Hispanic World, 1606–1661* (Oxford, 1982), pp. 109–34; Israel, *Dutch Primacy in World Trade, 1585–1740* (Oxford, 1989), chs 2–4.
24. Lockyer, *Buckingham*, pp. 268–85, 342–5; The council of war as an executive body in military affairs has been generally dismissed as ineffective and obstructive. However, its importance to a senior officer who may not have been a seaman, born and bred, was critical. For a discussion of this point see Perrin, *Boteler's Dialogues*, pp. 2–5. For a contemporary account of the Cadiz expedition see Glanville, J., *The Voyage to Cadiz in 1625*, ed. A.B. Grosart (1883). A narrative can be found in Penn, *The Navy Under the Early Stuarts*, pp. 139–66. This work footnotes other accessible contemporary sources of value.
25. For differing interpretations of Buckingham's war against France, see Lockyer, *Buckingham* and Young, M.B., 'Buckingham, War and Parliament: Revisionism Gone Too Far', *Parliamentary History*, IV (1985), 52. For the preparations for the La Rochelle expedition, see Lockyer, *Buckingham*, pp. 359–70. On the expedition itself, see ibid., pp. 378–402; Penn, *The Navy Under the Early Stuarts*, pp. 167–205; Herbert, E., *The Expedition to the Isle of Rhé* (1860).
26. Hebb, *The English Government*, pp. 268–74.
27. Penn, *The Navy Under the Early Stuarts*, pp. 205–16.
28. Cogswell, T., 'Prelude to Ré: The Anglo-French Struggle over La Rochelle', *History*, LXXI (1986), 8, 16.
29. Lockyer, *Buckingham*, pp. 282–5; Oppenheim, *Administration*, p. 229.
30. Oppenheim, *Administration*, pp. 229, 234–5
31. For an interpretation that leans towards this view see Stewart, R.W., 'Arms and Expeditions: the Ordnance Office and the Assaults on Cadiz (1625) and the Isle of Rhé (1627)', in Fissel, M.C. (ed.), *War and Government in Britain, 1598–1650* (Manchester, 1991), pp. 112–32.
32. Below is given the composition of the fleets on selected major operations, distinguishing between royal and hired vessels. The figures must be used with caution. They are intended to represent only those vessels

which were organised to act as battle fleets, although in some cases the Irish and other stations have been included. The figures are not strictly comparable, given the changes in naval vessels and tactical employment over these years. Nor are these figures the total number of vessels sent to sea in any given year. The list also contains some very small vessels or ships otherwise not intended for standard offensive operations. Nonetheless, the list indicates the gradual change in the composition of the fleet. Private warships continued to play an important role protecting convoys and cruising against privateers well into the eighteenth century.

		Royal ships	*Private vessels*
1588	Armada	23	79
1589	Lisbon	14	120
1625	Cadiz	14	30
1627	Ile de Ré	10	90
1635	Ship Money	19	6
1636	Ship Money	24	3
1637	Ship Money	19	9
1638	Ship Money	24	7
1639	Ship Money	28	11
1641	Summer Guard	15	10
1642	Summer Guard	16	16
1643	Summer Guard	24	23
1644	Summer Guard	30	55
1645	Summer Guard	36	16
1646	Summer Guard	25	4
1652	Mobilisation	39	0
1653	Gabbard	25	15
1666	Four Days Bat.	31	1
1672	Sole Bay	32	0
1673	Schoonveldt	49	0
1688	Dartmouth's Fleet	35	0
1690	Beachy Head	56	0
1692	Barfleur	55	0

Sources: Corbett, *Drake and the Tudor Navy*, II, 150, 300; Lockyer, *Buckingham*, p. 268; Oppenheim, *Administration*, p. 235; Powell, J. R. and Timings, E.K., *Documents Relating to the Civil War* (1963), pp. 8–9, 69–71, 138–9, 201–3, 244–5, 274–5; Gardiner, S.R. and Atkinson, C.T., *Letters and Papers relating to the First Dutch War*, I, 64–5, V, 16–17; Powell, J.R. and Timings, E.K., *The Rupert and Monck Letter Book*, pp. 196–7: Anderson, R.C., *Journals and Narratives of the Third Dutch War*, pp. 395–7;

Powley, E.B., *The English Navy in the Revolution of 1688* (Cambridge, 1928), pp. 57–9; Aubrey, P., *The Defeat of James Stuart's Armada, 1692* (Leicester, 1979), pp. 176–7; Colledge, J.J., *Ships of the Royal Navy*, 2 vols (1969), I; Anderson, R.C., *Lists of English Men-of-War, 1509–1649* (1959); *Anderson, Lists of English Men-of-War, 1650–1700* (1935).
For the development of English warships, see Lavery, B., *Ship of the Line*, 2 vols (1983), I, especially pp. 14–17. See also Thrush, 'In Pursuit of the Frigate'.

33. Lavery, *Ship of the Line*. The arguments about the size of vessels can be followed in the Navy Records Society volumes, cited in Lavery's notes.

34. Oppenheim, *Administration*, pp. 264–5; Alcala-Zamora, *España, Flandes*, p. 358; Israel, *The Dutch Republic*, p. 109.

35. Andrews, *Ships, Money and Politics*, pp. 135–7. For a general discussion of Charles's attitude to his navy, see Quintrell, B., 'Charles I and his Navy in the 1630s', *The Seventeenth Century*, III.(1988), pp. 159–79.

36. Aylmer, G.E., *The Struggle for the Constitution: England in the Seventeenth Century*, 4th edn (1975), p. 82.

37. Thrush, A., 'Naval Finance and the Origins and Development of Ship Money', in Fissel, *War and Government in Britain, 1598–1650*, pp. 133–62; Sharpe, K., *The Personal Rule of Charles I* (Yale, 1992), pp. 545–57.

38. For views on Ship Money see works quoted above and Andrews, *Ships, Money and Politics*, pp. 128–37; 140–2. Sources quoted here enable investigation of the Ship Money returns.

39. Ibid.; for Ship Money in the wider context of Charles's fiscal and administrative needs, see Sharpe, *Personal Rule*, pp. 88–104.

40. Lockyer, *The Early Stuarts*, pp. 233–5; Aylmer, *Struggle for the Constitution*, pp. 82–5.

41. Gordon, M.D., 'The Collection of Ship Money in the Reign of Charles I', *TRHS*, 3rd ser., IV (1910), 141–62.

42. Deitz, *English Public Finance*, p. 285.

43. Anderson, *English Men-of-War*, pp. 20–1.

44. Andrews, *Ships, Money and Politics*, p. 155.

45. Alcala-Zamora, *Espana, Flandes*, p. 346.

46. Ibid., p. 412.

47. Ibid., pp. 438–56.

48. Thrush, 'The Navy Under Charles I', particularly pp. 138–59. Oppenheim, *Sir William Monson*, especially III (1914); Hollond, *Two Discourses on the Navy*, passim.

49. Pollard, S., *The Genesis of Modern Management: A Study of the Industrial Revolution in Great Britain* (1965), passim. Pollard does not discuss the managerial problems of the navy, excluding it because the mainspring of modern capitalist organisation, competitive advantage, was missing (p.84). This is unfortunate because the financial constraints placed

upon naval administration required very similar administrative behaviours as in competitive organisations. There are a number of very good studies of naval administration but a comparative examination of administrative practices in the navy and contemporary large-scale private organisation remains to be written.

3   1642–1660: CIVIL WAR, THE REPUBLIC AND A STANDING NAVY

1. The narrative of the navy in the Civil War can be found in Powell, J.R., *The Navy in the English Civil War* (Hamden, 1962); Baumber, M.A., 'The Navy during the Civil Wars and Commonwealth, 1642–1651', unpublished MA thesis, University of Manchester, 1967. Additional information can be found in Powell, J.R. and Timings, E.K. (eds), *Documents Relating to the Civil War, 1642–1648* (1963). Details relating to Parliament's administration of the navy are in Dewar, A.C., 'The Naval Administration of the Interregnum, 1641–1659', *MM*, XII (1926), 406–30; Kennedy, D.E., 'The Establishment of and Settlement of Parliament's Admiralty, 1642–1648', *MM*, LXVIII (1962), 276–91. See also Andrews, K.R., *Ships, Money and Politics* (Cambridge, 1991), pp. 184–202.

2. Kennedy, D.E., 'Naval Captains at the Outbreak of the English Civil War', *MM*, XLVI (1960), 194; Chaplin, W.R., 'William Rainsborough and his Associates of the Trinity House', *MM*, XXXI (1945), 178–97.

3. Kennedy, 'Naval Captains', pp. 181–98; Andrews, *Ships, Money and Politics*, pp. 185–8.

4. Kennedy, 'Naval Captains', p. 198.

5. Powell and Timings, *Documents Relating to the Civil War*, pp. 2–3.

6. For the events leading to the surrender of the fleet to Parliament, see ibid., pp. 13–28; Powell, *The Navy in the English Civil War*, pp. 14–21.

7. Lewis, M., *The Navy of Britain: An Historical Portrait* (1948), p. 300. See also Lloyd, C., *The British Seaman, 1200–1860: A Social Survey* (1968), p. 52. For later studies of the seaman, see Andrews, K.R., 'The Elizabethan Seaman', *MM*, LXVIII (1982), 245–61; Scammell, G.V., 'Manning the English Merchant Service in the Sixteenth Century', *MM*, LVI (1970), 355; Scammell, 'The Sinews of War: Manning and Provisioning English Fighting Ships c.1550–1650', *MM*, LXXIII (1987), 351–67. Studies have been carried out on the eighteenth-century seaman, principally examined in the context of the North American labour market. Other studies emphasise the local connections between English seamen and officers. See Rediker, M., *Between the Devil and the Deep Blue Sea: Merchant Seamen, Pirates and the Anglo-American Maritime World, 1700–1750* (Cambridge, 1987); Howell, C. and Twomey, R.J.

(eds), *Jack Tar in History. Essays in the History of Maritime Life and Labour* (New Brunswick, 1991); Lemish, J., 'Jack Tar in the Streets: Merchant Seamen in the Politics of Revolutionary America', *William and Mary Quarterly*, XXV (1968), 375; Rodger, N.A.M., 'A little navy of your own making, Admiral Boscawen and the Cornish Connection in the Royal Navy', in Duffy, M. (ed), *Parameters of British Naval Power, 1650–1850* (Exeter, 1992), pp. 82–91.

8. Dewar, 'Naval Administration of the Interregnum', p. 417.

9. Ibid., pp. 406–30; Kennedy, D.E., 'The Establishment and Settlement of Parliament's Admiralty', 276–91.

10. Kennedy, 'Establishment and Settlement', p. 277; Reid, W., 'Commonwealth Supply Departments within the Tower', *Guildhall Miscellany*, II (1966), 319–52.

11. Richmond, H.W., *The Navy as an Instrument of Policy, 1558–1727*, ed. E.A. Hughes (Cambridge, 1953), p. 91; Kennedy, P., *The Rise and Fall of British Naval Mastery*, 2nd edn (1983), pp. 44–5. Others have viewed the navy's role as more decisive. Michael Lewis believed that: 'The briefest reflection leads to one stark conclusion. The navy's adherence to Parliament decided the issue.' See Lewis, *The History of the British Navy* (1957), p. 80.

12. Warwick to the Speaker, 18 Aug. 1642; Same to Same, 10 Feb. 1644; Same to Committee of Both Kingdoms, 31 Jan. 1645, in Powell and Timings, *Documents Relating to the Civil War*, pp. 35–6, 122, 184–5. On the financing of the war effort, see Morrill, J., *The Revolt in the Provinces. Conservatives and Radicals in the English Civil War, 1630–1650* (1976), pp. 55–6; Ashley, M., *Financial and Commercial Policy under the Cromwellian Protectorate* (1934).

13. Instructions to Batten, 7 Nov. 1646, in Powell and Timings, *Documents Relating to the Civil War*, p. 257.

14. This narrative is based principally upon Powell, *The Navy in the English Civil War* and Baumber, 'The Navy during the Civil Wars'.

15. On the politics of the New Model Army, see Kishlansky, M.A., *The Rise of the New Model Army* (Cambridge, 1979; 1983 edn), particularly, pp. 223–73.

16. Capp, B., *Cromwell's Navy: The Fleet and the English Revolution, 1648–1660* (Oxford, 1989), pp. 15–19.

17. Ibid., pp. 19–29.

18. Ibid., p. 31.

19. Ibid., pp. 36–41.

20. For details, see Underwood, D.E., *Pride's Purge: Politics in the Puritan Revolution* (Oxford, 1971).

21. Farnell, J.E., 'The Navigation Act of 1651, the First Dutch War, and the London Merchant Community', *Econ. H.R.*, 2nd ser., XVII (1964),

439–54; Jones, J.R., *Britain and the World, 1649–1815* (1980), pp. 54–7; Wilson, C., *Profit and Power: A Study of England and the Dutch Wars* (1957).

22. Capp, *Cromwell's Navy*, pp. 49–50. The records of Trinity House are now largely missing. G.E. Mainwaring, in his biography of Sir Henry Mainwaring, postulated that they were destroyed duing the Great Fire of London (*The Life and Work of Sir Henry Mainwaring*, 2 vols, 1920, I, 296). G. Harris, author of *Trinity House of Deptford, 1514–1660* (1969), however, believes that they were probably transferred to the House of Commons during the purge of 1649, and subsequently destroyed in the fire of 1834. I am grateful to Mr Harris for discussing this point.

23. Capp, *Cromwell's Navy*, p. 185. This view is shared by Baumber, 'The Navy during the Civil Wars', p. 53.

24. Brenner, R., *Merchants and Revolution. Commercial Policy, Political Conflict and London's Overseas Traders, 1550–1653* (Cambridge, 1993), pp. 577–632; Capp, *Cromwell's Navy*, p. 166.

25. Oppenheim, M., *A History of the Administration of the Royal Navy, 1509–1660* (1896; 1988 edn), pp. 314, 320–2. Financial abuses could work both to the advantage and disadvantage of the seaman, which makes a precise assessment of the real value of the seaman's income, let alone living standard, very difficult to establish. See Hollond, J., *Two Discourses on the Navy*, ed. J.R. Tanner (1896), pp. 128–52.

26. Capp, *Cromwell's Navy*, pp. 213–29, 284–8.

27. For Blake's campaigns, see Baumber, M., *The General at Sea: Robert Blake and the Seventeenth Century Revolution in Naval Warfare.* (1989); Powell, J.R. (ed.), *The Letters of Robert Blake* (1937); Powell, 'Blake's Reduction of Jersey in 1651', *MM*, XVIII (1932), 64–80; 'Blake's Reduction of the Scilly Isles in 1651', *MM*, XVIII (1932), 205–22. For the capture of Barbados and Virginia, see Baumber, 'The Navy and the Civil Wars', pp. 360–4.

28. For the history of Rupert's squadron, see Anderson, R.C,'The Royalists at Sea, 1648' *MM*, IX (1923), 34–46 and 'The Royalists at Sea, 1649', *MM*, XIV (1928), 320–38.

29. Capp, *Cromwell's Navy*, pp. 68–72; Howat, G.M.D., *Stuart and Cromwellian Foreign Policy* (1974), pp. 74–93; Prestwick, M., 'Diplomacy and Trade in the Protectorate', *Journal of Modern History*, XXII (1950), 103–21; Conquest, R., 'The State and Commercial Expansion: England in the Years 1642–1688', *Journal of European Economic History*, XIV (1985), 155–72.

30. The First Dutch War can be followed in the excellent series of volumes published by the Navy Record Society: *Letters and Papers Relating to the First Dutch War, 1652–1654*, vol. I, ed. S.R. Gardiner (1899): vol. II, ed. S.R. Gardiner (1900); vol. III, eds S.R. Gardiner and C.T.Atkinson (1906): vol. IV, ed. C.T. Atkinson (1910); vol. V, ed. C.T. Atkinson

(1912); vol. VI, ed. C.T. Atkinson (1930). J.R. Powell's *Letters of Robert Blake* (1937), gives a more sympathetic picture of Blake's tussle with Tromp in February 1653. Concise narratives can also be found in Wilson, *Profit and Power*, pp. 59–80; Baumber, *General at Sea*; Padfield, P., *Tides of Empire: Decisive Naval Campaigns in the Rise of the West*, 2 vols (1979 and 1982), I. Outlines of the causes of the war can also be found in the above. Additional interpretations which should be consulted are: Groenvald, S., 'The English Civil War as a Cause of the First Anglo-Dutch War', *HJ*, xxx (1987), 541–66: Taylor, H., 'Trade, Neutrality and the "English Road", 1630–1648', *Econ.H.R.*, xxv (1972), 236–60

31. Lavery, B., *The Ship of the Line*, 2 vols (1983), I, 18–27.

32. Corbett, J., *Fighting Instructions, 1530–1816* (1905), p. 95.

33. Guilmartin, J.F., *Gunpowder and Galleys: Changing Technology and Mediterranean Warfare at Sea in the Sixteenth Century* (Cambridge, 1974), pp. 85–94; Loades, D., *The Tudor Navy: An Administrative, Political and Military History* (Aldershot, 1992), p. 96; Martin, C. and Parker, G., *The Spanish Armada* (1988), pp. 165–6.

34. Perrin, W.G. (ed.), *Boteler's Dialogues* (1929), pp. 249–50. Lavery, *Ship of the Line*, I, 27; Lavery, 'The Revolution in Naval Tactics, 1588–1653', in M. Acerra, J. Merino and J. Meyer (eds), *Les Marines de Guerres Européenes, XVII–XVIII Siècles* (Paris, 1985), pp. 167–74; Baumber, *General at Sea*, pp. 182–6; Weber, R.E.J., 'Introduction of the Single Line Ahead as a Battle Formation by the Dutch, 1665–1666', *MM*, LXXIII (1987), 5–19. The instructions of 29 March 1653 can be found in Atkinson, C.T. (ed.), *Letters and Papers Relating to the First Dutch War, 1652–1654*, IV (1910), pp. 262–72. A detailed and well-illustrated history of tactical issues is Tunstall, B., *Naval Warfare in the Age of Sail: The Evolution of Fighting Tactics, 1650–1815*, ed. N. Tracy (1990).

35. For details of the outbreak of the war on Spain, see Prestwich, M., 'Diplomacy and Trade in the Protectorate', *Journal of Modern History*, xxii (1952), 103–21; Strong, F., 'The Causes of Cromwell's West Indian Expedition', *American Historical Review*, iv (1898), 228–45; Hill, C., *God's Englishman: Oliver Cromwell and the English Revolution* (1972), pp. 151–5; Taylor, S.A.G., *The Western Design* (Kingston, 1965). See also Baugh, D. 'Maritime Strength and Atlantic Commerce. The Uses of a "Grand Maritime Empire"', in Stone, L., *An Imperial State at War. Britain from 1689 to 1815* (1994), pp. 190–1.

36. Firth, C.H. (ed.), *The Narrative of General Venables* (1900), passim.

37. Powell, J.R., *Letters of Robert Blake*, pp. 322–92; Elliot, J.H., *Imperial Spain, 1469–1716* (1970 edn), p. 357.

38. Capp, *Cromwell's Navy*, p. 103.

39. For different views on the legacy of the Protectorate, see ibid., p. 114; Berckman, E., *Creators and Destroyers of the English Navy* (1974),

pp. 107–48. G. Parker's impressive overview of military change, *The Military Revolution. Military Innovation and the Rise of the West, 1500–1800* (Cambridge, 1989 edn), pp. 100–2, probably overstates the impact of the changes during the Interregnum. Although English ships did operate across European, Caribbean and North American waters, they did not yet have the support in place to maintain long-term operations at extreme distances from England.

40. Baumber, M., 'The Navy during the Civil Wars', p. 366, Parker, *The Military Revolution*, p. 102; Kennedy, *Rise and Fall of Naval Mastery*, pp. 55–7.

41. On the economic theories of the mid seventeenth century, see Wilson, C., *England's Apprenticeship, 1603–1763* (1965), pp. 57–65; Knorr, K., *British Colonial Theories, 1570–1850* (1963); Harper, L.A., *The English Navigation Laws* (New York, 1939). Despite the post-war depression in 1649, the trend for accelerating growth in English overseas trade, particularly long-distance trades to Asia and America, was marked. See Davis, R., *English Overseas Trade, 1500–1700* (1973), pp. 34–6; Clay, C.G.A., *Economic Expansion and Social Change: England 1500–1700*, 2 vols (Cambridge, 1984), pp. 141–54; Munck, T., *Seventeenth Century Europe, 1598–1700* (1990), pp. 112–28; Parker, G., 'The Emergence of Modern Finance in Europe, 1500–1730', in C. Cipolla (ed.), *The Fontana Economic History of Europe*, 6 vols (1974), II, 551.

42. Davis, J.D., *Gentlemen and Tarpaulins: The Officers and Men of the Restoration Navy* (Oxford, 1991), pp. 34–41.

43. Oppenheim, M. (ed.), *The Naval Tracts of Sir William Monson* (1913), V, 226–93; Elton, G., 'Piscatorial Politics in the early Parliaments of Elizabeth I', in McKendrick, N. and Outhwaite, R.B., *Business Life and Public Policy: Essays in Honour of D.C. Coleman* (Cambridge, 1986), pp. 1–20.

44. Schoerer, L.G., *No Standing Armies!* (Baltimore, 1974), particularly, pp. 52–66.

45. Capp, *Cromwell's Navy*, ch. 10.

4 1660–1713: CONSOLIDATION, CHALLENGES AND EXPANSION

1. Fox, F., *Great Ships. The Battlefleet of King Charles II* (1980), pp. 31–71. Also, the old idea of merchants hiring royal ships only died gradually. See Ellison, D., 'Lend Me a Frigate', *MM*, LXVIII (1982), 81–2.

2. For the changes in the size of European fleets see Glete, J., *Navies and Nations. Warships, Navies and Statebuilding in Europe and America, 1550–1860*, 2 vols (Stockholm, 1993), I, 173–255. For a statistical statement

of relative naval power based on the numerical changes (albeit with figures less reliable than Glete) see Modelski, G. and Thompson, W.R., *Seapower in Global Politics, 1494–1993* (1988), pp. 117, 218–19, 255–6, 278–9.

3. Davies, J.D., *Gentlemen and Tarpaulins. The Officers and Men of the Restoration Navy* (Oxford, 1991), pp. 139–42, 149–58; Davies, 'A Lover of the Sea and Skilful in Shipping. King Charles II and his Navy', *Royal Stuart Society Papers*, XII (1992); Hutton, R., *The Restoration: A Political and Religious History of England and Wales, 1658–1667* (Oxford, 1985; 1987 edn), p. 282.

4. Davies, J.D., 'Pepys and the Admiralty Commission of 1679–84', *Historical Research*, XLII (1989), 34–53; Hornstein, S.R., *The Restoration Navy and English Foreign Trade, 1674–1688* (Aldershot, 1991), pp. 12–21 . Contrast these views of the Admiralty commission with Aiken, W.A., 'The Admiralty in Conflict and Commission, 1679–84', in Aiken, W.A. and Henning, B.D. (eds), *Conflict in Stuart England. Essays in Honour of Wallace Notestein* (1960), pp. 205–25; Fox, *Great Ships*, p. 157. Despite the reservations about the objectivity of Pepys's views, his diaries and collected papers are indispensable for the historian. See Latham, R.C. and Matthews, W.(eds), *The Diary of Samuel Pepys* (1970–83), 11 vols; Tanner, J.R. (ed.) *Samuel Pepys' Naval Minutes* (1926) and *Pepys' Memoires of the Royal Navy, 1679–1688* (Oxford, 1906).

5. Davies, *Gentlemen and Tarpaulins*; Hornstein, *The Restoration Navy*; Le Fevre, P., 'Sir George Ayscue, Commonwealth and Restoration Admiral', *MM*, XLVIII (1982), 189–202, 'Arthur Herbert's Early Career in the Navy', *MM*, LXIX (1983), 91, 'John Tyrell (1642–1692): A Restoration Naval Captain', *MM*, LXX (1984), 149–60, 'Sir Cloudsley Shovell's Early Career', *MM*, XXX (1984), 92, 'Tangier, the Navy and its Connection with the Glorious Revolution of 1688', *MM*, LXXIII (1987), 183–90, 'Mathew Aylmer', *MM*, LXXIII (1987), 206–8 and 'Jasper Churchill: Another Naval Churchill', *MM*, LXXVI (1990), 67–9. Another biography of use is Ollard, R., *Man of War: Sir Robert Holmes and the Restoration Navy* (1969). Less useful is Street, L., *An Uncommon Sailor. A Portrait of Admiral Sir William Penn* (Bourne End, 1986). See also Holmes, G., *The Making of a Great Power. Late Stuart and Early Georgian Britain, 1660–1722* (1993), p. 93.

6. Fox, *Great Ships*, pp. 57–60, 116; Parry, J.R., *The Age of Reconnaissance; Discovery, Exploration and Settlement, 1450–1650* (1963), pp. 111–13. See also Robinson, A.H.W., *Marine Cartography in Britain. A History of the Sea Chart to 1855* (Leicester, 1962), pp. 35–46.

7. Bronowski, J. and Mazlish, B., *The Western Intellectual Tradition* (1960), pp. 180–9. See also Deacon, M., *Scientists and the Sea, 1650–1900. A Study of Marine Science* (1971). Although this book is largely concerned with

oceanography, it clearly illustrates the significant link between maritime affairs and emerging sciences. See particularly chs 4–9.

8. Fox, *Great Ships*, p. 139. See also Lavery, B., *The Ship of the Line* (1983), I, 30–9; Lavery, B. (ed.), *Deane's Doctrine of Naval Architecture, 1670* (1981).

9. Fox, *Great Ships*, p. 158.

10. Lewis, M., *The Navy of Britain. A Historical Portrait* (1948), pp. 251–6; Davies, *Gentlemen and Tarpaulins*, pp. 17, 40.

11. Rodger, N.A.M., *Articles of War* (Havant, 1982), pp. 7–19; Davies, *Gentlemen and Tarpaulins*, pp. 183–4. See also Merriman, R.D., *The Sergison Papers* (1950), pp. 16–22, The Navy Board to the Admiralty, 16 Mar. 1690.

12. For the organisational problems facing the Navy Board and its response to them, see Merriman, *The Sergison Papers*; Coad, J., *The Royal Dockyards, 1690–1815. Architecture and Engineering Works of the Royal Navy* (Aldershot, 1989); *Historic Architecture of the Royal Navy* (1983), pp. 48–86, 115–35.

13. For the problems posed by victualling, see Powell, J.R. and Timings, E.K. (eds), *The Rupert and Monck Letter Book, 1666* (1969), particularly, pp. 41–2, Rupert to Coventry, 13 May 1666; pp. 132–3, Same to Duke of York, 17 Aug. 1666; pp. 137–9, Same to Same, 22 Aug. 1666; p. 165, Same to Charles II, 3 Oct. 1666; Padfield, P., *Tides of Empire: Decisive Battles in the Rise of the West* (1982), II (1654–1763), 91. See also Shaw, J.J.S., 'The Commission of Sick and Wounded and Prisoners, 1664–1677', *MM*, xxv (1939), 306–27.

14. Harris, G.G., *The Trinity House of Deptford, 1514–1660* (1969), p. 220; Bromley, J.S., 'Away from Impressment: The Idea of a Royal Naval Reserve, 1696–1859', in Duke, A.C. and Tamse, C.A. (eds), *Britain and the Netherlands* (The Hague, 1977), pp. 168–88.

15. For different views on the importance of mercantilist ideology in naval strategy during the second half of the seventeenth century, see Wilson, C.H., *Profit and Power: A Study of England and the Dutch Wars* (1957); Pincus, S.C.A., 'Protestantism and Patriotism: Ideology and the Making of English Foreign Policy, 1650–1665', unpublished PhD thesis, Harvard, 1990. See also Harper, L., *The English Navigation Laws* (New York, 1939); Crump, H.J., *Colonial Admiralty Jurisdiction in the Seventeenth Century* (1931); Malone, J.J., *Pine Trees and Politics: The Naval Stores and Forest Policy in Colonial New England, 1691–1775* (Seattle, 1964).

16. Symcox, G., *The Crisis of French Sea Power, 1688–1697* (The Hague, 1974), pp. 23–4; Fox, *Great Ships*, pp. 115–17.

17. Symcox, *Crisis of French Sea Power*, pp. 33–55.

18. Brujn, J., *The Dutch Navy of the Seventeenth and Eighteenth Centuries* (Columbia, South Carolina, 1993), pp. 75–81.

19. Powell and Timings, *Rupert and Monck Letter Book*, pp. 201–88, docu-

ments relating to the Four Days Battle; Davies, *Gentlemen and Tarpaulins*, pp. 139–42, 160–3, 229; Davies, 'The Navy, Parliament and Political Crisis in the Reign of Charles II', *HJ*, xxxvi (1993), 271–88.

20. Minchinton, W.E., *The Growth of English Overseas Trade in the Seventeenth and Eighteenth Centuries* (1969), pp. 22–9; Albion, R.G., 'The Timber Problem of the Royal Navy, 1652–1862', *MM*, xxxviii (1952), 4–22; Steele, I.K., *The English Atlantic, 1675–1740* (Oxford, 1986), passim.

21. Padfield, *Tides of Empire*, pp. 22–3. Compare Wilson, *Profit and Power*, Seaward, P., 'The House of Commons Committee of Trade and the Origins of the Second Anglo-Dutch War, 1664', *HJ*, xxx (1987), 437–52; Pincus, S.C.A., 'Popery, Trade and Universal Monarchy: The Ideological Context of the Outbreak of the Second Anglo-Dutch War', *EHR*, cv (1992), 1–29. Details of the campaign are drawn from Padfield, Wilson, and Powell and Timings, *Rupert and Monck Letter Book*; Tedder, A.W., *The Navy of the Restoration. From the Death of Cromwell to the Treaty of Breda; its Work, Growth and Influence* (Cambridge, 1916), pp. 103–90. For the disaster in the Medway, see Rogers, P.G., *The Dutch in the Medway* (1970).

22. For the background to the Third Dutch War, see Howat, G.M.D., *Stuart and Cromwellian Foreign Policy* (1974), pp. 116–29; Black, J.M., *A System of Ambition ? British Foreign Policy, 1660–1793* (1991), pp. 126–9. The narrative of the war is based largely upon Anderson, R.C. (ed.), *Journals and Narratives of the Third Dutch War* (1946). The impact of the war on public opinion is traced in Boxer, C.R., 'Some Second Thoughts on the Third Dutch War, 1672–1674', *TRHS*, 5th ser., xix (1969), 67–94.

23. Hornstein, *The Restoration Navy*, pp. 99–150.

24. Le Fevre, P., 'Tangier, the Navy and its Connection with the Glorious Revolution of 1688', *MM*, lxxiii (1987), 183–90.

25. The role of the navy in the Revolution of 1688 is explored in Powley, E.B., *The English Navy in the Revolution of 1688* (Cambridge, 1928); Ehrman, J., *The Navy in the War of William III* (Cambridge, 1953), pp. 201–34; Davies, *Gentlemen and Tarpaulins*, pp. 199–227; Davies, 'James II, William of Orange and the Admirals' in Cruickshanks, E. (ed.), *By Force or Default ? The Revolution of 1688–1689* (Edinburgh, 1989), pp. 82–108; Anderson, J.L., 'Combined Operations and the Protestant Wind: Some Maritime Aspects of the Glorious Revolution of 1688', *The Great Circle*, ix (1987), 96–107.

26. Although Ehrman's *The Navy in the War of William III* remains the most important reference book for this period, recent scholarship has demonstrated the need for a new detailed analysis of the political and administrative consequences for the navy of the Revolution of 1688.

27. Ibid., pp. 266–7; Symcox, *Crisis of French Sea Power*, pp. 60–89.

Notes

28. Ehrman, *The Navy in the War of William III*, pp. 341–54; Symcox, *Crisis of French Sea Power*, pp. 91–100; Aubrey, P., *The Defeat of James Stuart's Armada, 1692* (Leicester, 1979), pp. 43–58.

29. Aubrey, *Defeat of 1692*, passim. For the reorientation of French naval policy, see Symcox, *Crisis of French Sea Power*, passim.

30. For the views of the nineteenth-century pro-battlefleet protagonists, see Columb, P.H., *Naval Warfare, Its Ruling Principles and Practice Historically Treated* (1891); Mahan, A.T., *The Influence of Sea Power upon History, 1660–1783* (1892); Spencer Wilkinson, H., *Command of the Sea* (1894); Corbett, J.S., *Some Principles of Maritime Strategy* (1911) . For the idea that the *guerre de course* was the only practicable strategy open to France, see Symcox, *Crisis of French Sea Power*, passim. For recent reassessments of the battlefleet strategy, particularly when applied to France, see Reynolds, C.G., *Command of the Sea. The History and Strategy of Maritime Empires* (New York, 1974), pp. 180–200; Hattendorf, J.B., 'Alfred Thayer Mahan and his Strategic Thought', in Hattendorf, J.B. and Jordan, R.S. (eds), *Maritime Strategy and the Balance of Power* (1989), pp. 83–94; 'Recent Thinking on the Theory of Naval Strategy' in ibid., pp. 138–9. For the privateering war, see Crowhurst, P., *The Defence of British Trade, 1689–1815* (Folkestone, 1977); Bromley, J.S., *Corsairs and Navies, 1660–1760* (1987); LePelley, J., 'The Privateers of the Channel Islands, 1688–1713', *MM*, xxx (1944), 22–37. For the eighteenth-century experience, see Starkey, D.J., *British Privateering Enterprise in the Eighteenth Century* (Exeter, 1990).

31. Duffy, M., 'The Establishment of the Western Squadron as the Linchpin of British Naval Strategy', in Duffy, M. (ed), *Parameters of British Naval Power, 1650–1850* (Exeter, 1992), pp. 60–81; Ryan, A.N., 'William III and the Brest Fleet in the Nine Years War', in Hatton, R. and Bromley, J.S. (eds), *William III and Louis XIV* (Liverpool, 1968), pp. 49–67.

32. For the war at sea 1702–13 see Hattendorf, J.B., *England in the War of Spanish Succession. A Study of the English View and Conduct of Grand Strategy, 1702–1712* (New York, 1987); Owen, J.H., *War at Sea Under Queen Anne, 1702–1708* (Cambridge, 1938); Bourne, R., *Queen Anne's Navy in the West Indies* (New Haven, Conn., 1939).

33. Lewis, M., *The Navy of Britain: A Historical Portrait* (1948), pp. 259–61.

34. Compare the concerns that emerge from the collections of papers edited by R.D. Merriman, *The Sergison Papers* (1950), and *Queen Anne's Navy* (1961).

35. The issues surrounding the almost concurrent emergence of the professional administrator and the naval officer have never been examined in any great detail. Studies of the professional naval officer can be found in Elias, N., 'Studies in the Genesis of the Naval Profession', *British*

Journal of Sociology, I (1950), 291–309; Holmes, G., *Augustan England: Professions, State and Society, 1680–1730* (1982), pp. 275–85; Roy, I., 'The Profession of Arms', in Prest, W. (ed.), *The Professions in Early Modern England* (1987), pp. 181–219. However, the only comparative study is with French and Dutch officers. See Teilter, G., *The Genesis of the Professional Officers Corps* (1977). For the administrators, see Holmes, *Augustan England*, pp. 243–56; Aylmer, G.E., 'From Office Holding to Civil Service: The Genesis of Modern Bureaucracy', *TRHS* (1979), 91–108. This last piece continues the author's studies of bureaucracy in the period 1625–60: *The King's Servants* (1961) and *The State's Servants* (1973).

36. Coleman, D.C., 'Naval Dockyards under the Later Stuarts', *Econ. H.R.*, VI, 2nd ser. (1953), 134–55; Lavery, *Ship of the Line*, I, 54–65.

37. Lavery, *Ship of the Line*, I, 53–63.

38. Ehrman, *The Navy in the War of William III*, pp. 59–64, 68, 149–51; Pool, B., *Navy Board Contracts, 1660–1832* (1966), p. 40.

39. For the gradual evolution of manning policies, see Bromley, 'Away from Impressment', in Duke and Tamse (eds), *Britain and the Netherlands*, pp. 168–88; Lloyd, C., *The British Seaman, 1200–1860: A Social Survey* (1968), pp. 136–89, and subsequent chapters. Impressment still remains an important area of study. The crude impression of a navy largely manned by compulsion has given way to a much more detailed picture of social relationships on board naval vessels. See particularly, Rodger, N.A.M., *The Wooden World: An Anatomy of the Georgian Navy* (1986), pp. 164–82; Gradish, S., *The Manning of the British Navy During the Seven Years War* (1980). The dominant view of impressment, drawn from official sources, is still in need of examination in the light of wider contemporary cultural attitudes. M. Rediker, *Between the Devil and the Deep Blue Sea; Merchant Seamen, Pirates, and the Anglo-American Maritime World, 1700–1750* (Cambridge, 1987) is an important addition to this debate, although heavily based upon the idea of the seaman as an industrial labourer.

40. For the wars in the Caribbean, see Moses, N.H., 'The British Navy in the Caribbean, 1689–1697', *MM*, LII (1966), 13–40: Bourne, R., *Queen Anne's Navy in the West Indies* (New Haven, Conn., 1939).

41. Gradish, S., 'The Establishment of British Seapower in the Mediterranean, 1689–1713', *Canadian Journal of History*, X (1975), 1–16; Dickinson, H.T., 'The Capture of Minorca 1708', *MM*, LI (1965), 195–204; Tunstall, B. (ed.), *The Byng Papers* (1930), I, 105–248; Martin-Leake, S., *The Life of Sir John Leake, Rear Admiral of Great Britain*, 2 vols (1920–1), passim.

42. For the war in North America, see Leach, D., *The Northern Colonial Frontier, 1607–1763* (New York, 1966); Graham, G.S., *The Walker*

Expedition to Quebec, 1711 (1953); Morgan, W.T., 'Queen Anne's Canadian Expedition of 1711', *Queen's Quarterly*, XXXV (1935), 460–89.

43. Johnson, J.A., 'Parliament and the Navy, 1688–1714', unpublished PhD thesis, University of Sheffield, 1968, pp. 26–68; Johnson, 'Parliament and the Protection of Trade, 1689–1694', *MM*, LVII (1971), 399–413.

44. Black, J.M., 'The British Navy and British Foreign Policy in the First Half of the Eighteenth Century', in K. Schweizer and J. Black (eds), *Studies in History and Politics* (1985), IV, 137–52; Black, 'Naval Power and International Commitments: Political and Strategic Problems, 1688–1770', in Duffy (ed.), *Parameters*, pp. 39–56; Black, J. and Woodfine, P. (eds), *The British Navy and the Uses of Naval Power in the Eighteenth Century* (Leicester, 1988), pp. 3–26.

45. Glete, *Navies and Nations*, I, 225.

46. Baugh, D., 'Great Britain's Blue Water Policy, 1689–1815', *International History Review*, X (1988), 33–58.

47. Denman, T.J., 'The Political Debate Over Strategy, 1689–1712', unpublished PhD thesis, University of Cambridge, 1985. For examples of the twentieth-century debate, see Liddell-Hart, B., *The British Way in Warfare* (1933); Howard, M., *The Continental Commitment: The Dilemma of British Defence Policy in the Era of Two World Wars* (1972).

48. Jones, D.W., *War and Economy in the Age of William III and Marlborough* (Oxford, 1988), pp. 37–61, 95–121, 130–5.

5 1713–1815: ESTABLISHMENT OF OCEANIC SUPREMACY

1. This period has inspired a stream of popular fiction dating from the publication of *Mr Midshipman Easy* in 1836 by Frederick Marryat (1792–1848). The Hornblower series by C.S. Forester gave the naval novel and short story a great boost. The form continues in the works of Dudley Pope, Alexander Kent and Patrick O'Brien. They remain popular, but unlike some other genres of modern literature they have not yet attracted scholarly critical appraisal. For perhaps the earliest example of the naval novel, in much more comic vein, see Davis, J., *The Post Captain* (1805; reprinted Sulhamstead, 1984).

2. Peter, M., *Pitt and Popularity. The Patriot Minister and London Opinion during the Seven Years War* (Oxford, 1980), passim; White, C., *Victoria's Navy: The End of the Sailing Navy* (Havant, 1981), pp. 57–92.

3. Hamilton, W. Mark, *The Nation and the Navy. Methods and Organisation of British Naval Propaganda, 1889–1914* (New York, 1986), passim.

4. Duffy, M., 'The Establishment of the Western Squadron as the Linchpin of British Naval Strategy', in Duffy, M. (ed.), *The Parameters of British*

Naval Power, 1650–1850 (Exeter, 1992), pp. 61–79; Saxby, R., 'The Blockade of Brest in the French Revolutionary War', *MM*, LXVIII (1992), 25–35; Partridge, M.S., 'The Royal Navy and the End of Close Blockade, 1885–1905: A Revolution in Naval Strategy?', *MM*, LXXV (1989), 119–36.

5. Baugh, D., *British Naval Administration in the Age of Walpole* (Princeton, NJ, 1965); Morgan, G.W., 'The Impact of War on the Administration of the Army, Navy and Ordnance in Britain, 1739–1748', unpublished PhD thesis, University of Leicester, 1977; Middleton, C.R., 'The Administration of Newcastle and Pitt: The Departments of State and the Conduct of the Seven Years War', unpublished PhD thesis, University of Exeter, 1968; Lewis, M., *The Navy of Britain. A Historical Portrait* (1948); Rodger, N.A.M., *Wooden World: Anatomy of the Georgian Navy* (1986); Mackay, R., *Admiral Hawke* (Oxford, 1965); Spinney, D., *Rodney* (1969).

6. On Anglo-Hanoverian relations, see Gibbs, G.C., 'English Attitudes towards Hanover and the Hanoverian Succession in the First Half of the Eighteenth Century', in Birke, A.M. and Kluxen, K. (eds), *England and Hanover* (1986), pp. 33–51. For the Baltic Campaigns, see Aldridge, D.D., 'Sir John Norris and the British Naval Expeditions to the Baltic Sea, 1715–1727', unpublished PhD thesis, University of London, 1972; Tunstall, B. (ed.), *The Byng Papers. Selected from the Letters and Papers of Admiral Sir George Byng, First Viscount Torrington and of his son Admiral the Honourable John Byng*, 3 vols (1930–3), III, 241–381; Miller, M.E., 'Naval Stores and Anglo-Russian Encounters in the Baltic: The English Expedition of 1715', in Runyan, T.J., *Ships, Seafaring and Society: Essays in Maritime History* (Detroit, 1987), pp. 167–82. Glete, *Navies and Nations*, I, 364, fn. 93. For background to operations in the Baltic and elsewhere, see Richmond, H.W., *The Navy as an Instrument of Policy, 1558–1727* (Cambridge, 1953), pp. 365–97.

7. Cranmer-Byng, J.L. (ed.), *Pattee Byng's Journal, 1718–1720* (1948), passim; Richmond, H.W., 'The Expedition to Sicily under Sir George Byng', *Journal of the Royal United Services Institution*, LXXX (1909), 1134–52; Hattendorf, J.B., 'Admiral Sir George Byng and the Cape Passaro Incident, 1718: A Case Study in the Use of the Royal Navy as a Deterrent', in *Guerres et Paix* (Vincennes, 1987). For background to the war, see Stugill, C., 'From Utrecht to the Little War with Spain: Peace at almost any Price had to be the Case', in Black, J. (ed.), *The Origins of War in Early Modern Europe* (Edinburgh, 1987).

8. For the diplomatic and military events of the 1720s, see Gibbs, G.C., 'Parliament and Foreign Policy, 1715–1731', unpublished MA thesis, University of Liverpool, 1953, passim; Black, J., *The Collapse of the Anglo-French Alliance, 1727–1731* (Gloucester, 1987); Scott, H. and

Mackay, D., *The Rise of the Great Powers, 1648–1815* (1983), pp. 94–137; Wilson, A. M., *French Foreign Policy during the Administration of Cardinal Fleury, 1726–1743* (Cambridge, Mass., 1936).

9. Woodfine, P., 'The Idea of Naval Power and the Conflict with Spain, 1737–1742', in Black, J. and Woodfine, P. (eds), *The British Navy and the Uses of Naval Power in the Eighteenth Century* (Leicester, 1988), pp. 72–3. See also Crewe, D.G., *Yellow Jack and the Worm. British Naval Administration in the West Indies, 1739–1748* (Liverpool, 1993).

10. Black, J., 'The British Navy and British Foreign Policy in the First Half of the Eighteenth Century', in Schweizer, K. and Black, J. (eds), *Studies in History and Politics*, IV (1985), pp. 144–8.

11. Woodfine, P. 'The Anglo-Spanish War of 1739', in Black, *Origins of War in Early Modern Europe*, pp. 185–209. For the war of 1739–48, the most comprehensive study remains Richmond, H.W., *The Navy in the War of 1739–1748* (Cambridge, 1920), 3 vols. The narrative which follows is based upon Richmond's work. For the French navy, see Bourland, R.D., 'Maurepas and his Administration of the French Navy on the Eve of the War of Austrian Succession, 1732–1742', unpublished PhD thesis, Notre Dame University, 1978. For the Spanish Navy, see Harbron, J.D., *Trafalgar and the Spanish Navy* (1988); Merino, J.P., *La Armada Española en el Siglo xviii* (Madrid, 1981). For the West Indian expedition of 1740–2, see Harding, R.H., *Amphibious Warfare in the Eighteenth Century: The British Expedition to the West Indies, 1740–1742* (Woodbridge, 1991). For a contemporary analysis of Britain's relative advantage in a war with France and Spain, see Richmond, H.W. (ed.), *Naval Miscellany*, vol. 3 (1927), pp. 51–81.

12. Richmond, *The Navy in the War of 1739–48*, II, 1–57; Luff, P.A., 'Mathews v. Lestock: Parliament, Politics and the Navy in Mid-Eighteenth Century England', *Parliamentary History*, x (1991), 45–62.

13. For contrasting views, see Richmond, *The Navy in the War of 1739–48*, II, 154–89; McLynn, F., 'Sea Power and the Jacobite Rising of 1745', *MM*, LXVII (1981), 163–72; Black, J., *Culloden and the '45* (Gloucester, 1990), pp. 119–27.

14. Good accounts of the battles can be found in Mackay, R., *Admiral Hawke* (Oxford, 1965), pp. 69–88; Pack, S.W.C., *Admiral Lord Anson* (1960), pp. 153–60.

15. For a recent view of the problem of the European land commitment, which lays great stress on the incompetence of Lord Carteret and his allies, see Massie, A.W., 'Great Britain and the Defence of the Low Countries, 1744–1748', unpublished DPhil thesis, University of Oxford, 1988. There are many biographies of William Pitt which chart his rise to power. Compare Williams, B., *The Life of William Pitt*, 3 vols (1915); Tunstall, B., *William Pitt, Earl of Chatham* (1938); Brown, P.D.,

William Pitt, Earl of Chatham: The Great Commoner (1978); Peters, M., *Pitt and Popularity. The Patriot Minister and London Opinion during the Seven Years War* (Oxford, 1980).

16. Swanson, C.E., 'American Privateering and Imperial Warfare, 1739–1748', *William and Mary Quarterly*, XLII (1985), 357–82; Starkey, D.J., *British Privateering Enterprise in the Eighteenth Century* (Exeter, 1990), pp. 117–53. The fullest history of Louisbourg is still McLennan, J.S., *Louisbourg: From its Foundation to its Fall, 1713–1758* (1918). See also Rawlyk, G.A., *Yankees and Louisbourg* (Orono, Maine, 1967): Gwyn, J. (ed.), *The Royal Navy and North America: The Warren Papers, 1736–1752* (1973). For a view on British policy regarding France on the North American littoral before 1756, see Douglas, W.A.B., 'The Sea Militia of Nova Scotia, 1749–1755: A Comment on Naval Policy', *Canadian Historical Review*, XLVII (1966), 22–37.

17. Rodger, N.A.M., *The Admiralty* (Lavenham, 1979), pp. 58–65; Haas, J.M., 'The Royal Dockyards: The Earliest Visitations and Reform, 1749–1778', *HJ*, XIII (1970), 191–215; Middleton, R., 'The Visitation of the Naval Dockyards, 1749', *MM*, LXXVII (1991), 21–30. See also Lavery, B., *The Ship of the Line: The Development of the Battlefleet*, 2 vols (1983), I, 90–5; Gardiner, R., *The First Frigates. Nine and Twelve Pounder Frigates, 1748–1815* (1992), pp. 14–17.

18. For the reappraisal of Pitt's role, see particularly Middleton, R., *The Bells of Victory. The Pitt–Newcastle Ministry and the Conduct of the Seven Years War, 1757–1762* (Cambridge, 1985), particularly pp. 211–27. The fullest narrative of the war is still Corbett, J.S., *England in the Seven Years War: A Study of Combined Strategy*, 2 vols (1907; reprinted 1973, 1992). See also Frazer, E.J.S., 'The Pitt–Newcastle Coalition and the Conduct of the Seven Years War', unpublished DPhil thesis, University of Oxford, 1976.

19. Corbett, *England in the Seven Years War*, I, 58.

20. On the Byng affair, see Richmond, H.W. (ed.), *Papers Relating to the Loss of Minorca* (1915); Tunstall, B., *Admiral Byng and the Loss of Minorca* (1928); Pope, D., *At Twelve Mr Byng was Shot . . .* (1962).

21. As well as Middleton, Corbett and Peters, see Hackman, W. Kent, 'The British Raid on Rochefort, 1757', *MM*, LXIV (1978), 263–75.

22. On the naval operations against Louisbourg, see Hitsman, J. and Bond, C., 'The Assault Landing at Louisbourg, 1758', *Canadian Historical Review*, XXXV (1954), 314–40.

23. Starkey, *British Privateering Enterprise*, pp. 161–92, Brown, J.W., 'British Privateering During the Seven Years War, 1756–1763', unpublished MA thesis, University of Exeter, 1978; Bamford, P.W., *Forests and French Sea Power, 1660–1789* (Toronto, 1956), pp. 58–67.

24. On the importance of the fiscal powers of the British and French states,

see Brewer, J., *The Sinews of Power. War, Money and the English State, 1688–1783* (1989); Dickson, P., *The Financial Revolution in England* (1967).

25. Marcus, G.J., *Quiberon Bay: The Campaign in Home Waters, 1759* (1960); Bosher, J.F., 'Financing the French Navy in the Seven Years War: Beaujon, Goosens et Compagnie in 1759', *Business History*, XXVIII (1986), 115–33; Pritchard, J., *Louis XV's Navy, 1748–1762. A Study of Organisation and Administration* (Quebec, 1987), pp. 185–202; Middleton, R., 'British Naval Strategy, 1755–1762: The Western Squadron', *MM*, LXXV (1989), 349–67.

26. Brewer, *Sinews of Power*; Kennedy, P., *The Rise and Fall of British Naval Mastery* (1976; 2nd edn 1983); Rodger, N.A.M., *The Wooden World. An Anatomy of the Georgian Navy* (1986), pp. 259–63, 273–302, 314–27. See also Baugh, D., 'Maritime Strength and Atlantic Commerce. The uses of a grand maritime empire', in Stone, L. (ed.), *An Imperial State at War. Britain, 1689–1815* (1994), pp. 185–223.

27. For studies of the Royal Navy's relationship with colonial society in America, see Clarke, D.M., 'The Impressment of Seamen in the American Colonies', in *Essays in Colonial History Presented to Charles McLean Andrews by his Students* (New Haven, Conn., 1931), pp. 198–224; Lax, J. and Pencak, W., 'The Knowles Riot and the Crisis of the 1740s in Massachusetts', *Perspectives of American History*, X (1976), 161–214; Swanson, C.E., 'The Competition for American Seamen during the War of 1739–1748', *Proceedings of the Canadian Society for Eighteenth Century Studies* (1982), pp. 119–29; Swanson, 'The Profitability of Privateering: Reflections on British Colonial Privateers during the War of 1739–1748', *American Neptune*, XLII (1982), 36–56; Stout, N.R., *The Royal Navy in America, 1760–1775: A Study of Enforcement of British Colonial Policy in the Era of the American Revolution* (Annapolis, 1973); Lemisch, J., 'Jack Tar in the Streets: Merchant Seamen in the Politics of Revolutionary America', *William and Mary Quarterly*, XXV (1968), 371–407; Ubbelohde, C., *The Vice-Admiralty Courts and the American Revolution* (Chapel Hill, 1960), pp. 25–43.

28. Tracy, N., *Navies, Deterrence and American Independence. Britain and Seapower in the 1760s and 1770s* (Vancouver, 1988); Roberts, M., *Splendid Isolation, 1763–1780* (Reading, 1970); Scott, H.M., 'The Importance of Bourbon Naval Reconstruction to the Strategy of Choiseul after the Seven Years War', *International Historical Review*, I (1979); Black, J., 'Naval Power, Strategy and Policy, 1775–1791', in Duffy, *Parameters*, pp. 93–120.

29. Pares, R., 'American versus Continental Warfare, 1739–63', *EHR*, LI (1936), 429–65. See also Pares, R., *War and Trade in the West Indies, 1739–1763* (Oxford, 1936).

30. Williams, E., *Capitalism and Slavery* (1948). For a recent collection of essays reflecting on Williams's thesis, see Solow, B.L. and Engerman, S.L., *British Capitalism and Caribbean Slavery: The Legacy of Eric Williams* (Cambridge,1987). This collection, especially Richardson, D., 'The Slave Trade, Sugar and British Economic Growth, 1748–1776', ibid., pp. 103–33; Hudson, P., *The Industrial Revolution* (1992), pp. 192–9.

31. See for example, Mackesy, P., *The War for America, 1775–1783* (1964); Black, J., *War for America. The Struggle for American Independence, 1775–1783* (Gloucester, 1991).

32. Syrett, D., *Shipping and the American War, 1775–1783* (1970), p. 243.

33. Ibid., passim; Syrett, *The Royal Navy in American Waters, 1775–1783* (Aldershot, 1989); Baugh, D., 'Why Did Britain Lose Command of the Sea during the War for America ?' in Black and Woodfine, *The British Navy and the Uses of Naval Power*, pp. 149–69; Baugh, D., 'The Politics of British Naval Failure, 1775–1777', *American Neptune*, LII (1992), 221–46; Bowler, R.A., *Logistics and the Failure of the British Army in America, 1775–1783* (Princeton, NJ, 1975); Tilley, J.A., *The British Navy and the American Revolution* (Columbia, South Carolina, 1987); Temple Patterson, A., *The Other Armada. The Franco-Spanish Attempt to Invade Britain in 1779* (Manchester, 1960).

34. Scott and Mackay, *Rise of the Great Powers*, p. 260; Baugh, 'Why Did Britain Lose Command of the Sea?', pp. 152–3.

35. An account of the case can be found in Barnes, G.R. and Owen, J.H. (eds.), *The Private Papers of John Earl of Sandwich, First Lord of the Admiralty, 1771–1782*, 5 vols (1932–38), II, 191–252.

36. Webb, P., 'Construction, Repair and Maintenance in the Battle Fleet of the Royal Navy, 1793–1815' in Black and Woodfine, *The British Navy and the Uses of Naval Power*, p. 208. See also Webb, P.L.C., 'The Rebuilding and Repair of the Fleet, 1783–93', *Bulletin of the Institute of Historical Research*, l (1977), 194–209.

37. For Middleton's administrative work, see Laughton, J.K. (ed.), *The Letters and Papers of Charles, Lord Barham, Admiral of the Red, 1758–1813*, 3 vols (1907–10), II (1909). Naval operations from the perspective of the First Lord of the Admiralty, the Earl of Sandwich, can be traced in Barnes and Owen, *The Private Papers*. For a reassessment of Sandwich, see also Rodger, N.A.M., *The Insatiable Earl. Life of John Montagu* (1993).

38. Jamieson, A.G., 'The War in the Leeward Islands, 1775–1783', unpublished DPhil thesis, University of Oxford, 1981, pp. 37–94; Spinney, *Rodney*. For contemporary opinions on health, disease and sanitation afloat, see Lloyd, C.C., *The Health of Seamen* (1965). For a much broader study, see Lloyd, C.C., Keevil, J. and Coulter, J.L.S., *Medicine and the Navy, 1200–1900*, 4 vols (Edinburgh, 1957–63).

39. Syrett, *Shipping and the American War*; Baker, N., *Government and Contractors*

(1971); Baugh, 'Why Did Britain Lose Command of the Sea?', pp. 152–3; Rodger, *The Admiralty*, pp. 74–5.

40. Spinney, *Rodney*, especially pp. 389–412. On the development of signals in this context, see Tunstall, B., *Naval Warfare in the Age of Sail: The Evolution of Fighting Tactics, 1650–1815*, ed. N. Tracy (1990), pp. 165–8; Corbett, J.S., *Fighting Instructions, 1530–1816* (1905), pp. 225–59.

41. Webb, 'Construction, Repair and Maintenance', p. 207.

42. Teitler, G., *The Genesis of the Professional Officers Corps* (1977), pp. 161–71; Rodger, N.A.M., 'Officers, Gentlemen and their Education, 1793–1860' in *Les Empires en Guerre et Paix, 1793–1860* (Vincennes, 1990), pp. 139–50.

43. The most detailed history of the plans to invade Britain remains Desbrière, E., *Projets de Débarquement aux Isles Britanniques*, 4 vols (Paris, 1900). British naval strategy can be followed in *The Keith Papers. Selected from the Letters and Papers of Admiral Viscount Keith*, 3 vols, I, ed. W.G. Perrin (1927), II and III ed. C. Lloyd (1950 and 1955); Bonner-Smith, D., *Letters of Admiral of the Fleet, the Earl of St Vincent, whilst First Lord of the Admiralty, 1801–1804*, 2 vols (1922 and 1927); *Private Papers of George, Second Earl Spencer, First Lord of the Admiralty, 1794–1801*, 4 vols, I and II ed. J.S. Corbett (1913–14), III and IV ed. H.W. Richmond (1923–4). Important narratives and analyses of strategy up to 1815 can be found in Mackesy, P., *Statesmen at War: The Strategy of Overthrow, 1798–1799* (1974), *War without Victory: The Downfall of Pitt, 1799–1802* (Oxford, 1984) and *The War in the Mediterranean, 1803–1810* (1957); Glover, R., *Britain at Bay: The Defence against Bonaparte, 1803–1814* (1973); Hall, C.D., *British Strategy in the Napoleonic Wars, 1803–1815*, (Manchester, 1992); Duffy, M., *Soldiers, Sugar and Seapower: The British Expeditions to the West Indies and the War against Revolutionary France* (Oxford, 1987). For the navy in this period, see Lavery, B., *Nelson's Navy. The Ships, Men and Organisation, 1793–1815* (1989). Except where stated, the following narrative has been drawn from these sources.

44. For an account of the First of June 1794, see Barrow, J., *The Life of Richard Earl Howe, K.G., Admiral of the Fleet and General of Marines* (1838), pp. 223–52.

45. Harbron, J.D., *Trafalgar and the Spanish Navy* (1988), pp. 115–19; Bruijn, J.R., *The Dutch Navy of the Seventeenth and Eighteenth Centuries* (Columbia, South Carolina, 1993), pp. 211–14; Lloyd, C., *St Vincent and Camperdown* (1963); Palmer, M.A.J., 'Sir John's Victory: The Battle of Cape St Vincent Reconsidered', *MM*, LXVII (1991), 31–46.

46. Northcote Parkinson, C., *Britannia Rules: The Classic Age of Naval History, 1793–1815* (1977; Gloucester, 1987), pp. 60–7.

47. There are many accounts of Trafalgar available. Many are listed in Warner, O., *Lord Nelson: Guide to Reading* (1955). For the debate over the

battle at the beginning of this century, see Schurman, D.M., *Julian S. Corbett, 1854–1922* (1981), pp. 114–30.

48.   Glover, *Britain at Bay*, pp. 15–19; Hall, *British Strategy*, pp. 153–65, 175–9; Ryan, A.N., 'The Navy at Copenhagen in 1807', *MM*, xxxix (1953), 201–10; Bond, G.C., *The Grand Expedition: The British Invasion of Holland in 1809* (Athens, Georgia, 1979).

49.   Duffy, *Soldiers, Sugar and Seapower*, pp. 368–93; Mackesy, *War in the Mediterranean*, p. 9. See also O'Brien, P.K., 'The Political Economy of British Taxation, 1660–1815', *Econ. H.R.*, 2nd ser., xli (1988), 1–32. See also Black, R.A. and Gilmore, C.G., 'Crowding Out during Britain's Industrial Revolution', *Journal of Economic History*, 1 (1990), 109–31; O'Brien, P.K., 'The Impact of the Revolutionary and Napoleonic Wars, 1793–1815, on the Long-Run Growth of the British Economy', *Review Fernand Braudel Center*, xii (1989), 335–95.

50.   Hall, C.D., 'The Royal Navy and the Peninsula War', *MM*, lxxix (1993), 403–18.

51.   Corbett (ed.), *Private Papers of George, Second Earl Spencer*, II, 103–76; Mainwaring, G.E. and Dobrée, B., *Mutiny; The Floating Republic* (1935; reprinted 1987); Wells, R., *Insurrection: The British Experience, 1795–1803* (Gloucester, 1983), pp. 79–109.

52.   Crimmin, P.K., 'Admiralty Administration, 1783–1806', unpublished MPhil thesis, University of London, 1965, pp. 311–12; Morriss, R., *The Royal Dockyards during the Revolutionary and Napoleonic Wars* (Leicester, 1983), pp. 189–222; Rodger, *The Admiralty*, pp. 93–6.

SELECT BIBLIOGRAPHY

The following are only some of the most significant works available. For the whole period, readers should seek out the volumes of the Navy Records Society, which are not listed here individually. Despite being rather elderly in some cases they do provide a good mix of informed introduction and original documents. Reference should be made to the footnotes to pursue specific issues. Biographies, which can also include important material, have been excluded.

General Histories

There are a number of modern general histories of the navy that repay examination. P. Kennedy, *The Rise and Fall of British Naval Mastery* (1976) is very important. J. Glete, *Navies and Nations. Warships, Navies and State Building in Europe and America, 1500–1860*, 2 vols (Stockholm, 1993) is extremely valuable for the comparative evolution of navies. For the ships, see B. Lavery, *The Ship of the Line: The Development of the Battlefleet*, 2 vols (1983); R. Gardiner (ed.), *The Line of Battle. The Sailing Warship, 1650–1840* (1992). For naval tactics, B. Tunstall, *Naval Warfare in the Age of Sail: The Evolution of Fighting Tactics, 1650–1815*, ed. N. Tracy (1990), is well illustrated and informative. The best single volume on the strategic management of the navy in this period is N.A.M. Rodger, *The Admiralty* (Lavenham, 1979).

1509–1603

The period is not well served by recent works, but the early Tudor navy is well covered by D. Loades, *The Tudor Navy. An Administrative, Political and Military History* (Aldershot, 1992). A. McGowan's *The Ship. Tiller and Whipstaff. The Development of the Sailing Ship* (1981), is a straightforward and brief introduction to a complex subject. K. Andrews, *Trade, Plunder and Settlement: Maritime Enterprise and the Genesis of the British Empire, 1480–1630* (Cambridge, 1984), puts the navy into the context of an expanding economy. G. Parker and C. Martin, *The Spanish Armada* (1988) is an excellent and well illustrated account of the famous campaign.

1603–1640

Some of the best work on the early Stuart navy remains unpublished, but naval affairs can be followed in works dealing with other subjects. R. Lockyer, *Buckingham. The Life and Political Career of George Villiers* (1981), covers the period 1618–28. Some details of earlier years can be found in M. Young, *Servility and Service. The Life and Work of Sir John Coke* (Woodbridge, 1986), and L.L. Peck, *Court Patronage and Corruption in Early Stuart England* (1991). Ship Money is discussed in K. Sharpe, *The Personal Rule of Charles I* (Yale, 1992), and K. R. Andrews, *Ships, Money and Politics. Seafaring and Naval Enterprise in the Reign of Charles I* (Cambridge, 1991). See also A. Thrush, 'Naval Finance and the Origins and Development of Ship Money' in M.C. Fissel (ed.), *War and Government in Britain, 1598–1650* (Manchester, 1991).

1640–1660

The Civil War is not very well covered at all by modern published works. J.R. Powell, *The Navy in the Civil War* (1962), remains the most accessible single volume. The political relationship between the merchant community and parliamentary naval power is dealt with in R. Brenner, *Merchants and Revolution. Commercial Change, Political Conflict and London's Overseas Traders, 1550–1653* (Cambridge, 1993). B. Capp, *Cromwell's Navy: The Fleet and the English Revolution, 1648–1660* (Oxford, 1989), provides excellent coverage of the later part of the period. For operational studies, the Navy Record Society volumes on the First Dutch War remain indispensable.

1660–1689

This period has recently received more attention, particularly the political and social context of naval development. J.D. Davies, *Gentlemen and Tarpaulins: The Officers and Men of the Restoration Navy* (Oxford, 1991), is an important social and political study. S. Hornstein's *The Restoration Navy and English Foreign Trade, 1674–1688. A Study in the Peacetime Use of Sea Power* (Aldershot, 1991), provides a good analysis of the importance of naval power in the development of English commerce in the Mediterranean. Both Davies and Hornstein provide useful correctives to the reputation of Samuel Pepys. Histories of the Second and Third Dutch Wars require updating.

1689–1713

J. Ehrman, *The Navy in the War of William III, 1689–1697* (Cambridge, 1953), remains the standard text. D.W. Jones, *War and Economy in the Age of William III and Marlborough* (Oxford, 1988), has put the navy into the context of the wider economic and strategic aspects of the war. Much work is needed to bring together and extend recent scholarship on this period.

1713–1763

The period before 1739 is on the whole very poorly covered. D. Baugh's *British Naval Administration in the Age of Walpole* (Princeton, NJ, 1965) is an excellent administrative history. D.G. Crewe, *Yellow Jack and the Worm. British Naval Administration in the West Indies, 1739–1748* (Liverpool, 1993), is an excellent regional study. H.W. Richmond's *The Navy in the War of 1739–1748* (Cambridge, 1920), 3 vols, remains the main text on operations. Although a fine piece of scholarship, it is now in need of replacement. The diplomatic background to naval affairs in this period can be traced in the works of Jeremy Black. Naval affairs during the Seven Years War can be drawn from a variety of sources, including biographies of politicians and seamen, and accounts of specific actions. R. Middleton, *The Bells of Victory. The Pitt–Newcastle Ministry and the Conduct of the Seven Years War, 1757–1762* (Cambridge, 1985), is the best single-volume history. J.S. Corbett, *England in the Seven Years War: A Study in Combined Strategy* (1907), 2 vols, is dated, but still repays attention. N.A.M. Rodger's *The Wooden World. An Anatomy of the Georgian Navy* (1986), is indispensable as a history of the internal workings of the navy during this period.

1763–1783

Although the diplomatic history of the period before 1775 is well covered by H.M. Scott, M. Roberts and J. Black, the naval history has received little attention. N. Tracy, *Navies, Deterrence and American Independence. Britain and Seapower in the 1760s and 1770s* (Vancouver, 1988), is a sound analysis of the navy's diplomatic role. The navy in the War of American Independence is covered by D. Syrett in *The Royal Navy in American Waters, 1775–1783* (Aldershot, 1989).

1783–1815

The first ten years of this period are in need of more research, but for the period after 1793 there is extensive coverage. B. Lavery's *Nelson's Navy. The Ships, Men and Organisation, 1793–1815* (1989), is fairly comprehensive and well illustrated. M. Duffy, *Soldiers, Sugar and Seapower: The British Expeditions to the West Indies and the War against Revolutionary France* (Oxford, 1987) and P. Mackesy, *The War in the Mediterranean, 1803–1810* (1957), are excellent studies of naval operations. R. Morriss, *The Royal Dockyards during the Revolutionary and Napoleonic Wars* (Leicester, 1983), provides a valuable study of organisational change and stasis. Trafalgar and Nelson can be followed in a vast literature of their own.

INDEX

Aboukir Bay, battle of (1798), 138
Admiralty, Board of, 106–7, 114, 118, 126, 133, 136, 140
Africa, 6–7, 19–21
Aix-la-Chapelle, Treaty of (1748), 124
Albemarle, Earl of, *see under* George Monck
Alexandria, 138
America, North, 35, 69, 141
Amiens, Treaty of (1802), 139
Anson, Lord George, 123, 125
Armada, Spanish (1588), 21, 23–7, 35; (1597), 29
Artillery at sea, 7, 50
Austria, 111, 119, 121–2, 124, 137, 139–40
Ayscue, Sir George, 75
Azores, 25, 29

Bacon, Sir Francis, 29, 37
Baltic, 22, 35, 78, 94, 108, 110–11, 118–19
Bantry Bay, battle of (1689), 102, 113
Barbados, 35, 69, 72
Barbary, coast, 21, 33, 45, 47, 59, 78, 100, 110; Algiers, 37; Sallee, 59, 67
Barfleur, battle of (1692), 103, 113
Basque Roads, 139
Batten, William, 60, 66–8
Bavaria, 121
Bayonne, 13

Beachy Head, battle of (1690), 113
Beaujon and Gossens, 129
Bedford, Duke of (Regent of Henry VI), 5
Bedford, Duke of, *see under* Russell, John
Bergen, 95
Bergen-op-Zoom, 123
Bermuda, 35
Bertie, Robert, Earl of Lindsey, 47, 54
Berwick, 123
Biscay, Bay of, 10, 46, 54–5
Blake, Robert, General-at-Sea, 70, 72, 74–5, 78
Blenheim, battle of (1704), 117
'Blue Water' Strategy, 9, 111, 117, 124, 130
Bombay, 100
Boscawen, Edward, 127
Boteler, Nathaniel, 75
Boulogne, 10, 14, 139
Bourbon, Duke of, 13
Breda, Treaty of (1674), 96
Brest, 14, 93, 96, 102–3, 120, 122, 137
Bristol, 20, 65–6
Brittany, 10, 13
Buckingham, Duke of, *see under* Villiers, George
Burghley, Lord, *see under* Cecil, William
Burgundy, 5–6, 9–10
Butler, James, Duke of Ormonde, 65